Friends, & Fello

The period for a new elec
tion of a citizen to administer the Executive
government of the United States, being not
far distant, and the time actually arri
ved, when your thoughts must be employ
ed in designating the person who is to be
cloathed with that important trust ~~tion~~
~~than~~, it appears to me proper, especi
ally as it may conduce to a more distinct
expression of the public voice, that I should
now apprise you of the resolution I have
formed, to ~~decline being~~ considered among
the number of those, out of whom a choice is
to be made. —

I beg you, at the same time, to do
me the justice ~~to be~~ assured, that this resolu
tion has not been taken, without a strict
regard to all the considerations apper
ing to the relation, which binds a dutiful
citizen to his country — and that, in with
drawing the tender of service which silence
in my situation might imply, I am influen
ced by no diminution ~~of zeal~~ for your futur
interest; no deficiency of grateful respect
for your past kindness; but ~~am supported by~~ a full
convicti

conviction that the step is compatible with both.

The acceptance of, & continuance hitherto in, the office to which your suffrages have twice called me, have been a uniform sacrifice of inclination to the opinion of duty, and to a deference for what appeared to be your desire. — I constantly hoped, that it would have been much earlier in my power, consistently with motives, which I was not at liberty to disregard, to return to that retirement, from which I had been reluctantly drawn. —————— The strength of my inclination to do this previous to the last election, had even led to the preparation of an address to declare it to you; but mature reflection on the perplexed & critical posture of our affairs with foreign Nations, and the unanimous advice of persons entitled to my confidence, impelled me to abandon the idea. —

I rejoice that the state of your concerns, external as well as internal, no longer renders the pursuit of inclination incompatible with the sentiment of duty, or propriety; & am persuaded that whatever partiality any may yet retain for my services, in the present circumstances of our country, will not disapprove my determination to retire. —

The impressions, with which, I first undertook the arduous trust, were explained on the proper occasion. — In the discharge of this trust, I will only say, that I have with good intentions, contributed toward the Organization

A Sacred Union of Citizens

A Sacred Union of Citizens

GEORGE WASHINGTON'S
FAREWELL ADDRESS
AND THE
AMERICAN CHARACTER

Matthew Spalding and Patrick J. Garrity

INTRODUCTION BY DANIEL J. BOORSTIN

ROWMAN & LITTLEFIELD PUBLISHERS, INC.
Lanham • Boulder • New York • London

ROWMAN & LITTLEFIELD PUBLISHERS, INC.

Published in the United States of America
by Rowman & Littlefield Publishers, Inc.
4720 Boston Way, Lanham, Maryland 20706

3 Henrietta Street
London WC2E 8LU, England

Portrait of George Washington (1797) by Gilbert Stuart reprinted on cover courtesy of
The New York Public Library, Astor, Lenox and Tilden Foundations.

Pages from George Washington's Farewell Address manuscript reprinted on
endsheets courtesy of the George Washington Papers, Rare Books and Manuscripts
Division, The New York Public Library, Astor, Lenox and Tilden Foundations.

British Cataloging in Publication Information Available

Library of Congress Cataloging-in-Publication Data
Spalding, Matthew.
A sacred union of citizens : George Washington's farewell address
and the American character / Matthew Spalding and Patrick J. Garrity.
p. cm.
Includes bibliographical references and index.
1. Washington, George, 1732–1799. Farewell address. 2. National
characteristics, American. I. Garrity, Patrick J. II. Title.
E312.952.S67 1996   973.4'3'092—dc20   96-19644   CIP

ISBN 0-8476-8261-7 (cloth: alk. paper)

Printed in the United States of America

♾ ™ The paper used in this publication meets the minimum requirements of
American National Standard for Information Sciences—Permanence of Paper for
Printed Library Materials, ANSI Z39.48–1984.
Distributed by NATIONAL BOOK NETWORK

Contents

Acknowledgments   *vii*

Introduction   *ix*
George Washington and American Character
by Daniel J. Boorstin

1   Remembering Washington's Legacy   *1*

2   Establishing the National Character   *9*

3   Friends and Fellow Citizens   *45*

4   Our Interest, Guided by Our Justice   *91*

5   Washington and the American Political Tradition   *141*

6   Truths Important at All Times   *169*

Appendix: Farewell Address   *175*

Notes   *189*

Index   *213*

About the Authors   *217*

Acknowledgments

This book is the result of a year-long collaboration between the authors. Matthew Spalding would like to thank his teachers and colleagues who encouraged this project and his work on George Washington and the American Founding period. The generous support of the Henry Salvatori Foundation, the Earhart Foundation, and the Intercollegiate Studies Institute during his dissertation research on Washington, some of which made its way into this project, is greatly appreciated. Lastly, he expresses his thanks to his wife, Elizabeth, and his family for their confidence and inspiration.

Patrick Garrity would like to express his appreciation to the faculty and students of the Foreign Policy Institute of The Johns Hopkins University Paul H. Nitze School of Advanced International Studies (SAIS), especially Andrew Bacevich and Eliot Cohen. His contribution to the book was made while on sabbatical at SAIS, where he was provided with a stimulating intellectual environment as well as excellent research support.

Both authors wish to thank the following individuals in particular for reviewing various portions of the draft manuscript, or for otherwise providing useful ideas and insights: William B. Allen, Stephen Cambone, Christopher Flannery, Harry V. Jaffa, Charles Kesler, Steven Maaranen, and Ken Masugi. Lawrence Serewicl provided timely and valuable research and assistance.

Introduction

GEORGE WASHINGTON AND AMERICAN CHARACTER

George Washington has a centrality in the American national consciousness for which there is no close analogue in other great modern nations. John Adams wrote to Benjamin Rush in 1790: "The history of our revolution will be . . . that Dr Franklin's electric rod smote the earth and out sprang General Washington. That Franklin electrized him with his rod, and hence-forward these two conducted all the policy, negotiations, legislatures and war." This role of Washington is especially surprising, in view of his remote and rigid personality, which has been embellished only by heroic panoramas—Washington Crossing the Delaware or braving the snows of Valley Forge—or moralistic fabrications like the child George confessing that he had really cut down his father's prized cherry tree. But interest in the life of this unvivid, glacial person does not abate. During the last twenty-five years there has been an average of some four new biographies of him published in the United States every year—including many books for children.

Both the life and legend of George Washington reveal some large features of American culture. First, of course, is the remarkable brevity of the history of the United States, compared to other great Western nations. Nations with longer pasts have had their Romulus and Remus, Saint Joan or King Arthur—offering the opportunity and the temptation to make myth into history. But in the United States our recent and abbreviated history has led us into the opposite temptation—to make history into myth. Of this the story of George Washington is a good illustration. Also we in the United States have idealized the self-made man, and we have harbored a wholesome and enduring suspicion of government and of those who cling to positions of power.

The dominant American national heroes have not been charismatic figures but what I would call Representative Men. Figures most prominent in our national pantheon are not men of superhuman inspiration expressing a "divine essence" in the mold of Carlyle's *Heroes and Hero-Worship;* rather they seem to embody and illustrate the common virtues or what we like to believe are the common virtues of our society. A short list would surely include—besides George Washington—Andrew Jackson and Abraham Lincoln. Recent candidates might include Franklin Roosevelt and Harry Truman.

An American writer once plausibly observed that "England's greatest contribution to the world is the works of Shakespeare; America's greatest contribution is the character of George Washington." The word "character" (not too popular in the United States nowadays, except in the polemics of presidential campaigns!) recurs again and again in the best remembered eulogies of Washington—so Thomas Jefferson, who worked closely with him observed. Daniel Webster, not given to understatement, declared that "America has furnished to the world the character of Washington, and if our American institutions had done nothing else, that alone would have entitled them to the respect of mankind." The unprecedented opportunities for Washington's display of character may not really have been a peculiar product of American institutions, but were provided also by British misjudgment, imprudence and doctrinaire politics. Still, William E. Gladstone, not backward in assessing other peoples' characters, placed Washington on the highest pedestal "supplied by history for public characters of extraordinary nobility and purity." An especially grudging recognition of the force of Washington's character was Oscar Wilde's observation that "The crude commercialism of America, its materialising spirit . . . are entirely due to the country having adopted for its national hero a man who was incapable of telling a lie."

The appeal of Washington's character is the more conspicuous when we see him in the panorama of the remarkable men of his age—what historians have called the Age of the Enlightenment. Paragons of that age, Benjamin Franklin and Thomas Jefferson, were his contemporaries and collaborators in public affairs. But they were men of surpassing wit and eloquence, at home in the cosmopolitan world of French philosophers and in the heritage of Western humanism, familiar with the history of empires, proud citizens of the international Republic of Letters. Franklin, a founder of the American Philosophical Society, and Jefferson, its longtime president, were colleagues on the frontiers of knowledge. It is hard to fit Washington into their company and imagine what they might have talked about beyond the pressing daily problems of defending colonial rights and organizing for the defense and survival of a new transatlantic nation.

Washington had almost no formal education. He appears to have had some schooling between the ages of seven and eleven. But, unlike his elder half brother Lawrence, he was never sent to England to school. When he was eleven his father died and the family could not afford it. Anyway his possessive and difficult mother probably would not have tolerated the separation. As a young man he had a reputation as a good marksman and a skillful horseman. Unlike Franklin and Jefferson, who were at home in the Paris salons, and John Adams, who served on diplomatic missions to Britain, France and the Netherlands, Washington never visited Europe. In fact, the only time he went outside the future boundaries of the United States was a brief trip to Barbados when he was nineteen to accompany his ailing half brother in search of a mild climate. He did not read Latin, and was embarrassed by his lack of knowledge of French, which once discouraged him from accepting an invitation to France.

Although Washington remained provincial in his experience and his domestic tastes, he never lost his transatlantic awe of things European. For example, when the question arose of the design for the proposed capitol building for the new republic, he wrote to Secretary of State Thomas Jefferson that the Capitol "ought to be upon a scale far superior to anything in *this* country." Only a domed building, Washington insisted, would have the required grandeur and elegance. Since there were no large domed structures in the United States at the time, Washington could only have seen them in illustrations. Still his hopes would eventually be amply fulfilled. About the same time, "beauteous Dome" became a hyperbolic metaphor for how the new Federal Constitution covered and protected all the states. For this dome too Washington would have some responsibility.

Washington's duties as commander required that he compose many letters, scores of which survive in his own clear hand. But he was never fluent or eloquent. "That Washington was not a scholar is certain," observed the acid New Englander John Adams, who served as his vice president, "That he was too illiterate, unlearned, unread for his station and reputation is equally past dispute." Washington himself seems to have been well aware of his intellectual limitations, and for his important state papers, he turned to more skillful pens. His intellectual interests and reading, apart from the pressing concerns of war and government, seem to have been focused on farming, which he called "the most delectable" of occupations. He exchanged advice on seeds and fertilizers with his fellow planter Thomas Jefferson, sought advice too from the English expert Arthur Young, put up a barn according to Young's instructions, and imported an English farmer to superintend operations at Mount Vernon.

Washington's biographers have been careful to note that his account books do reveal his purchase not only of books on military affairs and agriculture, but also newly popular English novels like *Tom Jones*. He seems to have read Pope and Addison, and he quoted the Bible. But the eminent American contemporaries with whom he dealt on equal terms were at home in the Greek and Latin classics and the heritage of English and continental philosophy, which was the main subject of the lively correspondence between Jefferson and Adams in their last years. Having first made his own reputation as a commander of frontier militia, Washington found his earliest heroes among military men. In 1759, to embellish Mount Vernon he ordered six portrait busts of his heroes from London. These were Alexander the Great, Julius Caesar, Charles XII of Sweden, Frederick II of Prussia, Prince Eugene, and the Duke of Marlborough. When his agent was unable to provide them, Washington did not accept the busts of poets and philosophers offered in their place.

As president, Washington revealed both his character and his good sense by willingly enlisting those who excelled him in expertise and experience. For fiscal matters and problems of the national debt, he relied on Alexander Hamilton, and for international relations on Thomas Jefferson. Even for the everyday questions of dignity and decorum, which he was aware would shape his public image, long before the age of public relation consultants, he leaned on Hamilton. When the new government was formed under the Federal Constitution, Washington complained that under the old Congress presidents had been "considered in no better light than a maitre d'hotel . . . for their table was considered as a public one and every person who could get introduced conceived that he had a right to be invited to it." Some advised him to protect himself with the trappings of royal pomp and inapproachability that might have been congenial to his natural reticence. But Hamilton helped him strike the shrewd balance that would increase public awe and admiration—between what Washington called "too free intercourse and too much familiarity."

The admiration for Washington's "character" was not illusory. It was rooted in qualities that were characteristically American—nurtured in the peculiar circumstances of a new transatlantic nation, on a sparsely populated continent, barren of ancient institutions.

The not inaccurate popular picture of the mature Washington as the slaveholding squire of spacious Mount Vernon plantations obscures the fact that his career was in many ways a parable of the American "Self-made Man." When his father died and George was only eleven, most of his father's estate was inherited by his two half brothers. Not until he came of age would he inherit his only portion, Ferry Farm. Meanwhile, George lived there with his mother, who was possessive in more senses than one, and actually delayed his possession of the farm until some thirty years later. Still, land, the obsession and the measure of things in colonial Virginia, was, one way or another, to dominate Washington's private fortunes.

By the time he was sixteen he had picked up enough mathematics to begin a career as a surveyor and he joined in a survey of Fairfax family lands. The next year (1749) he was assistant surveyor laying out the new town that was to be called Alexandria, a few miles north of Mount Vernon, and then he became surveyor of Culpepper County. At eighteen he used his surveying skills to claim some 1450 acres in the lower Shenandoah. When his half brother Lawrence died, he finally inherited Mount Vernon. But then his military ambitions, stimulated by Lawrence's example, drew him into the Virginia militia in the French and Indian War to defend English interests in the back country. He soon made his own reputation by leading a risky expedition to the French outposts on the shores of Lake Erie. By the age of twenty-three (1755) his courage and initiative in fighting to defend English landed interests against the French brought him appointment as colonel and commander in chief of all Virginia's forces. By the time Washington retired from the Virginia military service, his courage and energy had earned him a considerable reputation. But he never secured the royal commission that was his ambition. What might have been the course of history if he had! Incidentally, he had seen enough of the inflexible British military command to nourish his doubts of their military effectiveness.

Washington was only twenty-seven years old when he first retired from military life to Mount Vernon (1759) and married the wealthy widow Martha Custis, with two children. His ambition, courage and taste for "preferment" had already brought him a reputation that he never ceased to cherish. He took a seat in the House of Burgesses where he regularly attended and personally experienced some of the painful and costly consequences of British colonial policy. In a characteristically homely phrase he objected to the Stamp Act, because, he said, the British Parliament "hath no right to put their hands into my pocket, without my consent, than I have to put my hands into yours for money." He interrupted his life at Mount Vernon for an expedition to the frontier down the Ohio River, to locate bounty lands for the Virginia men he had recently commanded.

By the time Washington attended the first Continental Congress (1774) as Virginia delegate, he had definitely earned his right to command. After his efforts in military planning for the second Continental Congress in 1775, they put him in charge of all the American armies. By the age of 43, he had established his stature for courage and initiative in colonial military affairs. He was known to be a man of wealth, which also commended him to the delegates. The New York delegation thus felt reassured "that he may rather communicate lustre to his dignities than receive it, and that his country in his property, his kindred, and connections, may have sure pledges that he will faithfully perform the duties of this high office, and readily lay down his power when the general weal shall require it."

Washington informed the Congress that as commander he required no salary, and would accept only reimbursement of expenses. Congress had already decided on an allowance of $500 a month for his pay and expenses. Again in his first inaugural address as president in 1789, he declared that he would accept no salary, but only expenses. Luckily for him and his successors, the Congress did not take up his suggestion. The costs of the presidency would have ruined him. Instead, the Congress fixed his annual salary at $25,000, then a considerable sum, when cabinet members were receiving $3,500 and members of Congress $6 a day. The Washington story has scant resemblance to the log cabin to White House clichés or the self-help litany of Samuel Smiles. But he was an authentic early example of the American self-made man where he was born—into the Virginia colonial planter aristocracy.

That was a slaveholding aristocracy. And the peculiar institution was a touchy subject. Washington himself did not fail to note the parallel between the arbitrary rule of Britain over the American colonies and the "arbitrary sway" of Virginians over slaves. As the war was ending, Washington corresponded with Lafayette over a possible program of emancipation by setting up small estates where the Negroes would be employed as free tenants. In this plan Washington indicated his willingness to join, and he gave a friendly reception to British Methodist evangelists who came to petition the Virginia General Assembly to legislate gradual emancipation.

Washington expressed his agreement with them. Still he refused to sign their petition, saying only that if the matter came before the assembly he would write a letter of support. The laws of Virginia limited the freedom of slaveholders to emancipate their slaves. The law made it mandatory to provide freed slaves with support, and it is doubtful that another Virginia shareholder, Thomas Jefferson, who was increasingly in debt, could have afforded to free his slaves if he had determined to. After Jefferson's death his slaves, like his other possessions, were sold. But Washington did provide for the freeing of his slaves at his wife Martha's death and guaranteed their support with a fund he had been long accumulating. In the 1830s payments were still being made to his aging freedmen.

Washington's two principal aides in his presidency—Thomas Jefferson and Alexander Hamilton—both became icons of the political parties that were just forming. Their ideas perpetuated their influence. Although American political life would be conspicuously (and happily) weak in ideology, the influence of these nation-founders would survive in their words and doctrines. But this was not true of Washington. With the exception of a few state papers, his written legacy is letters on the practical affairs of the war or the presidency.

The heirs of Jefferson and Madison would be the Democratic-Republicans, the heirs of Hamilton and Adams would be the Federalists. But the heirs of Washington would be all Americans. His achievement was recorded in history and biography, not in political ideals and ideas. When generations praised Washington for "character," they were praising his personal achievement as the commander of an ill-equipped, poorly supplied, rag-tag militia on short-term enlistment fighting against the strongest power in the Western world. As president of the momentous Constitutional Convention of 1787, again he drew disparate forces together. He was notable for his overshadowing persuasive influence toward compromise and agreement on workable plans. Only reluctantly had he gone to the convention. He was aware of charges that he had violated his recent Cincinnatus pledge to return to private life when he resigned his command of continental forces. His final support of the Constitution transcended the sectional and ideological partisanship that had characterized the debate. He defended the Constitution simply as the best plan obtainable at the time, and because provision had been included for its amendment. His personal prestige was crucial in securing the adoption of the Constitution in the pivotal state of Virginia.

In two terms as president of the new nation Washington helped give shape to the vaguely defined office. And to give it a character that in times of crisis would transcend politics. He showed his ability to mediate the acrimonious disputes between Hamilton and Jefferson and their partisans—without himself becoming a doctrinaire advocate. The issues raised by the French Revolution and then the war between Britain and France sorely tested his ability to stand above partisan enthusiasms. While he leaned to the Federalists and a strong central government, he avoided the new party broils or involvement in the war in Europe, aiming as he explained in his Farewell Address, "to endeavour to gain time to our country to settle and mature its yet recent institutions and to progress without interruption to that degree of strength and consistency, which is necessary to give it humanly speaking, the command of its own fortunes."

This continual awareness of his own limitations and of the perils of doctrinaire politics reinforced Washington's reputation for character. By transcending the party divisions of his time he helped set the stage for a national politics that was conspicuously interest-oriented and unideological. So too he was a personal symbol of the new American ideal of independence. And he remained wary of revolutionary enthusiasms like those that had disrupted France. When his friend the Marquis de Lafayette sent him, as a token of their common opposition to tyranny, the key of the Bastille, he did not respond with a "hurrah" but with the return token of a pair of shoe buckles manufactured in the city of Washington.

Despite, or perhaps because of, his diffidence in taking on offices of great power—the command of the continental forces and the presidency—he earned his reputation of character by his steadfastness and adeptness. Finally, by the end of his life he attested his character by his exemplary readiness to yield power. In his command of the poorly drilled and transient American militia forces, Washington, as Professor Edmund S. Morgan has observed, revealed an uncanny sense of the geography of power and for the frugal use of the limited colonial resources. His experience of the American terrain made him resist the temptation to erect elaborate stationary defenses and he saw the mistake of General Howe in exaggerating the military importance of urban centers like Philadelphia. He knew that he needed to keep his small force concentrated and mobile. And this feel for the feasible American uses of power helped explain his climactic defeat of Cornwallis at Yorktown. American weakness required frugality and independence of judgment against British power and the conventional military wisdom. These were as much virtues of character as of intelligence.

The dominant metaphor in the traditional portrait of Washington is the image of Cincinnatus—the legendary Roman farmer called from the plough in 458 B.C. to save the blockaded Roman army. He was made dictator, defeated the enemy, and then quietly returned to his farm. The figure of the Cincinnatus hero—in George Washington—illustrates still another feature of American character. As we have noted, the cult of the hero, celebrated by Carlyle and Nietzsche, would exalt the charisma and vehement energy of the bold leader over more placid satisfactions. But Jefferson (and other Americans after him) amended Locke's "Life, Liberty and Property" to read "Life, Liberty and the Pursuit of Happiness." Washington's career surely showed how property might be a prop of character. Washington's career as the "Cincinnatus of the West" (in Byron's phrase) dramatized the third item in the American trinity, "the pursuit of happiness." Washington never lost his eagerness for the relaxed life of Mount Vernon and its domestic responsibilities, which he always preferred when life and liberty did not urgently call him elsewhere. "Pursuit" meant not merely the chasing after, but the active practice of a profession or recreation (as in the pursuit of law or medicine). In that sense too, Washington at Mount Vernon was a paragon.

Americans' deep-rooted suspicions of military and political power would be expressed in the fact that our prime national hero would be celebrated not only for his leadership, but equally for his impressive willingness to yield the reins of power and return to his community.

On October 19th, 1781, Cornwallis surrendered at Yorktown, and the final Peace Treaty with Great Britain was signed in Paris on September 3rd, 1783. In an emotional scene Washington bid farewell to his officers at Fraunces' Tavern in New York City. Then on December 23rd, he ceremoniously resigned his commission as commander in chief. He stood before the Congress in Annapolis "to surrender the trust committed to me, and to claim the indulgence of our Independence and Sovereignty, and pleased with the opportunity afforded the United States of becoming a respectable Nation, I resign with satisfaction the Appointment I accepted with diffidence." "Having now finished the work assigned me, I retire from the great theatre of Action . . . and take my leave of all the employments of public life." So it was that Washington's modesty, self-control and reluctance to reach for power became proverbial. It was picturesquely—if vulgarly—expressed in the metaphor of the popular humorist Artemus Ward, who said, "The prevailin' weakness of most public men is to Slop Over. . . . G Washington never slopt over."

Washington plunged into the daily affairs of Mount Vernon, but soon was president of a company to build canals and exploit the lands beyond the Allegheny. Incidentally, he was now selected president of the new Society of the Cincinnati. By May 1787, he was a Virginia delegate to the Constitutional Convention in Philadelphia, where he was elected president. In September, when the Constitution had been drafted, he returned again to Mount Vernon. Then, in March 1789, came "the event which I have long dreaded"—unanimous election as the first President of the United States. Though he greeted the news with "a heart filled with distress," "foreseeing the ten thousand embarrassments, perplexities and troubles to which I must again be exposed," it was a call which he could not refuse. On completion of his first term as president (in 1792) he was not eager for another term. But the festering partisan spirit led others to believe that only Washington—known for his character and not his ideas—could mediate the partisan bitterness. Again he was unanimously elected. His remarkable four-sentence Second Inaugural Address suggested, in its formality, his lack of enthusiasm for the assignment. This second term was to be even less comfortable than the first had been. He was under attack from all sides for his neutrality stand, in his belief that two decades of peace were needed to make the nation strong enough to defend its independence. He became the target of personal abuse to which he was not accustomed, but which is familiar in the presidential politics of our time.

As he completed his second term, Washington was still being solicited to stand for a third term. But he had long since indicated his desire not to run for the presidency again. This time he was not to be persuaded. And it is poetically appropriate that his enduring legacy to our American political literature should have been a Farewell Address collaboratively produced by representatives of the opposing parties of his time. Above all other considerations, Washington set the independent spirit of the nation to which he had devoted much of his life. And his willingness, even his insistence, on giving up coveted positions of power to allow others to take their turn, became an American tradition.

On its two-hundredth anniversary, it is appropriate for Americans to remember and reconsider this great document. *A Sacred Union of Citizens* is a contribution not only to the current renaissance in Washington scholarship but also to contemporary debates about citizenship and the American character.

Daniel J. Boorstin

1

REMEMBERING WASHINGTON'S LEGACY

"*O*ur Washington is no more! The hero, the patriot, and the sage of America, the man on whom, in times of danger, every eye was turned, and all hopes were placed, lives now only in his own great actions, and in the hearts of an affectionate and afflicted people." With these words, drafted by James Madison and Henry Lee, John Marshall offered resolutions in Congress calling for a national period of mourning and the creation of an appropriate memorial to honor the memory of President George Washington after his death in December 1799.

"Ancient and modern names are diminished before him. Greatness and guilt have too often been allied, but his fame is whiter than it is brilliant," read the official message of the Senate, addressed to President John Adams. "Let his countrymen consecrate the memory of the heroic General Washington, the patriotic statesman and the virtuous sage. Let them teach their children never to forget that the fruit of his labors and his example are their inheritance." Washington's successor answered in turn: "The life of our Washington can not suffer by a comparison with those of other countries who have been most celebrated and exalted by fame. The attributes and decoration of royalty could only have served to eclipse the majesty of those virtues which made him, from being a modest citizen, a more resplendent luminary. . . . For his fellow citizens, if their prayers could have been answered, he would have been immortal."[1]

Congressman Henry Lee—Lighthorse Harry of Revolutionary War renown—was chosen to deliver the official eulogy, which included these memorable words:

> First in war, first in peace, and first in the hearts of his countrymen, he
> was second to none in humble and enduring scenes of private life. Pious,

1

just, humane, temperate, and sincere; uniform, dignified, and commanding; his example was as edifying to all around him as were the effects of
that example lasting. . . . Correct throughout, vice shuddered in his presence and virtue always felt his fostering hand. The purity of his private
character gave effulgence to his public virtues. . . . Such was the man for
whom our nation mourns.[2]

Two centuries later, Washington remains one of the most recognized
figures in all American history. But is Washington still alive in the hearts of
his countrymen? In recent years, there has been a major revival of interest
in, and renewed respect for, the man described by Henry Lee as America's
first citizen. We suspect that this is no accident. At present, Americans
increasingly question their national purpose and role in the world. They
have won the Cold War; but they are uncertain how to live in a world
without a clear and present danger. They express pride in their citizenship
and heritage; but they doubt the ability of government, and politics, to
address the very real problems of society. They celebrate and try to enlarge
their individual freedom; but they fear the breakup of community and
family, and the deeper loss of morality, that seem to result from unrestrained
individualism. Under these circumstances, it is no wonder that Americans
might look to the father of their country for guidance and inspiration.

Remarkably, this renaissance has paid relatively little attention to
Washington's most famous writing. The Farewell Address of 1796 was long
considered to be a major contribution to American political thought; and,
along with the Declaration of Independence, the Constitution, and *The
Federalist Papers*, it was considered one of the great documents of American
history. Washington's own objective, expressed in the Farewell Address,
was "to offer to your solemn contemplation and to recommend to your
frequent review, some sentiments which are the result of much reflection,
of no inconsiderable observation, and which appear to me all important to
the permanency of your felicity as a People."[3] To be sure, Washington
would not have insisted that he or his generation held a monopoly on
political wisdom; he fully expected that experience and new circumstances
would lead to changes in the form and substance of American politics. And
the Farewell Address certainly cannot be read or understood in isolation
from the events and personalities that confronted Washington in 1796—
any more than can, say, the Gettysburg Address be understood apart from
the Civil War.

But Washington was not alone in claiming some "permanency" for
the Farewell Address. John Quincy Adams expressed his hope that the
American people "may not only impress all its admonitions upon their
hearts, but that it may serve as the foundation upon which the whole sys-

tem of their future policy may rise, the admiration and example of future time." When Thomas Jefferson and James Madison were designing the primary reading list for the University of Virginia in 1825, they described the Farewell Address as one of "the best guides to the distinctive principles" of American government. In their biographies of Washington, John Marshall and Parson Weems saw fit to reprint the Farewell Address in its entirety. Marshall described it as a "last effort to impress upon his countrymen those great political truths which had been the guides of his own administration," and argued that it contained "precepts to which the American statesman can not too frequently recur." Weems thought that "this little piece, about the length of an ordinary sermon, may do as much good to the people of America as any sermon ever preached, that DIVINE ONE on the mount excepted."[4]

Daniel Webster, speaking at the centennial of Washington's birth in 1832, recounted at length the principles that animated the first president. According to Webster, those principles were to be found in the Constitution itself, the great measures recommended and approved by Washington, his speeches to Congress, and in "that most interesting paper, his Farewell Address to the People of the United States." The Address was "full of truths important at all times," and Webster called for "a renewed and wide diffusion of the admirable paper, and an earnest invitation to every man in the country to reperuse and consider it."[5]

To see why American statesmen of all political persuasions placed such emphasis on the Farewell Address, we need to place it in the context of Washington's view of, and role in, the Founding. The Address has become popularly viewed as being concerned primarily with foreign policy; we recall Washington's great rule of conduct—to have with other nations "as little political connection as possible . . . to steer clear of permanent Alliances, with any portion of the foreign world."[6] But as we shall see, the Address is actually much more comprehensive than this. The two great themes of the Address are union at home and independence abroad. But union and independence were not sought for their own sake. They were necessary preconditions for, and the consequence of, the development of what Washington called a "national character."

Washington did not believe that by establishing and vindicating their national existence as an independent, free-standing people and political community Americans would automatically assume a certain type of character. It must, or at least could, be a consciously chosen identity within the limits of the humanly possible. Neither the American nor the republican dimension of Washington's project was assured by the environment of the New World or the predispositions of the people. The formation of the national character was above all to be determined by "reflection and choice" (in the famous words of *The Federalist Papers*). To be sure, America was not a tabula rasa. Washington frequently referred to the material abundance of the New World, which was the fortunate "stage" or "theater" on which the American drama would be played. He was aware that the American people had certain preexisting attributes of character, both good and bad, and that major differences of view existed among the various sections and interests of the new country. All of these facts importantly shaped and limited the choices available to Washington and his colleagues at the time of the Founding.

In fact, Washington believed that there were strong tendencies toward a different and dangerous type of public and private character for the nation. For the common man, Washington feared that indolence, drunkenness, and licentiousness would replace the republican virtues of industriousness, sobriety, and private virtue. The potential dark side of the American character would call forth leaders with attributes very much different from those that Washington believed essential if the experiment in popular government was to succeed. These men would enter into politics to satisfy private and selfish concerns rather than by an ambition to do public good. Experience during and after the Revolution had taught Washington that such leaders tended to attach themselves to the politics and interest of the states, where they could more easily flatter and support the degradation of the "yeomanry."

In Washington's judgment, by the middle of the 1780s the corruption of public and private character had reached a point where a decisive choice had to be made. Either the republican experiment would be revitalized through a renewed commitment to good government and public justice or anarchy would ensue. If anarchy was the outcome, despotism would not be far behind. The good men of society would then have to decide whether they would be ruled by despots, or themselves rule despotically. This Hobson's choice would weigh most heavily of all on Washington, who would inevitably be considered as the best and probably the only possible "benign despot" or monarch who could still assure some sort of justice. These thoughts are unstated but painfully evident in Washington's private correspondence of the period.

Such an outcome would be unnecessary if Americans could strengthen the better elements of the national character. This strengthening was a process of political deliberation about the proper relationship between rulers and ruled in an extended republic. By exercising reflection and choice through the drafting, ratification, and implementation of a well-ordered national constitution, the American people vindicated their own rights and the rights of mankind. Washington believed that good political choices, in turn, had critical and salutary effects on private behavior.

To be sure, the initial agreement on the Constitution did not foreclose further controversy over the American character. During Washington's own presidency, two distinct views of the meaning of "American" and "republican" emerged under the intellectual and political leadership of Thomas Jefferson and Alexander Hamilton. Washington never believed it necessary to choose publicly between the two, although for many he became identified with the latter. His role was rather to help define the boundaries of acceptable choice for his friends and fellow citizens, and to provide the grounds of reconciliation.

For Washington, there was an inseparable relationship between individual character, or virtue, and the national character. This relationship suggests the existence of a regime, or a true political community: that is, not merely a certain form of government but a distinct way of life, a commitment to justice of a certain sort. In a regime, the soul—the animating principle—of the political community reflects, and is reflected by, a distinct type of individual. The regime, through its laws and institutions, endeavors to form the character and inculcate the virtues that are appropriate to its peculiar way of life. In classical political philosophy, democracy was regarded as a defective regime in large part because it was not a true regime: it was open to all types of characters, vicious as well as virtuous. In more modern times, liberal democracy (which is not the same as ancient democracy) has likewise been criticized—or praised, depending on one's taste— for its lack of character, its moral permissiveness, its allowance for excessive individualism.

The national character, according to Washington, was to be both American and republican. The national character would reflect, and in turn would depend upon, the character, or virtue, of individual citizens. In Washington's public and private writings, he constantly elaborated on the idea of character and defined not only what it meant to be a man of good character but also a nation of good character. In the First Inaugural he said that "there is no truth more thoroughly established than that there exists in the economy and course of nature, an indissoluble union between virtue and happiness; between duty and advantage, between the genuine maxims of an honest and magnanimous policy, and the solid rewards of public prosperity and felicity." In the Farewell Address the connection between private and public happiness made religion and morality "a necessary spring of popular government" and an indispensable support to political prosperity.[7] Maintaining the proper dispositions and good habits of citizenship was central to achieving the collective national ends of safety and happiness. Far from being based on the separation of rights from duties, the American character was based on the idea that these rights required a commitment to moral virtue, in individuals and in the republic as a whole.

Washington set out his public understanding of the American character most notably in his Circular Address to the States in 1783, upon his retirement from the army, and in his First Inaugural Address of 1789. The final and most mature statement from Washington came on 19 September 1796, when he addressed his "friends and fellow citizens" and announced his retirement from public life. Despite the partisan turmoil and lack of civility that characterized Washington's last days in office, he nevertheless wrote in the Farewell Address as if the Founding were complete, as if what remained were the perpetuation of the regime and its character. To be sure, this was no small task. Abraham Lincoln thought it to be an even greater one than that of the Founding itself. The task of perpetuation remains with us today, in no less demanding albeit in much different circumstances.

It is in this spirit that we review the teachings of the Farewell Address. The reader will find that this volume is something more than a narrow commentary on the Address itself but something less than a comprehensive assessment of Washington's statesmanship. We feel compelled to go beyond the text because Washington himself invites us to do so by referring in the Address to his previous speeches and deeds. In various public statements and private correspondence, Washington went into greater detail about many of the central themes of the Address, and we rely heavily on those sources to help understand and illuminate his arguments. (By using the Farewell Address as something of an index, or guide, to Washington's plans and policies, we also dispel the notion that the first president was merely a cypher for more intelligent men or that the Address was simply a partisan political tract.) But we are equally conscious of the limits of our enterprise: to do full justice to Washington and the Founding would require an account of Plutarchean (or Thucydidean) magnitude. We only hope that ours will serve as a modest but useful contribution toward that eventual and more complete assessment.

We have divided our assessment into chapters dealing with Washington's overall view of, and contribution to, the American Founding; the composition and content of the Address, focusing on how Washington hoped to shape the proper habits and dispositions of the people; Washington's views on foreign policy and the possibility of an American approach to the world that comprehended interest and justice; a review of the uses, and misuses, of the Farewell Address by statesmen and scholars throughout American history; and a short concluding chapter on the contemporary applicability of the Address. Because some readers may want to concentrate on specific issues associated with the Address (for example, religion and morality), the chapters have been written largely as self-contained essays. This has unavoidably resulted in some overlap and repetition in the text, for which we apologize to our more diligent interlocutors. We have quoted faithfully from the original sources, including any misspellings or odd punctuation.

As we reach the two-hundredth anniversary of Washington's great valedictory, then, let us accept Webster's invitation to "reperuse and consider" the Farewell Address, to see if in fact it contains "truths important at all times." Let us go beyond the Washington of legend and historical partisanship. Let us see how Washington recognized that most men are governed most of the time by the prospect of some interest or reward, yet proposed to define a regime that proclaimed itself to be the best hope of mankind for decent and even elevated political life. Let us see if there is any validity to the judgment of John Adams upon Washington's death: "His example is now complete, and it will teach wisdom and virtue to magistrates, citizens, and men, not only in the present age, but in future generations, as long as our history shall be read."[8]

2

ESTABLISHING THE
NATIONAL CHARACTER

*T*hroughout his adult lifetime there was hardly a period when George Washington was not in a position to bring his deep-seated ideas and the lessons of his experience into fruition, influencing not only events but also the men around him. We constantly see him with his hand on the political pulse of the nation, all the while urging, counseling, warning, bolstering, and leading his fellow patriots in their common efforts. He was the de facto leader of the colonial struggle and the personification of the American Revolution. As commander of continental forces during the Revolution, General Washington led a rag-tag army to victory against the strongest and best-trained military force in the world. In retirement he was the hub of correspondence among the most thoughtful men of the day. He was crucial to the success of the Constitutional Convention, and his personal support of the resulting document, more than anything else, assured its final approval. His election to the presidency, the office designed with him in mind, was absolutely essential to the establishment of the new nation. So dominant was this one figure that many spoke of the Founding era as nothing less than "the Age of Washington."[1]

Yet Washington is best known not for his long resume but for his solid character. The Continental Congress appointed him to be commander in chief of all continental forces in 1775 because he had military experience and was from Virginia, to be sure, but most of all because he displayed the qualities of character—courage, integrity, loyalty, dedication—that were needed to build and lead a republican army. Washington's character was the symbolic glue that held the other Founders together when they weakened or strayed from course and gave them reassurance and confidence in their efforts to build a republican government. The vast powers of the presidency, as one delegate to the Constitutional Convention of 1787 noted, would not have been made as great "had not many of the members cast their eyes towards General Washington as president; and shaped their ideas of the powers to be given to a president, by their opinions of his virtue."[2]

Washington's understanding of moral character did not stop with George Washington, but extended to his countrymen as well. He believed that the formation of character—whether of a man or a nation—was the first and most important step toward independence and greatness. "[T]he first transactions of a nation, like those of an individual upon his first entrance into life," Washington wrote at the time of the ratification of the Constitution, "make the deepest impression, and are to form the leading traits in its character."[3] The success of the American experiment in self-government would require good laws and good citizens, and Washington set out to establish a nation of both. The way to do so, he concluded, was to establish rightly from the very beginning not only a sense of character as a nation but also a nation of character.

Washington's own understanding of character as a political principle, then, should not be overlooked when it comes to exploring his view of the American Founding. Indeed, the cornerstone of Washington's statesmanship was the formation of an independent, national American character. Washington sought to establish the nation—to found a new order of the ages—in the hearts and minds of the people by personifying, defining, and encouraging what he believed ought to be the leading habits and dispositions of this national character. This lifelong project, as it developed throughout every aspect of his career, forms the background to the Farewell Address of 1796.

The best portrait of Washington left by a close associate was written by Thomas Jefferson, erstwhile opponent of Federalist policies and some-time critic of Washington. Jefferson gave this more considered view of the man in 1814: "His mind was great and powerful, without being of the very first order; his penetration strong, though not so acute as that of Newton, Bacon or Locke; and as far as he saw, no judgment was ever sounder. It was slow in operation, being little aided by invention or imagination, but sure in conclusion." Though Washington was no abstract thinker—at least not of the type of Jefferson's favorite political philosophers—his judgment was both sound and sure. He followed his best judgment under particular circumstances, often pursuing what was at the time a bold course, one that seemed obvious only in hindsight. In short, he displayed the practical wisdom of statesmanship, guiding his people through the dangers of establishing their own freedom, remaining alive to the difficulties and challenges of founding a new nation. "To inveigh against things that are past and irremediable," Washington wrote in 1781, "is unpleasing; but to steer clear of the shelves and rocks we have struck upon, is the part of wisdom, equally incumbent on political, as other men, who have their own little bark, or that of others to navigate through the intricate paths of life, or the trackless Ocean to the haven of secury. and rest."[4]

"Perhaps the strongest feature in his character was *prudence*," Jefferson continued in his portrait, "never acting until every circumstance, every consideration, was maturely weighed; refraining if he saw a doubt, but when once decided, going through with his purpose, whatever obstacles opposed." Prudence, in the classical sense, is the virtue of deliberating well on the proper means to the ends set by moral virtue. As prudence presupposes the presence of moral virtue, the measure of the prudent man is good character. Jefferson concluded:

> His integrity was pure, his justice the most inflexible I have ever known, no motives of interest or consanguinity, of friendship or hatred, being able to bias his decision. He was, indeed, in every sense of the words, a wise, a good, and a great man. On the whole, his character was, in its mass, perfect, in nothing bad, in few points indifferent; and it may truly be said, that never did nature and fortune combine more perfectly to make a man great, and to place him in the same constellation with whatever worthies have merited from man an everlasting remembrance.

Washington's moral sense was the compass of both his private and public life, having become for him a "second" nature. The accumulation of the habits and dispositions, both good and bad, that one acquired over time defined one's character. In the eighteenth century "character" was also shorthand for the persona for which one was known and was tied to one's public reputation. Indeed, many historians today argue that "character" was largely synonymous with "reputation" for men of affairs in the eighteenth century and that concern for character was driven by the need to create, and protect, one's good name. In an important sense, this was true: for example, in financial matters, the reputation for being able to meet one's obligations was essential for getting credit in a society that lacked modern devices for money transactions. But for Washington what mattered was that the reputation of good character be deserved: self-respect preceded public respect, and self-respect required virtuous intentions and behavior. Individuals with self-respect were motivated by honor in the highest and best sense. The best way to establish a good reputation, Washington knew, was to be, in fact, a good man. "I hope I shall always possess firmness and virtue enough to maintain (what I consider the most enviable of all titles) the character of an honest man," he told Hamilton, "as well as prove (what I desire to be considered in reality) that I am."[5]

That Washington was known for his good character was no accident or coincidence. All his life Washington worked hard at being a gentleman. This was already evident in one of his earliest writings, an adolescent copybook record of one hundred and ten "Rules of Civility and Decent Behavior in Company and Conversation." Drawn from an early etiquette book, these social maxims taught lessons of good manners concerning everything from how to treat one's superiors ("In speaking to men of Quality do not lean nor look them full in the face") to how to moderate one's own behavior ("Let your recreations be manful not sinful"). It ended with a more significant expression of civility: an admonition to "keep alive in your breast that little spark of celestial fire called conscience."[6] Simple rules of decent conduct, Washington always held, formed the backbone of good character.

Washington constantly warned of "the necessity of paying due attention to the moral virtues" and avoiding the "scenes of vice and dissipation" often presented to youth. Because an early and proper education in both manners and morals would form the leading traits of one's life, he constantly urged the development of good habits and the unremitting practice of moral virtue. "To point out the importance of circumspection in your conduct, it may be proper to observe that a good moral character is the first essential of man, and that the habits contracted at your age are generally indelible, and your conduct here may stamp your character through life," he advised one young correspondent. "It is therefore highly important that you should endeavor not only to be learned but virtuous." The first object of education was to acquire as much knowledge as one could, thereby establishing the habits of earnestness, industry, and seriousness. And while the beginnings of education depended upon it, the end product of education was never unattached in Washington's mind from moral character. The "advantages of a finished education," Washington wrote, were both a "highly cultivated mind, and a proper sense of your duties to God and man."[7]

Washington's life was a constant striving to control the passions and habituate the qualities of good character. As a young man, Washington displayed high ambitions and a desire for military glory. When he began his military career in 1752 he set out to prove himself a dedicated and patriotic soldier of the British crown. In accepting one early military command, for instance, he noted that he would have to give up "what at present constitutes the chief part of my happiness; i.e., the esteem and notice the country has been pleased to honour me with." He quickly learned, however, that mere reputation was no match for the requirements (and rewards) of duty, principle, and honor. When he took control of the

American continental forces in 1775, he told his wife that he could not avoid the position without exposing his character to censures that would reflect dishonorably upon himself, yet he sensed a "kind of destiny" and hoped his appointment was "designed to answer some good purpose." When his close friend Henry Lee urged him in 1788 to accept the presidency out of a regard not only for the happiness of the American people but also for his own fame and reputation, Washington responded that he would not act for the sake of the latter: "Though I prize, as I ought, the good opinion of my fellow citizens; yet, if I know myself, I would not seek or retain popularity at the expense of one social duty or moral virtue. . . . And certain I am, whensoever I shall be convinced the good of my country requires my reputation to be put in risque, regard for my own fame will not come in competition with an object of so much magnitude." [8] Thomas Jefferson understood Washington to be risking all of his fame by becoming president:

> Nobody who has tried public & private life can doubt that you were much happier on the banks of the Potowmac than you will be in New York. But there is nobody so well qualified as yourself to put our new machine into regular action, nobody the authority of whose name could have so effectually crushed opposition at home, and produced respect abroad. *I am sensitive of the immensity of the sacrifice on your part. Your measure of fame was full to the brim: and therefore you have nothing to gain. But there are cases wherein it is a duty to risk all against nothing, and I believe this was exactly the case.* [9]

The Lessons of War

During the American Revolution, General Washington fully expected his soldiers and officers to follow the rules of moral behavior and conduct themselves as patriots deserving of freedom and independence—in short, to display the character of republicans. In fact, his political and military leadership turned on the sense of character and common purpose that he imparted and encouraged in the continental army as a way of building the diverse forces under his command into a unified and committed fighting force. As the first means of advancing the larger project of making seemingly disparate groups into one nation, Washington made the army not just an instrument of war but also a mechanism for demonstrating and transmitting a national character.

Early in his tenure as commander in chief Washington observed that the men of the continental army were brave and good, men "who with pleasure it is observed, are addicted to fewer Vices than are commonly found in Armies." In his private correspondence, however, he reflected deep misgivings about relying on patriotism, bravery, and virtue alone to build an army for a long and bloody war. Once the patriotic passions of the moment had settled down, Washington noted, most soldiers were motivated by their self-interest. In order to act as a unit it was necessary for that narrow interest to be directed, if not transcended, by a common interest compatible with the principles and ends of the Revolution. Thus, the first element of Washington's wartime policy stemmed from a general reform of the existing army and centered on encouraging discipline and the basic civility needed to build camaraderie and teach the greater good of their common cause. "If we would pursue a right System of policy," Washington believed, "there should be none of these distinctions. We should all be considered, Congress, Army, etc. as one people, embarked in one Cause, in one interest; acting on the same principle and to the same End."[10]

Over the first six months of the war Washington reorganized the existing forces under his command with the intent of creating a disciplined army. "Men accustomed to unbounded freedom, and no controul," Washington averred, "cannot brook the Restraint which is indispensably necessary to the good order and Government of an Army; without which, licentiousness, and every kind of disorder triumphantly reign." General Washington's initial orders are especially instructive, for in them he laid out the rules by which he "expected and required" his army to act and around which the new army would be built. The orders make clear that, for Washington, moral as well as physical discipline was necessary for good order. First, he expected all geographic distinctions to be laid aside "so that one and the same Spirit may animate the whole." The Continental Congress had placed the troops of the several colonies under their pay and service, making them the army of "the United Provinces of North America." The only competition between various individuals and states should be over who would render the most essential service to "the great and common cause in which we are all engaged." Second, he expected that exact discipline and due subordination be observed, the failure of which would lead to "shameful disappointment and disgrace." Third, he expected a "due observance" of the rules that forbade profane cursing, swearing, and drunkenness. Fourth, he expected all officers and soldiers not on actual duty punctually to attend divine services "to implore the blessings of heaven upon the means used for our safety and defense." Fifth, he expected his officers to pay attention to the neatness and cleanliness of the soldiers.[11]

Washington hoped that "every officer and man, will endeavor so to live, and act, as becomes a Christian Soldier defending the dearest Rights and Liberties of his country." His first thought in his orders to commence the reorganized continental army in January 1776 concerned the importance of his example to the officers and soldiers. Washington expected that "a laudable Spirit of emulation, will now take place, and pervade the whole of it; without such a Spirit, few Officers have ever arrived to any degree of Reputation, nor did any Army ever become formidable." The character that Washington wished to have emulated and encouraged—the reputation for which the army was to be known—was high indeed: "Our own Country's Honor," Washington wrote in his General Orders of 2 July 1776, "all call upon us for a vigorous and manly exertion, and if we now shamefully fail, we shall become infamous to the whole world. Let us therefore rely upon the goodness of the Cause, and the aid of the supreme Being, in whose hands Victory is, to animate and encourage us to great and noble Actions."[12]

Washington's officer corps played a unique role in this character-building effort. Time, effort, and an uncommon degree of attention were required to acquaint men with the duties of the soldier and habituate them to the discipline of the army. It was necessary that the officers attend to Washington's orders, obey them rigidly, communicate and explain their meaning to the troops, and, if necessary, punish their neglect. In addition to ensuring the discipline of the army, however, the officers also had the important job of being role models for their soldiers: "Enjoin this upon the Officers, and let them inculcate, and press home to the Soldiery, the Necessity of Order and Harmony among them, who are embark'd in one common Cause, and mutually contending for all that Freemen hold dear." This would serve to raise the tone and character of recruits, who Washington knew were often influenced by concerns of narrow self-interest, by substituting for self-interest an enlarged sense of the common good. "Discourage vice in every shape," Washington told one of his officers, "and impress upon the mind of every man, from the first to the lowest, the importance of the cause, and what it is they are contending for." Thus, Washington sought men of good character, motivated by the gentlemanly virtues, as officers in his army.[13] To be sure, many of the old, established elite had prior military training, and thus were a natural base to recruit from, but Washington wanted men of talent and ability (such as Alexander Hamilton) above those of wealth and family.

At the end of the war, in his Farewell Orders to the Armies of the United States in November 1783, Washington posited that the victory in the Revolutionary War was "little short of a standing miracle." Few besides Washington could have imagined from the beginning that "the most violent local prejudices would cease so soon, and that Men who came from

different parts of the Continent, strongly disposed, by the habits of education, to despise and quarrel with each other, would instantly become one
patriotic band of Brothers." With the end of the war and the establishment
of independence, it was now necessary for this united patriotism and common dedication to republican government to infuse the general populace.
Washington expected all of his officers and soldiers to become loyal and
productive citizens and play a role in firming up and establishing the new
government. His "last injunction to every Officer and Soldier" was that
they—now "his worthy fellow Citizens"—support the principles of the
federal government and an increase of the powers of the union. He hoped
that his troops would "carry with them into civil society the most conciliating dispositions; and that they should prove themselves not less virtuous
and useful as *Citizens*, than they have been perservering and victorious as
Soldiers."[14] By bringing their good habits and dispositions to the new nation, Washington's soldiers would now be models of citizenship for the rest
of their countrymen. Note that while Washington understood that martial
pursuits were one of the classical means of inculcating civic virtue, he did
not propose using the army to bring specifically military virtues, which
were incompatible with republicanism, to civil society.

The Critical Period

Having finished the work he had been assigned, Washington resigned
his military commission to Congress to return to private life as a farmer and
concerned citizen. Doing so in a clear and public manner, Washington
not only proved his loyalty to the country he served, by recognizing the
sovereignty of the people, but also testified that republican citizenship was
nobler than dictatorial rule. "The moderation and virtue of a single character," Jefferson later wrote of Washington, "probably prevented this Revolution from being closed, as most others have been, by a subversion of that
liberty it was intended to establish."[15]

During the war, Washington was never reluctant to point out the
weaknesses and failings of the existing political system in meeting the military requirements of the Revolution. Each colony had a militia, but they
were untrained and could only be called to service with the consent of
the particular state legislature. The troops that did fall under Washington's
command were subject to short enlistments. As a result, volunteers went
home as their enlistments expired or whenever their pay was not forthcom-
ing, leading to a constant ebb and flow of recruits. Washington, dependent
on the whims of state legislatures for the strength of his army and faced

with a weak and unwilling Congress, was forced to spend much of his time writing to governors, begging for men and supplies. "I believe I may, with great truth affirm," Washington noted, "that no Man perhaps since the first Institution of Armys ever commanded one under more difficult Circumstances, than I have done. To enumerate the particulars would fill a volume."[16]

Congress, unable to directly levy taxes and collect revenue to meet the demand for personnel and material, at first relied on the printing press to pay the war debt, increasing the supply of continental currency and issuing credit certificates in depreciating continental dollars. Once France entered the war, Congress turned more to loans from foreign countries, banks, and domestic lenders, building up a continental debt that threatened the war effort and that would cause serious economic problems after the war. "More than half the perplexities I have experienced in the course of my command," Washington later wrote, "and almost the whole of the difficulties & distress of the Army, have their origin here." Under circumstances of inflation and uncontrollable price increases, by 1778 Washington doubted whether the war could be carried on much longer and feared that the conflict would be lost by the failure of American finances.[17]

The root cause of America's political distresses, Washington believed, lay in the thirteen individual states. Mired in their own local concerns and prejudices, the states had become hotbeds of political corruption and poor management. As a result of their disagreements and refusal to work together, the common interests of America were moldering and sinking into irretrievable ruin, a situation that would eventually and necessarily undermine the states as well. Washington feared that the best men would be content with places of honor and profit in their home states instead of becoming involved in national affairs and serving "the good of the common weal." The financial situation, meanwhile, encouraged speculation on the part of the creditors and financiers. Contemplating "the gloomy side of things" in 1779, Washington saw "a very disagreeable train" of events: "The rapid decay of our currency, the extinction of public spirit, the increasing rapacity of the times, the want of harmony in our councils, the declining zeal of the people, the discontents and distresses of the officers of the army; and I may add, the prevailing security and insensibility of danger, are symptoms, in my eye of a most alarming nature." In Washington's mind the breakdown of political and economic order, and the activities of those seeking to profit at the expense of the already strapped war effort, "afford too many melancholy proofs of the decay of public virtue."[18]

The Articles of Confederation, drafted in late 1777 but not approved until early 1781, created little more than a league of friendship and quickly proved both insufficient to the task of supporting the war effort and an obstacle to the establishment of a stronger union that Washington and other nationalists supported. Each state remained sovereign and independent and, although Congress was given authority over foreign affairs, it could neither levy taxes nor regulate commerce and was still completely dependent on the states for revenue. The fatal flaw of the Articles was the requirement that any amendments secure the unanimous approval of state legislatures. As a result, all attempts to amend the Articles to give Congress some sort of coercive authority over the states or an independent source of revenue failed.

From the beginning, Washington saw fundamental political reform as the best and only way to restore and legitimate the principles of the Revolution and bring the nation back to its republican roots, for "unless the bodies politick will exert themselves to bring things back to first principles, correct abuses, and punish our internal foes, inevitable ruin must follow." Marginal changes and administrative improvements would not be enough to correct these problems: "nothing therefore in my judgment can save us but a total reformation in our own conduct." Washington advocated a permanent union of the states upon republican principles under a well-defined, national structure. The American people, Washington believed, must be convinced of the "more liberal and extensive plan of government which wisdom and foresight, freed from the mist of prejudice, would dictate." He was convinced that "the honor, power, and true Interest of this Country must be measured by a Continental scale" and feared that local prejudices and state politics would distract the people and prevent them from realizing their potential as a nation. Every departure from this idea weakened the union and might "break the band, which holds us together." The only way to avoid this problem was "to form a Constitution that will give consistency, stability and dignity to the Union; and sufficient powers to the great Council of the Nation for general purposes." To form such a constitution was "a duty which is incumbent upon every Man who wishes well to his Country."[19]

Reforming America's conduct, however, depended on much more than radical changes in the financial or legal structure. The narrow, local prejudices that previously dominated the confederation had to be replaced by a sense of interest in and patriotism for a common, national good. This depended on developing a sense of national character—a sense of character as a nation. The successful outcome of the Revolutionary War, and the recognition of America's independence as a nation, afforded the opportunity for such a venture. "We now stand an Independent People, and have yet to learn political tactics," Washington wrote matter-of-factly in the spring of 1783. "We are placed among the Nations of the Earth, and have a character to establish." Washington believed that having increased power and authority in a national government—an idea many thought repugnant to the principles of republicanism—was necessary for establishing a workable republican government. Yet republican government at a national level required (and allowed) a national character that would build a nation out of the loose and disorganized confederation that then existed. A new constitution would be an important part of a larger reformation of the political culture because it would serve to bind the people formally to each other and to the principles of the Revolution. The larger challenge was to form a republican people and encourage the dispositions and habits necessary for self-government. "In a word the Constitution of Congress must be competent to the general purposes of Government; *and of such a nature as to bind us together*. Otherwise, we may well be compared to a rope of Sand."[20]

The Circular Address

During the war General Washington communicated with the state governors (who provided funds and personnel for the war effort) by way of official and virtually identical letters called "circulars." It was in his final and longest such communication in June 1783, the immediate purpose of which was to announce his own military retirement, that Washington first laid out his case for establishing a national character as the core of American nationhood. Its significance is further underscored by Washington's "final and only request" that the Circular Address, as it is now called, be communicated in turn to the various state legislatures and considered his "legacy" to the new nation.[21]

The Circular began simply enough by congratulating the state governors on the American military victory and announcing his intention to retire his military commission, the "great object" for which he had been appointed—independence—now "being accomplished." Then, in a move not welcomed by everyone, Washington went well beyond the purview of his immediate military responsibilities and presented his fellow countrymen with a momentous choice. This was the "moment," he announced, that would "establish or ruin the national Character forever. . . ." The peace had been won, political independence established, and a vast territory was now in their sole possession. Finding themselves in the most enviable of conditions, it was now in the power of the American people to decide their own future and choose to be a respectable and prosperous nation or a contemptible and miserable one.[22]

Emphasizing this moment all the more, Washington argued that the answer to this question would determine whether the Revolution would be "a blessing or a curse," not only for present and future generations of Americans but also for the rest of the world. "This is the time of their political probation," Washington wrote, echoing John Winthrop's famous sermon of 1630, for "this is the moment when the eyes of the World are turned upon them." This 1783 passage closely parallels his General Orders of 2 July 1776: then the question was whether Americans, as a people rather than a nation, were to be "Freemen, or slaves"; and it was "the eyes of all our Countrymen" that were upon them. Nevertheless, in both cases, the fate of millions was said to rest on their decision and their conduct. Washington thought the decisions of 1783 were as important as those of 1776. The idea of a unique American moment of universal significance—and the sense of a clear political choice—was strongly echoed as well in the opening essay of *The Federalist Papers* of 1787, where the American people was said to decide whether mankind is capable of establishing government "from reflection and choice" or is "forever destined to depend . . . on accident and force."[23]

Nothing better illustrated the significance of this moment, Washington asserted in the Circular Address, than an observation of the "happy conjuncture of times and circumstances" under which America had declared its independence and status as a sovereign nation. He was referring less to the physical conditions than to the intellectual and moral preconditions of the moment when America came into existence as a nation. In describing the times and circumstances in this broad way, Washington saw America's founding moment in line with the deeper philosophical and theological roots of the Revolution and America's place in the larger traditions of history and civilization. "The foundation of our empire was not laid in the gloomy age of Ignorance and Superstition," he wrote in one of his most striking statements,

> but at an Epocha when the rights of mankind were better understood and more clearly defined, than at any former period; the researches of the human mind, after social happiness, have been carried to a great extent; the Treasures of knowledge, acquired through a long succession of years, by the labours of Philosophers, Sages and Legislatures, are laid open for our use, and their collected wisdom may be happily applied in the Establishment of our forms of Government; the free cultivation of Letters, the unbounded extension of Commerce, the progressive refinement of Manners, the growing liberality of sentiment, and *above all*, the pure and benign light of Revelation, have had a meliorating influence on mankind and increased the blessings of Society.

Washington understood the intellectual and moral truths and traditions of history and civilization to provide the philosophical touchstones for the new American nation. Americans were described as "Actors on a most conspicuous Theatre, . . . peculiarly designed by Providence for the display of human greatness and felicity." By this grounding, limits were placed on government: the rights of mankind were better understood and more clearly defined than ever before. At the same time, duties were placed on every enlightened citizen to respect the principles of reason and revelation—the collected wisdom of the ages as well as the pure and benign light of revelation. Washington claimed that, far from being contradictory, the great truths of reason and revelation cooperated and collaborated at the practical level in the American moment. The occasion of the American Revolution afforded "infinite delight to every benevolent and liberal mind" regardless of whether it is viewed "in a natural, a political, or moral point of light." At its best, the character of the American people would reflect the best of these truths and traditions.

While these unique circumstances were favorable—previously, no nation had been given such an opportunity for political happiness—they did not guarantee success. Washington challenged Americans to "seize the occasion and make it your own." If they failed under these opportune circumstances, the fault would be entirely their own. In order to seize the moment and to establish the national character properly, Washington recommended a number of policies he regarded as essential to the well-being and continued existence of the United States as an independent nation: a permanent union of the states; a proper peace establishment; public justice; and the encouragement of the proper dispositions among the citizenry. These four ideas—building upon the foundation of political freedom, for "liberty is the basis"—made up the "Pillars on which the glorious Fabrick of our Independency and National Character must be supported."

Washington always understood union to be the substance of American nationhood. As early as 1756, he had advocated an association of the states for purposes of self-defense, foreseeing the necessity of "a union of the colonies in this time of eminent danger."[24] By 1783, he argued that union was essential to the liberty and independence of all Americans. The union was not only necessary for defense but also for the maintenance of civil liberty and the establishment of good government. Foreshadowing the Gettysburg Address, Washington argued that without union the "fruits of the Revolution" would be lost, and the suffering and bloodshed of the war "would have been made in vain."

Without a clear dedication to "the Spirit of the Union," Washington asserted, the United States would not be able to exist as an "Independent

Power." It was only by way of a "united Character of an Empire" that the rest of the world acknowledged America's independence, regarded its power, and supported its credit. Dissolution of the union would give treaties with foreign nations no validity and, worse, would leave America nearly in a "state of Nature" and anarchy, open to the extremes of tyranny and arbitrary power. Thomas Paine had made a similar argument in the last of his *Crisis Papers*: a national character based on union gave Americans "importance abroad and security at home."[25]

The nation must also fulfill its public contracts and pay the debts acquired during the war. The "path of our duty is plain," Washington averred: "Honesty will be found on every experiment, to be the best and only true policy; let us then as a Nation be just." This public responsibility was to be built upon the same good faith that was found in private engagements. Contracts, Washington always maintained, must be seen as final and sacred. (The "only way to make men honest," he told one correspondent, "is to prevent their being otherwise, by tying them firmly to the accomplishments of their contracts."[26]) In pursuing public justice, Washington wrote, let a "cheerful performance of their proper business, as Individuals, and as members of Society, be earnestly inculcated on the Citizens of America." Washington had in mind to encourage private justice as the ground and model of public justice.

Washington's sentiments in the Circular Address regarding the adoption of a proper peace establishment were shorter and to the point. It was necessary for the defense of the republic that the continental militia— which should be considered "the palladium of our security"—be placed on "a regular and respectable footing" and that the army be built upon a single system of organization with its formation, discipline, arms, and supplies uniform throughout the Union. Experience taught the difficulty, expense, and confusion that resulted from any other arrangement.

Lastly, Washington observed that republican government required "a pacific and friendly Disposition among the People of the United States, which will induce them to forget their local prejudices and policies, to make those mutual concessions which are requisite to the general prosperity, and in some instances, to sacrifice their individual advantages to the interest of the Community." To have a national character, citizens must acquire the habits and dispositions to overcome local prejudices and self-interest in favor of the common good and an interest in the national community. What were the specific aspects of this friendly disposition? As befitting a man retiring from public life, Washington left it to "the good sense and serious consideration" of others. Nevertheless, he returned to this theme in his conclusion in the form of a prayer for the nation. The sentiments expressed show Washington's concern for the formation of the character and the virtues of the people, without which the establishment of a republican nation would be impossible:

> I now make it my earnest prayer, that God would have you, and the State over which you preside, in his holy protection, that he would incline the hearts of Citizens to cultivate a spirit of subordination and obedience to Government, to entertain a brotherly affection and love for one another, for their fellow Citizens of the United States at large, and particularly for their brethren who have served in the Field, and finally, that he would most graciously be pleased to dispose us all, to do Justice, to love mercy, and to demean ourselves with all that Charity, humility, and pacific temper of mind, which were the Characteristicks of the Divine Author of our blessed Religion, and without an humble imitation of whose example in these things, we can never hope to be a happy Nation.

To Washington the American Founding was much more than the chronology of events normally associated with the period. It was an auspicious moment that would prove the viability of republican government and determine the political future of mankind. The crucial act in the formation of the new nation was the establishment of the habits of good government and citizenship that would stamp the nation with an indelible character and make its people capable of ruling themselves. And the national character—as in any nation where the institutions of government are based on the consent of the governed—ultimately turned on the disposition of the American people to transcend their local prejudices and to overcome their self-interest in favor of the common good: to practice the habits and virtues of self-government.

A More Perfect Union

As he retired from public life in 1783, Washington had no doubt that the many problems faced by the nation would in due time be corrected. America would "work its own cure, as there is virtue at the bottom." The "good sense of the people" would eventually "get the better of their prejudices," and order and sound policy would grow out of the "present unsettled and deranged state of public affairs." Washington wrote Lafayette in 1784 of his confidence that good sense would prevail and reported that "the spirit of meanness is beginning to subside." Nevertheless, Washington was increasingly pessimistic about the actual road to political reform. He doubted whether the Articles of Confederation was sufficient to establish a strong and stable nation like the one he had envisioned in the Circular

Address, and he feared that the current path—based on jealousy and bickering between the states and their continued refusal to grant adequate powers to the federal government—would eventually lead to the downfall of the nation. "This is as clear to me as the A, B, C," Washington wrote in January 1784. He was afraid that "like a young heir, come a little prematurely to a large inheritance, we shall wanton and run riot until we have brought our reputation to the brink of ruin."[27] As Congress failed to act and the states continued to bicker the situation worsened.

In March 1785 commissioners from Virginia and Maryland met in Alexandria to consider problems dealing with the navigation of the Chesapeake Bay and the Potomac River. They soon moved the meeting to Mount Vernon to be under the watchful eye of Washington, who had long shown a keen interest in inland navigation. The commissioners not only agreed on the jurisdictional questions but also recommended uniform commercial regulations, a uniform currency, and an annual meeting on commercial problems. It was proposed that Pennsylvania and Delaware be invited to these meetings as well. Based on the success of the Mount Vernon Conference, the Virginia legislature invited all the states to meet in Annapolis to discuss their commercial relations. Unfortunately, only five of thirteen states sent representatives to the Annapolis Conference, and they decided that it would be politically useless to proceed. They did take the step of adopting a statement (drafted by Alexander Hamilton) calling for a new convention at Philadelphia in May 1787 to discuss all matters necessary "to render the constitution of the Federal Government adequate to the exigencies of the Union."[28]

By late 1785 Washington himself had concluded that the confederation was "a shadow without the substance" and that Congress was but "a nugatory body." He wondered whether Americans had enough wisdom and justice to realize the opportunities before them and prevent the collapse of the new nation. Washington's optimism and high expectations were slowly being replaced by astonishment and despair. So far had things declined that, "from the high ground on which we stood, we are descending into the vale of confusion and darkness."[29]

All of the jealousies, vices, and narrow opinions that Washington considered the root causes of the problem continued to engulf greater portions of the public mind, especially the political leadership. Washington was mortified by what he saw and told John Jay that "virtue, I fear has, *in a great degree*, taken its departure from us; and the want of a disposition to do justice is the source of the national embarrassments." Three months later, writing again to Jay, Washington lamented that "we have probably had too good an opinion of human nature in forming our confederation." America could not long exist as a nation unless an energetic government with adequate powers given to Congress was formed to meet national obligations and purposes. "We must take human nature as we find it," Washington wrote. "Perfection falls not to the share of mortals." Only a vigorous, national, republican government could demonstrate to the advocates of despotism that Americans were capable of governing themselves and that governments "founded on the basis of equal liberty" were not "ideal and fallacious."[30]

In late 1786 events turned violent in western Massachusetts in what became known as Shays's Rebellion. A group of ex-soldiers and officers led by Daniel Shays forcibly prevented the sitting of the law courts and threatened the continental arsenal at Springfield. Now debt-ridden farmers, they were fearful of losing their property to creditors and were attempting to prevent the courts from foreclosing on their land. Although the insurrection quickly collapsed, it proved the weakness of the confederation: the Continental Congress could raise neither the money nor the manpower to mount a response; there was no state militia to call up, and private funds had to be used to raise even a small volunteer force. Thomas Jefferson, then in Paris, took a nonchalant point of view: "A little rebellion now and then is a good thing," he wrote. "The tree of liberty must be refreshed from time to time with the blood of patriots & tyrants." But for many in the United States, the troubles in Massachusetts confirmed their gravest fears and raised doubts about the very possibility of popular government. How the rebellion was dealt with, Washington argued, was crucial not only for the reform effort but also for the rule of law and the whole republican project. If the insurgents had real grievances, they should be redressed. Otherwise, the full force of the government must be used against them at once. The insurgents, Washington reluctantly admitted, "exhibit a melancholy proof of what our trans-Atlantic foe has predicted," namely, that mankind was not fit for self-government. Yet he did not believe that the majority of the American people were "so shortsighted, or enveloped in darkness, as not to see rays of a distant sun thro' all this mist of intoxication and folly." Nevertheless, Washington wrote to his friend and personal aide David Humphreys that the event "is so unaccountable, that I hardly know how to realize it, or to persuade myself that I am not under the illusion of a dream."[31]

Washington considered one of the great evils of democratic government to be that "the people, not always seeing and frequently misled, must often feel before they can act right." The remedies that some saw early and clearly were often slow in coming and not practicable until the people were directly affected, for only then did they feel the need for change. As of

spring 1786, although a growing number of nationalist leaders knew what
needed to be done, Washington observed that the time was "not yet sufficiently ripe for such an event." With Shays's Rebellion, the situation
quickly changed. By making manifest the threat to popular self-government, the rebellion pushed forward the need for reform: "Influence is no
Government. Let us have one by which our lives, liberties, and properties
will be secured; or let us know the worst at once. Under these impressions,
my humble opinion is, that there is a call for decision."[32]

Washington forwarded to James Madison information (that later
proved exaggerated) describing events in Massachusetts from General
Henry Knox, who had been sent by Congress to deal with the rebellion.
"What stronger evidence," Washington asked, "can be given of the want
of energy in our governments than these disorders?" More than ever,
Washington believed, the issue of the federal government must be given
calm and deliberate attention: "Let prejudices, unreasonable jealousies, and
local interest yield to reason and liberality. Let us look to our National
character, and to things beyond the present period. . . . Wisdom, and good
examples are necessary at this time to rescue the political machine from the
impending storm." Thirteen competing sovereignties would soon bring
ruin to the whole nation, Washington argued, but "a liberal and energetic
Constitution, well guarded and closely watched to prevent encroachments,
might restore us to that degree of respectability and consequence, to which
we had a fair claim, and the brightest prospect of attaining." The upcoming
convention in Philadelphia, Washington observed to Madison, "is a measure of equal necessity and magnitude; and may be the spring of reanima-
tion" that was needed to save the country.[33]

In November 1786, when Madison informed Washington that the
Virginia legislature had decided to send a delegation to the upcoming convention and had nominated Washington as its head, Washington hesitated.
At first he told Governor Edmund Randolph that he would not attend
because of a scheduling conflict with the Society of the Cincinnati. He
asked Henry Knox whether his nonattendance would be seen as a dereliction of his republican duty. Finally, at the strong behest of his associates, he
said that he would attend if his health permitted. Even then Washington
delayed. Aware of the failure of the Annapolis Convention, he worried that
all the states would not be represented and that those that were would so
constrain their delegates that the whole proceeding would be jeopardized.
If either were the case, Washington did not want to take part in the convention: "If the Delegates come with such powers as will enable the Convention to probe the defects of the Constitution to the bottom, and point
out radical cures, it would be an honourable employment; but otherwise it

is desirable to avoid it." When it became clear that the delegates would have sufficient freedom to provide for serious changes, Washington moved to ensure that radical reform be proposed at the start of the convention. He recommended to Madison that the convention adopt "no temporizing expedient" but instead "probe the defects of the Constitution to the bottom, and provide radical cures." Any new constitutional structure must give adequate powers and energy to the federal government. It must allow the secrecy and dispatch characteristic of all good government. Finally, it must have the confidence and ability to exercise national powers and pursue national policies. Washington doubted whether any new system could be established without some sort of coercion in the sovereign to enforce the law, although the form of coercion, he noted, would require some thought. Regardless of whether such reforms were ultimately approved, this should be the plan from the beginning: "a conduct like this, will stamp wisdom and dignity on the proceedings."[34]

James Madison replied by submitting to Washington his outline of a new system based on the creation of a supreme national government and a change in the principle of representation.[35] With the Virginia delegation, which included Madison, committed to presenting a plan for a radical cure, Washington could now confidently proceed to the convention. While they waited at Philadelphia for a quorum of delegates, Washington presided over daily morning meetings of the Virginia delegation to consider strategy and refine Madison's proposals, which became the Virginia Plan presented by Governor Randolph at the outset of the convention.[36]

It is often wrongly assumed that Washington was a silent delegate at the Philadelphia convention, yet both inside and outside the convention Washington urged bold action. Gouverneur Morris quoted Washington at the opening of the convention: "It is too probable that no plan we propose will be adopted. Perhaps another dreadful conflict is to be sustained. If, to please the people, we offer what we ourselves disprove, how can we afterwards defend our work? Let us raise a standard to which the wise and the honest can repair. The event is in the hand of God." Having been immediately and unanimously elected president of the convention, Washington presided over the enterprise for the next four months. With his ability to take part in the open discussion limited by this official role, he contributed to formal debate only once at the end of the Convention. (Even then, his support for an amendment concerning Congressional apportionment had more to do with magnanimity and consensus-building than with the particulars of the last-minute change. "It was much to be desired that the objections to the plan recommended might be as few as possible," Madison recorded Washington as saying.) Yet his leadership position and formal silence only served to increase his moral authority over the work of the convention. The dignified tone that he gave to the proceedings maintained the secrecy and seriousness of the debates; so respected was Washington that the convention placed all the papers and notes of the convention in his care. He worked actively and voted with his state delegation throughout the proceedings, and an examination of his voting record shows his consistent support for a strong executive and strong national powers—two issues on which he was a leading advocate.[37]

Although he did not publicly participate in the ratification debate, Washington staunchly supported the Constitution in private correspondence. Just after the convention's close, Washington told Patrick Henry that while he wished that "the Constitution that is offered had been made more perfect," he sincerely believed that it was "the best that could be obtained at this time" and that with its process for amendment, its adoption was clearly desirable. To his allies Washington was unequivocal and decided on the issue of ratification; he increased his correspondence with key political leaders, especially in Virginia, and invited others to circulate and communicate his strong support for the new Constitution. Washington also monitored the political debates and voting in each state and closely followed the pamphlet debate for and against the proposed Constitution— praising and encouraging the dissemination of *The Federalist Papers*. His prestige and backing were essential to its eventual approval. "Be assured," James Monroe wrote to Jefferson, "his influence carried this government."[38]

Washington had good reasons to support the resulting document: it established a national government, created a strong executive, and formed the legal framework necessary for a commercial republic. In doing so it opened the door, in Washington's mind, to restoring the national character. This restoration began, he believed, as the nation went through the process of constitution-making:

> Upon the whole I doubt whether the opposition to the Constitution will not ultimately be productive of more good than evil; it has called forth, in its defence, abilities which would not perhaps have been otherwise exerted that have thrown new light upon the science of Government, they have given the rights of man a full and fair discussion, and explained them in so clear and forcible a manner, as cannot fail to make a lasting impression upon those who read the best publications on the subject, and particularly the pieces under the signature of Publius.[39]

In a letter to Lafayette in February 1788, Washington—fully aware that his words would "become known to all the world"—gave his primary reasons for supporting the Constitution and at the same time imparted his larger concerns. First, the new government was invested with no more power than was absolutely necessary for good government; it was to be a limited government with powers restricted by a written constitution. Second, these powers were distributed into the three branches of government—legislative, executive, and judicial—so as to prevent the degeneration of the government into a monarchy, oligarchy, aristocracy, or other despotic or oppressive form. The Constitution provided for energetic government, yet at the same time the separation of powers preserved its republican form, and frequent elections kept it close to the people. But the Constitution could prevent degeneration into despotism only "... so long as there shall remain any virtue in the body of the people." The new government took advantage of the progress of the science of politics by proposing more checks and barriers against tyranny than any government "hitherto instituted among mortals." A good constitution, no matter how well constructed, did not remove the need for good citizens and sound morals. Washington continued:

> I would not be understood my dear Marquis to speak of consequences which may be produced, in the revolution of ages, by corruption of morals, profligacy of manners, and listlessness of the preservation of the natural and unalienable rights of mankind; nor of the successful usurpations that may be established at such a juncture, upon the ruins of liberty, however providently guarded and secured, as these are contingencies against which no human prudence can effectually provide.[40]

A similar argument is made in the seventy-three-page inaugural address that Washington drafted but decided against delivering. In this "discarded inaugural," Washington viewed the Constitution as the completion and the fulfillment of the Revolution, forming a purely republican government: "that is to say, a government in which all the power is derived from [the people], and at stated periods reverts to them—and that, in its operation . . . is purely, a government of Laws made and executed by the fair substitutes of the people alone." After having heard and read all the arguments for and against the new Constitution, Washington concluded that the new government was superior to those that previously existed. The new government had powers adequate to its purposes, these being the safety and happiness of the people. It was also clear that no previous government had had as many checks and restraints to prevent it from degenerating into tyranny and oppression. Washington was equally convinced that the republican form of government, based as it was on popular opinion and suffrage, depended upon certain characteristics above and beyond its constitutional arrangements. Indeed, those arrangements depended on the degree of virtue and character in the people. Washington wrote:

> The blessed Religion revealed in the word of God will remain an eternal and awful monument to prove that the best Institutions may be abused by human depravity; and that they may even, in some instances be made subservient to the vilest purposes. Should, hereafter, those who are entrusted with the management of this government, incited by the lust of power and prompted by the Supineness or venality of their Constituents, overleap the known barriers of this Constitution and violate the unalienable rights of humanity: it will only serve to shew, that no compact among men (however provident in its construction and sacred in its ratification) can be pronounced everlasting and inviolable, and if I may express myself, that no Wall of words, that no mound of parchment can be so formed as to stand against the sweeping torrent of boundless ambition on the one side, aided by the sapping current of corrupted morals on the other.[41]

Washington believed that the hard task of demonstrating and maintaining popular government depended in the end not on any written document but on the morals, manners, and character of the people. Rejoicing at every step that was taken to preserve the union and establish good government, Washington recognized that it still remained to be seen whether "there is good sense and virtue enough left to recover the right path."[42]

Washington as President

From the time of the Constitutional Convention, if not before, it was widely assumed that Washington would be the first President of the United States. "Had any character of less popularity and celebrity been designated to this high trust, it might at this period have endangered, if not proved fatal to the peace of the union," wrote one anti-Federalist historian in 1805. "Though some thought the executive vested with too great powers to be entrusted to the hand of any individual, Washington was an individual in whom they had the utmost confidence."[43]

In the congressional elections of 1788 Washington encouraged Federalists to run for office and warned against anti-Federalist machinations. He considered the favorable outcome of those contests—which overwhelmingly elected supporters of the Constitution—to be proof of the good disposition and the good sense of the American people. He believed that the people were just then "ripened by misfortune for the reception of a good government" and knew that whoever was entrusted with the administration of the new government would be in a position to "do justice to the public creditors and retrieve the National character." Washington quickly began to lay out his plan to do just that. When he wrote Lafayette in January 1789 that nothing short of a conviction of duty would induce him to become President, it was clear that he was already thinking about that likelihood. He wrote that "in that case, if I can form a plan for my own conduct [as President]" it would be to "extricate my country from the embarrassments in which it is entangled" and "establish a general system of policy" that would lead to permanent happiness for the country. "I think I see a *path*," Washington went on to tell Lafayette,

> as clear and as direct as a ray of light, which leads to the attainment of that object. Nothing but harmony, honesty, industry and frugality are necessary to make us a great and happy people. Happily the present posture of affairs and the prevailing disposition of my countrymen promise to co-operate in establishing those four great and essential pillars of public felicity.[44]

Departing Alexandria for the trip to New York to become president, Washington gave four reasons for accepting the office. The first three—the unanimity of the choice, the opinion of his friends, and the wishes of those who were not completely satisfied by the Constitution—rested on the opinions of others. The fourth reason indicated Washington's larger plan and expressed his own motivation: "an ardent desire on my own part, to be instrumental in conciliating the good will of my countrymen towards each other."[45]

Washington knew that he was in a position to shape the office of president and define the character of a republican executive and, to a large extent, the character of the whole government. He was well aware and often noted that the customs, manners, and traditions that emerged at the beginning of the government would be of enduring and crucial importance, and he knew that his every word and action, small or large, would serve as a precedent. "As the first of everything, in our situation will serve as a Precedent, it is devoutly wished on my part, that these precedents may be fixed on true principles," Washington told Madison.[46] These precedents, rightly established, would serve to legitimate not only the presidency but also the Constitution and thereby the nation.

While his primary responsibility would be to fulfill the constitutional responsibilities and obligations of the presidency, Washington also saw the office as an opportunity further to establish and define the character of the nation. He realized the office's great potential for raising the moral tone of the government and the citizenry. By encouraging the virtues appropriate for republican government, Washington could further his goal of evincing the goodwill of his countrymen and founding a people in the fullest sense. In order to make the proper impression on the nation, then, it was important for Washington to begin the government by encouraging the proper characteristics and habits. Washington hoped that all those chosen to administer the new government would have the wisdom to realize "the influence which their example as rulers and legislators" would have on the people, and the virtue to act so as to increase public happiness. As "the first transactions of a nation, like those of an individual upon his first entrance into life, make the deepest impression, and are to form the leading traits in its character," the nation's leaders must pursue measures that would restore public and private faith and promote national respectability and individual welfare.[47]

That a concern for the character of both the rulers and the ruled was the first theme of his presidency is seen in the much shorter and more general Inaugural Address that Washington did deliver to Congress on 30 April 1789. By being more direct and succinct in his message, Washington underscored all the more those ideas he chose to express. Washington began by noting that he had "greater anxieties" about becoming president than any other event in his life. On the one hand, he was summoned by his country to leave a retirement he had chosen with "the fondest predilection." On the other, the vast responsibilities of the office would "awaken in the wisest and most experienced" of men a consciousness of deficiency. Only a sense of duty based on an appreciation of the circumstances motivated him to accept the office. Then, rather than laying out an understanding of the Constitution or the challenges ahead, Washington paid homage to "that Almighty Being who rules over the universe; who presides in the councils of nations; and whose providential aid can supply every human defect." He made a point of noting that "in this first official act" it would be "peculiarly improper" to neglect "fervent supplications" to "the Great Author of every public and private good." Every step of the American people toward independence reflected "providential agency," just as the peaceful establishment of government demanded "some return of pious gratitude." In his first official communication as president, Washington chose to underscore the importance of national humility and pious reflection, emphasizing the solemnity of the Founding.

While it was within his duties to recommend specific policy measures to Congress for consideration, Washington did no more than point the new representatives toward the objects defined in "the great constitutional charter." He spoke of "the talents, the rectitude, and the patriotism, which adorn the characters selected to devise and adopt" national measures. He highlighted these characteristics, instead of the measures themselves, because it was here that he saw the "surest pledges" of wise policy. These virtues would ensure that neither local prejudices nor party animosities would misdirect their efforts. They would also guarantee that "the foundation of our national policy will be laid in the pure and immutable principles of private morality." Encouraging the proper moral characteristics on the part of those in government would prove that free government might be "exemplified" by attributes worthy of the affections of its citizens. Washington was moved to "dwell on this prospect," he explained, for three reasons:

> since there is no truth more thoroughly established than that there exists in the economy and course of nature, an indissoluble union between virtue and happiness; between duty and advantage, between the genuine maxims of an honest and magnanimous policy, and the solid rewards of public prosperity and felicity: since we ought to be no less persuaded that the propitious smiles of Heaven can never be expected on a nation that disregards the external rules of order and right, which Heaven itself has ordained: and since the preservation of the sacred fire of liberty, and the destiny of the republican model of government, are justly considered as deeply, perhaps as finally, staked on the experiment entrusted to the hands of the American people.

Although the connection between private morality and national policy, between virtue and happiness, might seem utilitarian, "the external rules of order and right" clearly suggest moral principles that are both inflexible and permanent. This implied that some degree of virtue according to the rules of order and right is necessary for the preservation of the "sacred fire of liberty." (In its response to Washington, the Senate concurred: "If Individuals be not influenced by moral principles, it is vain to look for public virtue; it is therefore, the duty of legislators to enforce, by both precept and example, the utility, as well as the necessity, of a strict adherence to the rules of distributive justice.") After advising care and moderation in amending the Constitution and refusing any compensation for his services as President, Washington concluded by "resorting once more to the benign Parent of the human race." After referring again to the providence and tranquillity of the Founding, Washington ended with his hope that "his divine blessing may be equally conspicious in the enlarged views, the temperate consultations, and the wise measures, on which the success of the Government must depend."[48]

Washington had always been an advocate of strong executive leadership. From the beginning of his military command in 1775, he pushed for more energy and responsibility in government. He was most concerned, however, with the creation of a clear and authoritative executive power. The Articles of Confederation allowed for no such leadership. When it came to the new federal constitution, Washington supported a strong and independent president. He urged this position throughout the Constitutional Convention. While he supported checks on the president's power, Washington advocated an energetic executive over the anarchy, gridlock, and weakness associated with the Articles of Confederation. "No man is a warmer advocate for proper restraints and wholesome checks in every department than I am," Washington wrote in 1789, "but I have never yet been able to discover the propriety of placing it absolutely out of the power of men to render essential Services, because a possibility remains of their doing ill."[49]

As president, Washington was aware of the constitutional limits placed on his office. He was reluctant to use the veto power, and when he did it was for *constitutional*, not policy, reasons. On several occasions—over the assumption and bank bills, for instance—Washington raised constitutional questions about policies that he supported and sought contrary advice before approving the legislation. In contemplating the policy of neutrality, Washington not only sought the opinions of his cabinet and close advisors but also queried the Supreme Court for its views of the constitutionality of the matter.

It would be incorrect to speak of Washington as the leader on questions of national policy; he did not propose a legislative agenda and generally deferred to the authority of Congress on such matters. Nor can it be said that he was a party leader, a role closely associated with modern presidents. Nonetheless, he was a strong, energetic president. This was because he understood the office first and foremost from the perspective of the Constitution. Washington saw the presidency as an equal branch of government and thus an equal defender of the Constitution. He always acted within the confines of the document, but aggressively defended his prerogatives and position when challenged. He understood the precedents that his actions set for the country and future executive officeholders.

Washington was also aware of the unique characteristics of the presidency: he was the sole spokesman for the people as a whole and the official representative of the nation for the rest of the world. Finally, Washington knew that he symbolized the new government as well as the whole American project. His words and deeds would be considered a timeless legacy to his country and the supporters of republican government everywhere. The Farewell Address would subsequently be prepared and issued with all of these ideas in mind.

Washington's First Term

After their inauguration in 1789 George Washington and John Adams comprised the sole elements of the executive branch of the new government. As a result, for the first five months Washington conducted government operations with holdovers from the previous government. When Congress authorized the creation of the first executive departments to assist the President in carrying out his responsibilities, he quickly brought in the ablest individuals he could find. His first appointment was that of Alexander Hamilton to head the Treasury Department, a move urged by Madison after Robert Morris, who held the job under the Articles of Confederation, proved unavailable. He next reappointed Henry Knox as secretary of war, the job he held during the Confederation. John Jay was Washington's first choice to head the State Department, but Jay preferred to be chief justice of the Supreme Court, and Washington obliged. Instead, Washington turned to Thomas Jefferson, who had just completed his tour as minister to France. He completed his team—the Constitution made no provision for a cabinet—by appointing Edmund Randolph to be attorney general. Washington, by expertise and interest, was more involved in foreign and defense policy, often working with Jefferson and Knox in these areas. The President played a lesser role in designing financial and commercial policy, partially because Hamilton's plans were in accord with general opinions that Washington had long held, but also because Washington was neither expert nor interested in the finer points of finance.

The chief policy issues of Washington's first term concerned the fiscal proposals made by Hamilton at the request of Congress, submitted in a series of four reports over two years. Together the reports formed the administration's financial program, intended as much to build confidence in and strengthen the federal government as to salvage the public credit. Controversy over the proposals marked the first political divisions in the new government. The first two reports dealt with the debt inherited from the Confederation. Hamilton urged that the national debt (both foreign and domestic) be funded at full value, that the federal government assume the liabilities incurred by the states during the Revolution, and that a system of taxation be established to pay the bills. While the proposal to pay the foreign debt was virtually unopposed, the scheme to pay the domestic debt was controversial. Madison, elected to Congress from Virginia, unsuccessfully opposed paying the debt in full, proposing instead to discriminate between the original holders of debt and speculators. Madison and others also inveighed against the assumption of state debts by the federal government. While it is possible that Washington preferred discrimination of the debt, it is known that he favored assumption of the state debts. Throughout his career, Washington advocated paying national debts as a matter of simple justice. He had prepared his own plan for addressing the debt problem at the beginning of his presidency but turned the matter over to Hamilton. As the cause of the expenses was "a Common Cause" to which all the states were pledged, so the debt was common to all. Had hard-pressed states thought otherwise during the Revolution, opposition to Great Britain would have given way to submission "and given a different termination to the War." Ultimately, the assumption question was settled in a political compromise brokered by Hamilton, Madison, and Jefferson to place the national capital eventually on the Potomac River. With the compromise agreed to by both sides, Washington hoped that simmering political divisions were settled.[50]

Hamilton's third contribution was *The Report on a National Bank* of December 1790. Legislation to create a national bank to service the debt passed easily in the Senate but met opposition in the House. The Bank Bill passed the House as well, but not before Madison raised the question of its constitutionality. Washington had long seen the practicality and importance of establishing a national bank. In 1781 the Continental Congress had incorporated the Bank of North America to offer credit to pay for the war effort, a situation with which Washington was familiar. Indeed, when Madison first raised objections to the national bank proposal, Washington referred to this earlier example as precedent.[51]

While Washington supported the intention of the Bank Bill, he was concerned about the objections raised about its constitutionality and sought the opinions of his closest advisors. Madison was opposing the bank in contradiction to the argument he had made in a report to Congress in 1781 and in *The Federalist Papers* in 1788. When Washington turned to his attorney general and then to his secretary of state, both also thought the bank unconstitutional. Jefferson argued for a "strict construction" of the Constitution based on the yet-to-be-adopted Tenth Amendment. A national bank was not among the specific powers delegated to Congress. At the end of his opinion, however, Jefferson argued that if the President was undecided, he should defer to the will of the legislature and support the measure. Washington was concerned enough to ask Madison to begin preparing a message just in case a veto was required. When the President turned to Hamilton for a response, he received a long exposition on constitutional interpretation that set forth a broad view of government based on a doctrine of implied powers. A bank was related to the ability of government to collect taxes and regulate trade. It was perfectly constitutional as an implied *means* to the *end* of government's delegated powers and therefore was within the compass of national authority. Already convinced of the bank's necessity to the restoration of American finances and now convinced of its constitutionality, Washington signed the bill. The legal question settled, Washington believed that the bank not only played a crucial role in establishing the public credit and building confidence in the government but also provided an "unexpected proof" of the resources of the American people.[52]

In the last element of the financial system, the *Report on Manufactures*, Hamilton proposed that the government aid and encourage the growth of young industries through various protective laws. Although Congress did not act on the plan, it was another idea that Washington had long advocated. By encouraging domestic manufacturers, Washington hoped to break the hold of foreign goods, especially British goods, on the American market. This would further nourish independence and build an appreciation of American-made goods. (Washington had informed Lafayette that he had ordered "homespun broad cloth" from Connecticut for his inaugural clothing and would serve no port or cheese "but such as is made in America.") Nevertheless, Washington doubted, as did Jefferson, that the issuance of bounties for this purpose fell within the public welfare powers of the government.[53]

Although Washington never liked political parties, it was nevertheless during his administration that the first political parties came into being, along with the first party newspapers and the rudiments of party organization. And while Washington never considered himself a party man, the seeds of party dispute sprouted within his administration. The secretary of the treasury, Alexander Hamilton, came to lead the Federalist Party, which had grown out of the successful pro-constitution movement of the 1780s. The opposition within the administration was led by the secretary of state, Thomas Jefferson. Jefferson, along with James Madison in Congress, began what became the Republican Party. Within the Cabinet, Hamilton could rely on having the support of Secretary Knox, while Attorney General Randolph often supported Jefferson. Despite this web of partisanship and the fact that Washington often and knowingly sided with Hamilton over the protestations of Jefferson, Washington tried to stay outside and above the fray, moderating the disputes to keep party divisions within the confines of constitutional government and prevent the development of the darker side of political parties: factionalism. It was no surprise that Washington had pledged in his First Inaugural that "no local prejudices, or attachments; no separate views, nor party animosities, will misdirect the comprehensive and equal eye which ought to watch over this great Assemblage of communities and interests." He always saw himself as an impartial executive, standing above the narrow prejudices and self-interested animosities associated with parochialism and partisanship. "I presume it will be unnecessary for me to say that I have entered upon my office without the constraint of a single *engagement*," Washington wrote James Wilson, "and that I never wish to depart from that line of conduct which will always leave me at full liberty to act in a manner which is befitting an impartial and disinterested magistrate."[54]

One of the first signs of party division came in the spring of 1791 when the reprinted edition of Thomas Paine's *Rights of Man*, written in response to Edmund Burke's *Reflections on the Revolution in France*, appeared in the United States. Paine's treatise was prefaced by a note penned by Jefferson (published without his permission) praising the book for responding to Burke and the "political heresies" springing up in the United States. Jefferson, who was allegedly referring to Vice President John Adams's *Discourses on Davila*, denied the charge to Washington but not without referring to Adams's "apostasy to hereditary monarchy." In May and June—after Washington had failed to veto the Bank Bill—Jefferson and Madison went on their infamous botanical tour of New York State, with an excursion into New England, to sound out anti-Federalist opinion about forming a national coalition. Madison laid out their position in his *National Gazette* essays of 1791–92, and together they hoped to affect the congressional elections of 1792. It was later that year that Philip Freneau, under pay of Jefferson as a State Department translator, began publishing the *National Gazette*, opposing administration policies in general and Hamilton's financial scheme in particular as corrupt and monarchical.[55]

In mid-1792 Jefferson wrote at length to Washington, laying out an extensive indictment of Hamilton and his policies, decrying them as the first steps toward destroying republicanism and establishing a monarchy along the British model. Washington must have had trouble understanding this claim. While he had been present for Hamilton's speech to the Constitutional Convention—in which Hamilton praised the British constitution and the energetic leadership associated with the British monarchy—Washington never doubted Hamilton's dedication to the Constitution or believed that Hamilton aimed to replace it with a monarchy. Now Jefferson was arguing that Washington was surrounded by dedicated monarchists, bent on destroying the Republic. Nevertheless, Washington wrote a long and frank letter to Hamilton asking for a response to twenty-one specific points of complaint made by Jefferson and inquiring specifically whether Hamilton wanted to change the current republican form of government into a monarchy. Hamilton replied in typical fashion, defending in detail and at length the integrity of his motives and conduct. He gave a "flat

denial" to the charge of monarchism. The path to subverting republicanism, he argued, was not the establishment of a monarch but the encouragement of the prejudices, jealousies, and apprehensions of the people. As a
result, Hamilton, who had been writing anonymously in the pro-Federalist
Gazette of the United States, stepped up his attack against Jefferson as an
opponent of the government.[56]

In the fall of 1792, Washington wrote to his bickering cabinet secretaries, calling for forbearance and yielding on both sides. Without their cooperation, Washington told Hamilton, he could not see how the government
was to be managed or how the union of the states could be preserved much
longer. While he recognized that differences in political opinions were unavoidable, he regretted that "men of abilities, zealous patriots, having the
same general objects in view" could not discuss their differences with moderation and propriety. "How unfortunate," he told Jefferson, that with foreign enemies and insidious friends all around, "internal dissensions should
be harrowing and tearing at our vitals." If these divisions continued they
would weaken the government, tear asunder the Republic, and allow the
enemies of America to triumph, thereby forfeiting the greatest prospect yet
for republican government.[57]

At the end of his first term in 1792, with the strengthening of the
public credit and the brightening of the financial picture, Washington considered retiring. The government was working, and the issues of foreign
policy were just beginning to unfold. The only problem that stood in the
way of his stepping down was the looming political divisions that he so
lamented that could disrupt the larger task of building the nation. Washington hoped his cabinet would stay on to allow for continuity with the new
president and appealed mightily to Jefferson, who wanted to step down, to
remain in the government. When he told Madison of his plans to retire,
Washington noted that he would continue only if his departure would
leave the country in a serious political crisis resulting from "the divided
opinions which seem to prevail at present." When Washington consulted
Jefferson, Hamilton, Knox, and Randolph, they all—as had Madison—
argued against his retiring. Jefferson and Hamilton both viewed Washington as their only shield against the partisan intrigues of the other. Jefferson
argued that Washington was the only person who could keep Hamilton's
policies from fracturing the Union: "North & South will hang together, if
they have you to hang on," he wrote. Hamilton thought that Washington
was the only person who could protect the maturing Union against its
growing political enemies, meaning the Republicans. In the end, Washington agreed that his leadership was necessary to maintain a moderate and
stable course until, as Madison argued, "public opinion, the character of

the Govt., and the course of its administration shd be better decided, which could not fail to happen in a short time."[58] Washington was inaugurated for a second term of office in March 1793.

Washington's Second Term

Toward the end of Washington's first year as president, news of a revolution in France began arriving in America, beginning the first great foreign policy controversy of the young Republic. Like many others, Washington at first was optimistic about events in France. In 1789, during the period of a limited monarchy under the Estates-General and the Constituent Assembly, Washington wrote that the revolution was of "so wonderful a nature that the mind can hardly realize the fact." Lafayette seemed to be a major figure in French politics, and the revolution was following a moderate course. Lafayette even sent Washington the key to the Bastille as "a tribute which I owe as a son to my adoptive father, as an aide-de-camp to my general, as a missionary of liberty to its patriarch."[59]

From the beginning, however, Washington had reservations about the revolution, its direction, and the possibility of it ending in the establishment of free government. Unless it could be prevented from moving from one extreme to another, the revolution would end in "a higher-toned despotism" than the previous regime. Washington warned Lafayette—who was part of the moderate promonarchy group—of the terrible consequences of "indiscriminate violence" and those "wicked and designing men" who might take advantage of the turmoil and confusion that abounded in Paris. Until a proper constitution was established, with the French government organized and the legislature reformed, Washington cautioned that tranquillity could not be expected. In the fall of 1792 and the spring of 1793, worse news reached America: mobs had stormed the Tuileries, Lafayette had fled and been captured, and the king executed. Even more significant, France declared war on England, Spain, and Holland in February 1793, presenting the United States with the possibility of war under the Franco-American treaties of 1778. While Washington's cabinet unanimously supported a general neutrality, Hamilton's sympathies lay with Great Britain—he wanted to repeal or suspend the treaties of 1778—and those of Jefferson with France. Washington wanted a completely independent course and issued a strong proclamation calling for "a conduct friendly and impartial toward the belligerent powers." If the United States was to assist France in any significant way, it would immediately be at odds—if not at war—with Great Britain, and again caught in the middle of the historic rivalry between the two most powerful nations in Europe. Washington's fear was that either of the two powers would draw America into the arena of European politics and European war, a circumstance Washington opposed at all costs.[60]

Washington's neutrality policy initially caused more problems at home than it did abroad. It further divided American political opinion and was assailed in the opposition press. The controversy led to the debate between Hamilton, under the pseudonym "Pacificus," and Madison, under the pseudonym "Helvidius," over the president's constitutional authority to declare such a policy without Congressional approval. A deeper debate occurred over the nature and significance of the French Revolution itself. Some, such as Thomas Jefferson and James Monroe, saw those events as a great battle against monarchical despotism that deserved American support. Others, like Hamilton, saw the violence as the result of a radical social upheaval that threatened freedom and republicanism. A more important question, in Washington's mind, concerned foreign influence in domestic politics and the threat that this posed to American independence. After his arrival in April 1793 the new French minister, Edmund Charles Genet ("Citizen Genet"), went about commissioning privateers against British shipping, organizing activities against British interests in North America, and threatening to circumvent Washington's authority in order to favor French interests. Washington took the initiative in defending his position and the independence of the United States. "Is the Minister of the French Republic to set the Acts of this Government at defiance, with impunity? and then threaten the Executive with an appeal to the People," Washington asked Jefferson. "What must the World think of such conduct, and of the Governmnt. of the U. States in submitting to it?" Within a few months, Washington requested the French minister's recall. When a foreign power tells America "what we shall do, and what we shall not do, we have Independence yet to seek, and have contended hitherto for very little," Washington later wrote Hamilton.[61]

Relations with the British, which had always been a difficult matter, became particularly dangerous with the outbreak of war with France. During the summer and again in the fall of 1793 the British adopted orders-in-council interfering with neutral American shipping, which resulted in the seizure of American vessels and the impressment of American citizens. Madison and Jefferson proposed economic retaliation, while Hamilton, as more news of maritime seizures reached America, proposed recruiting and fitting a federal army. Washington knew that the nation must take that prudent step of preparing for war but at the same time decided to send a special envoy to London—Chief Justice John Jay—to seek a negotiated settlement. Although the resulting treaty was far from perfect, Washington reluctantly supported and eventually signed the agreement. The most important accomplishment of the Jay Treaty was the withdrawal of the British from the northwest posts by mid–1796. It also opened American trade on a limited basis to British East and West Indies ports, referred pre-Revolutionary debts, boundary questions, and compensation for maritime seizures to a joint commission, and placed British trade with the United States on a most favored nation status. It did not, however, address impressment, British relations with the Indians, slaves illegally removed by the British after the war, or loyalist claims against the United States.[62] Nevertheless, Washington believed that the treaty did settle a number of important questions and prudently postponed others. Above all, it prevented war at a point when America was weak and disunited and bought time for the growth of American strength and prosperity.

Washington believed that the Jay Treaty presented a grave political and strategic dilemma: if the treaty should be approved, the French and their partisans would be excited to hostility against the American government; if it should be rejected, there most likely would be war with Great Britain, threatening the very existence of the nation. He could only hope that his decision to accept the treaty would be appreciated in the long run. "In time, when passion shall have yielded to sober reason, the current may possibly turn," Washington wrote Edmund Randolph in 1795, "but in the mean while, this government, in relations to France and England, may be compared to a ship between the rocks of Scylla and Charybdis."[63]

The Jay Treaty put an end to the foreign occupation of American territory north of the Ohio River. This meant greater security to settlers because of a decreased threat from the Indians, who depended on the British forts for supplies and provisions. This fact and the American victory over the Indians at the Battle of Fallen Timbers led to the Treaty of Greenville in 1795 by which the Indian tribes ceded large sections of Ohio to the Americans. At the same time Spain, initially the ally of Britain against France, had now made peace with Paris. In light of the Jay Treaty, the Spanish chose to lessen the number of their potential enemies while protecting their flank in North America. In a treaty negotiated by Thomas Pinckney, Spain recognized the boundaries as set out in the U.S.-British peace treaty of 1783 (the Mississippi in the west and the thirty-first parallel in the south) and gave Americans free navigation of the Mississippi River.[64]

For most of Washington's second term, the party struggle—intertwined with these foreign-policy issues—dominated the public mind and seemed to be on the verge of consuming the whole structure of government. Washington suffered personally from the growing bitterness of the party struggles, as he had become the object of much of its aggression. During Jay's negotiations in London, Washington told Jay that he was endeavoring to maintain the status quo at home until the conclusion of a treaty with Great Britain, but that this was not an easy task with the "many hot heads and impetuous spirits among us who with difficulty can be kept within bounds." Washington regretted but was not surprised that the Jay Treaty was caught up in the partisan debates of the party newspapers. Under these heated conditions Washington saw an even stronger duty "to do what propriety, and the true interest of this country" required. When the terms of the treaty became generally known in March 1795, the Republicans led the popular opposition. Coming on the heels of disagreements with Hamilton's financial plans and objections to American neutrality in the wars of the French Revolution, this opposition to the Jay Treaty permanently established the Republican Party, caused the first clear party divisions in Congress, and began a true party system in the United States. The Senate narrowly ratified the treaty, and the Republicans in the House attempted to block funding for its provisions by requesting the executive to provide the instructions and other documents from the negotiations. Washington refused the request, based on his constitutional authority on foreign policy, and noted that the House of Representatives had no authority in the matter unless it were conducting an impeachment investigation.[65]

For his role in the agreement, Washington was roundly vilified by his political enemies. Long immune from such personal attacks, Washington as early as 1793 was openly being charged with gambling, reveling, niggardliness, foul language, and blasphemy. It is not surprising that when Washington decided to retire in 1796, he gave as one of the reasons a disinclination to be attacked by the "set of infamous scribblers" who wrote for the party presses. Thomas Jefferson credited the treaty's success to Washington's great influence over the people and their great trust in his judgment: "Republicanism must lie on its oars, resign the vessel to its pilot, and themselves to the course he thinks best for them." Jefferson even told a foreign correspondent—who quickly published his indiscreet remarks—that a monarchical party in America was bent on changing the government to the British form and complained of the "apostates who have gone over to these heresies, men who were Samsons in the field and Solomons in the council, but who have had their heads shorn by the harlot England."[66]

In their last correspondence, Washington told Jefferson that he had "no conception that Parties would, or even could go, the length I have witness to." He could not believe his administration was being attacked in such "exaggerated and indecent terms as could scarcely be applied to a

Nero; a notorious defaulter; or even a common pickpocket." While he said that he did not accuse Jefferson of being the source of the scurrilous attacks from the opposition newspapers, Washington nevertheless realized the association between Mr. Jefferson's "particular friends" (he referred to Jefferson here in the third person) and the arguments they made that the President had fallen under the sway of Hamilton. From almost the very beginning of Washington's presidency Jefferson believed that Washington, though a fellow Virginian, favored Hamilton to the detriment of the policies Jefferson advocated. Jefferson was all the more convinced when war broke out in Europe, and Washington took a position that Jefferson viewed as being pro-British and anti-French. (This despite the fact that Washington's policy of neutrality was unanimously supported by the cabinet, including Jefferson.) Eventually, Jefferson concluded that he could no longer serve in Washington's administration and resigned, leaving Hamilton (who left the following year) to make policy while Jefferson pursued influence by other, more partisan means. From that moment Washington, so the argument goes, was surrounded by the biased opinions of Federalists and was prevented from receiving alternative, Republican viewpoints. Suffering from what Jefferson believed to be the onset of senility, Washington was accused of being a tool of the Federalist Party. As ironic proof of Jefferson's contention, historians point to the words of Hamilton himself, who wrote just after the first President's death: "Perhaps no man in this community has equal cause with myself to deplore the loss. I have been much indebted to the kindness of the General, and he was *an Aegis very essential to me.*"[67]

That Hamilton played a notable role in preparing Washington's Farewell Address at the height of these partisan divisions, a fact that was suspected at the time, may be considered further evidence of Hamilton's predominance and Washington's reliance on others. The implication is that Washington, old and tired, was little more than a respectable name under which to publish the latest salvo in the growing controversy between the Federalists and the Republicans.

3

FRIENDS AND FELLOW CITIZENS

*P*resident Washington rose unusually early on the morning of 19 September 1796. He had been in the capital to confer with Charles Cotesworth Pinckney, the new minister to France, and was anxious to be on his way before Philadelphia's largest newspaper, the *American Daily Advertiser,* was delivered. Having quickly signed a batch of naval commissions and reviewed the day's official paperwork, he was in a carriage traveling home to Virginia before most of the city had even awakened. Little did they know that the journey would be his last official trip home as President of the United States; the next time he headed for Mount Vernon he would be George Washington, private citizen.

The *American Daily Advertiser* carried an exclusive and momentous story that Monday morning, but without banner headline, introductory explanation, or editorial comment. On page two was a seemingly innocuous article introduced under the simple heading: "To the PEOPLE of the United States" and then "Friends and fellow Citizens," all in slightly enlarged type. The reader discovered the lengthy article's famous author and realized the historic significance of the work only at the end, where, again in enlarged type and indented, there appeared the words: "G. Washington, United States." Such an inauspicious and simple delivery—it was not communicated to Congress, delivered on a grand occasion, or given any official fanfare—emphasized Washington's intent to speak directly and simply to the American people. The first-of-its-kind presidential statement received immediate and widespread popular attention and quickly spread throughout the nation and much of civilized Europe. Although the address was reprinted by virtually every major newspaper in America, only one—the *Courier of New Hampshire*—can claim the credit for reprinting it under the title by which it is now known: "Washington's Farewell Address."[1]

Forming the Address

Before looking closely at the final text of the Address, it is useful to review the process of its creation. Washington had considered retiring at the end of his first term in May 1792, going so far as to ask James Madison for advice on the "mode and time most proper" for announcing his intention to step down. Ignoring Madison's pleas against his retirement, Washington wrote Madison on 20 May to ask that he turn his thoughts to the preparation of a "valedictory address." The letter then presented a number of points that Washington wanted to express in "plain and modest terms" to the public. In a typically dense statement, he told Madison that he wanted to assert

> that having been honored with the Presidential Chair, and to the best of my abilities contributed to the organization & administration of the government—that having arrived at a period of life when the private walks of it, in the shade of retirement, becomes necessary, and will be most pleasing to me;—and the spirit of the government may render a rotation in the Executive officers more congenial with their ideas of liberty & safety, that I take my leave of them as a public man;—and in bidding them adieu (retaining no other concern than such as will arise from fervent wishes for the prosperity of my Country) I take the liberty at my departure from civil, as I formerly did at my military exit, to invoke a continuation of the blessings of Providence upon it—and upon all those who are supporters of its interests, and the promoters of harmony, order & good government.

In phrases reminiscent of those found in his earlier writings, especially from the early days of the Revolution, Washington proceeded to express the ideas that he wished to relate to the American people. He continued:

> That to impress these things it might, among other things be observed, that we are *all* the Children of the same country—a Country great & rich in itself—capable, & promising to be, as prosperous & as happy as any the annals of history have ever brought to view—That our interest, however diversified in local & smaller matters, is the same in all great & essential concerns of the Nation.—That the extent of our Country—the diversity of our climate & soil—and the various productions of the States consequent of both, are such as to make one part not only convenient, but perhaps indispensably necessary to the other part;—and may render the whole (at no distant period) one of the most independent in the world.— That the established government being the work of our own hands, with the seeds of amendment engrafted in the Constitution, may by wisdom, good dispositions, and mutual allowances; aided by experience, bring it as near to perfection as any human institution ever aproximated; and

therefore, the only strife among us ought to be, who should be foremost in facilitating & finally accomplishing such great & desirable objects; by giving every possible support, & cement to the Union.—That however necessary it may be to keep a watchful eye over public servants, & public measures, yet there ought to be limits to it; for suspicions unfounded, and jealousies too lively, are irritating to honest feelings; and oftentimes are productive of more evil than good.

Washington noted that the incorporation of these ideas "would require thought" but felt confident that Madison would "comprehend all that would be proper." He did not want to touch on any specific parts of the Constitution; this would be a broad statement of principle rather than a resume of particular policies. Washington intended not only to announce his retirement, but also to express his sentiments for the future happiness of the nation. His theme was clear: despite the diversity of the nation, all Americans should by their wisdom, good dispositions, and mutual allowances work to bring the new government nearer to perfection and thus give every possible support to cementing the Union. In closing, Washington asked that Madison consider the propriety of such an address, its contents, and the time it should appear.[2]

On 20 June 1792, Madison sent to Washington a short draft, based on Washington's instructions. Madison "aimed at the plainness & modesty of language" that Washington requested. He noted that he had "had little more to do, as to the matter, than follow the just and comprehensive outline" that Washington had sent him and assumed that "much improvement" would be made before the "last form" of the address. In style and substance, the short draft that Madison penned followed closely the points made by Washington. Not surprisingly, Madison used many of Washington's own phrases in expressing the President's sentiments. This draft, in amended form, would make up the first part of the 1796 address.[3]

In the spring of 1796, Washington again thought of retirement and the preparation of a valedictory statement. In February, Washington discussed his intended address with Alexander Hamilton, who was in Philadelphia to argue before the Supreme Court. This was the first time that Hamilton was aware of the statement that Washington had begun to develop when he considered retiring four years earlier. While the extent of the discussion is not known, at some point Washington must have inquired if Hamilton would be interested in helping to revise the work. In May, Washington sent Hamilton his rough draft of the address. The Washington Draft, as it is now called, was made up of the paragraphs written by Madison in 1792 and an additional, lengthier section written by Washington.

The "considerable changes" at home and abroad, Washington wrote in his draft, induced him to add his wishes for the future of the nation. The nature of his comments, however, show that he was not only speaking to immediate circumstances but also addressing posterity. Washington hoped that party disputes would subside, and (using a phrase from a letter to Jefferson in 1792) that the cup of beneficence offered by posterity would not be dashed by party division. Nevertheless, as it was man's nature not to think alike, Washington first wished that "charity and benevolence" would replace "illiberal prejudices and jealousy." He wanted the nation to fulfill all its domestic and foreign engagements and quoted himself from the Circular Address: "Honesty will forever be found to be the best policy."[4]

In the new section of his draft Washington also introduced a number of points on foreign affairs, a topic that had dominated his second term as President. He recommended that the nation avoid any political connections with foreign nations other than those necessary for trade and commerce. Every citizen, Washington argued, should "take pride in the name of an American," motivated by a sense of distinct nationhood independent from the influences and intrigues of any foreign nation. Here Washington took liberally from the letter that he wrote to Patrick Henry in October 1795 expressing his desire for an independent American character that would check partisanship toward foreign nations and prevent the destruction of "the cement wch. binds the nation." Political alliances, he warned, would involve the young nation in disputes and eventually lead to war, whereas a policy without such alliances would leave the nation always at liberty "to act from circumstances, and the dictates of Justice—sound policy—and our essential Interests."[5]

While the nation must always be prepared for war, Washington wrote, it should only turn to force when necessary to defend justice, essential rights, and national honor. If the country could remain at peace for at least twenty years, during which time population, commerce and resources would increase its strength, "the nation could bid defiance, in a just cause, to any earthly power whatsoever." This paragraph paralleled the argument Washington laid out in his letters to Gouverneur Morris (in December 1795) and Charles Carroll (in May 1796). For now, the United States should be neutral, that is, without partialities or prejudices. A contrary policy would be full of mischief, embarrassing, divisive, and "productive of all the evils and horrors which proceed from faction."[6]

Above all, Washington, returning to the theme of many of his earlier writings, hoped that the Union would be "as lasting as time." If they remained collected in "one band," Americans would possess the strength of a giant, while divided they would become the prey of foreign intrigue and internal discord. Instead of being "enviable and happy," they would become "miserable and contemptible." (A similar choice had been posed in the Circular Address, whether to be "respected and prosperous, or contemptable and miserable.") Washington added two paragraphs arguing that the departments of the government be preserved in their "utmost Constitutional purity," that the general and state governments be maintained in their proper orbits, and that the public not withdraw their confidence in the government or its officers without just cause.[7]

Washington's last four paragraphs form a summation of his presidency and his own role as president. After referring to the partisan invectives of the press that had misrepresented his politics and affections and after noting the virulent abuse that he had suffered, Washington wrote that he would "pass them over in utter silence" as he had done on every other occasion. His politics were "unconcealed; plain and direct," to be found in the Neutrality Proclamation of 1793. The acts of his administration were of public record, he noted, and open for judgment. If they did not acquit him he could only hope that charity would throw a mantle over his want of abilities and that he be allowed, after having spent all the prime of his life in the service of his country, to retire.

Returning to the modest language of his First Inaugural, Washington noted that infallibility was not an attribute of man and that it was his constant endeavor to avoid intentional error. The circumstances that Washington faced as the first president of an infant nation were "as delicate, difficult, and trying as may occur again in any future period of our history." Throughout, Washington did the best he could to follow "the true and permanent interest" of his country "without regard to local considerations, to individuals, to parties, or to Nations." He was proud that he had not served his country because of "ambitious views," or a desire for reputation, or the expectation of compensation. His only reward was the benefit of the peace and prosperity with which the country was blessed while other nations had fallen into the horrors of war. He concluded: "I leave you with undefiled hands, an uncorrupted heart, and with ardent vows to heaven for the welfare and happiness of that country in which I and my forefathers to the third or fourth progenitor drew our first breath."[8]

In transmitting this draft to Hamilton, Washington noted that he was attached to the portion prepared by Madison and wanted it to remain. This was partially for reasons of content, based as it was on Washington's own sentiments. It was probably also for reasons of politics. Washington surely hoped that allowing both Madison and Hamilton a part in his valedictory would affirm his belief that partisan differences could be overcome by recourse to common principles. As both Madison and Jefferson would recognize Madison's contribution, party tensions might be reduced. At the same time, Washington's reuniting of Madison and Hamilton would serve to recreate the common purpose and success of Publius—their pseudonym as authors, along with John Jay, of *The Federalist Papers*—whose writings Washington so greatly admired.

Washington asked Hamilton that his draft be returned amended, corrected, "curtailed, if too verbose; and relieved of all tautology." He wanted the whole in a plain style that could be given to the public in "an honest; unaffected; simple garb." When Washington gave directions to Hamilton about removing certain passages and discarding the egotisms in this draft, he also gave him permission, if he thought best, "to throw the whole into a different form." Regardless of whether he gave a different shape to the address, Washington instructed Hamilton that the new form should be "predicated upon the Sentiments contained in the enclosed paper," meaning his own draft.[9]

Washington's draft included eight of the paragraphs developed by Madison, introduced by two paragraphs pointing out that this section had been written when Washington considered retiring in 1792. Washington then added fourteen new paragraphs intended to express "the most ardent wishes" of his heart. These wishes became the core sentiments expressed in the final Farewell Address. Indeed, a comparison of the ideas expressed in the final Address with those of Washington's first draft shows that there are no ideas in it that are not to be found in this early draft.[10] It is this draft that establishes Washington's intellectual paternity of the Farewell Address.

The Final Draft

Upon receiving the draft, Hamilton immediately went to work revising Washington's materials. After reviewing Washington's draft Hamilton decided to form a new address before redressing the existing work. In order to do this, Hamilton prepared for himself an "abstract of points to form an address." The order of this document does not follow Washington's order but is an outline of what would become Hamilton's draft. The abstract shows, however, that Hamilton implemented the President's instruction that the new form be "predicated upon the Sentiments" in Washington's draft. Hamilton's abstract was organized into twenty-two roman numeral points, corresponding to twenty-two paragraphs in the Washington draft. Of these points, fifteen come directly from or are paraphrased language from Washington's draft. The ideas expressed in the remaining seven points, while expanded upon by Hamilton, can be traced to or logically follow from ideas expressed in Washington's draft.[11]

A month and a half later Hamilton sent to Washington "a certain draft" of the address, which he hoped would be "importantly and lastingly useful," embracing "reflections and sentiments as will wear well, progress in approbation with time, & redound to future reputation." Hamilton left the final determination of this newly formed and expanded address to the President: "How far I have succeeded you will be the judge." He also informed Washington that he was at work revising Washington's first draft, though he expressed reservations about this version. Hamilton believed that it had "a certain awkwardness" and contained some ideas that would "not wear well" over time. In particular, Hamilton saw a problem in presenting one section (that penned by Madison) within the address, identifying it as a statement initially prepared in 1792. When he had both drafts before him, Hamilton averred, Washington could better decide this question. In either case Hamilton would shape the address however Washington desired, improving the expression and condensing its length.[12]

Hamilton's original Major Draft, as it is now called, is much longer and more in depth than the Washington Draft. The first eight paragraphs followed Washington's rendering, using much from the 1792 draft, just as the last six paragraphs closely followed the last paragraphs of Washington's version. The rest of Washington's work is to be found distributed throughout the other thirty-four paragraphs of Hamilton's draft. Of these paragraphs, each one elaborates a point made by Washington, sometimes a point made only in a sentence or a phrase. The overall movement of the address followed the design of Washington's draft, as the wishes that Washington expressed in his draft are made more extensive and elaborated to become general sentiments and advice. For instance, Washington expressed the concise wish that in order to stabilize its commerce and avoid the disputes and wars of Europe, the nation should not connect itself with the politics of any other nation farther than was necessary to regulate its trade. In Hamilton's draft this recommendation formed the basis of four or five paragraphs, all of which develop from Washington's original point. Washington's two paragraphs lamenting party disputes became four paragraphs in Hamilton's draft. The President's crisp paragraph warning against the political intrigues of foreign nations Hamilton elaborated in two lengthy and three short paragraphs. In comparing the two drafts it is clear, however, that Hamilton, while embellishing and eloquently developing Washington's ideas, did not add new material or depart from Washington's original design.

When he received Hamilton's draft, Washington's initial reaction was that it was too long. Yet after only a cursory reading he could see that "the Sentiments therein contained" were "extremely just, & such as ought to be inculcated." On the same day Hamilton sent Washington another shorter draft (the Draft for Incorporating) that revised but did not reshape Washington's own draft. Hamilton dropped language that might be construed as partisan self-justification, added a better introduction to Madison's section, and strengthened the ideas Washington had proposed. Almost all of the paragraphs, not surprisingly, were the same as those of Hamilton's reshaped draft. (Indeed, Hamilton's second draft was intended to be the first part of much of the reshaped address and, if incorporated in this way, would have been just as long.) The main difference was a shortened section on the idea of union and its geographic advantages. Also absent was the paragraph on religion and morality. Having delivered the two drafts as requested—and self-conscious of his relationship to Washington and his secondary role in preparing the address—Hamilton told Washington affectionately (and obediently) that "if there be *any* part you wish to transfer from one to another, *any* part to be changed—or if there be *any* material idea in your own draft which has happened to be omitted and which you wish introduced—in short if there be *any* thing further in the matter in which I can be of *any* service, I will with great pleasure obey your commands."[13]

After "several serious & attentive readings" Washington decided that he preferred Hamilton's main draft. It was "more copious on material points; more dignified on the whole; and with less egotism." It was less open to criticism and "better calculated to meet the eye of discerning readers." Hamilton's draft, Washington noted, comprehended most if not all of his own draft and was "better expressed." Because it was a rewritten version of his own work, Washington saw no reason for major revision or addition, but he did make some editorial points. Nevertheless, Washington sent the draft back to Hamilton because Hamilton wanted to work on it again. Washington explained his own editing of the Hamilton draft: "I shall expunge all that is marked in the paper as unimportant etc. etc. and as you perceive some marginal notes, written with pencil, I pray you to give the sentiments so noticed mature consideration. After which, and in every other part, if change or alteration takes place in the draught, let them be so clearly interlined, erased, or referred to in the Margin as that no mistake may happen in copying it for the Press."[14]

In early September 1796, Washington wrote Hamilton to say that, after further considering the contents of the address, he regretted that the important subject of education had been omitted. After pointing out that education not only served to advance knowledge but also assumed the political task of uniting disparate individuals, Washington directed Hamilton to his (Washington's) letter to the Virginia governor, and the resolves of the Virginia legislature responding to the same, as sources for his thought on the subject. In response, Hamilton recommended that a fuller statement on education be reserved until Washington's upcoming Message to Congress, but he promised to add a general comment on education to the main draft. Hamilton returned the draft to Washington on 5 September without revisions or abridgment. Hamilton's health prevented the additional work he had intended. Although he told Washington that he had included a short paragraph on the subject, nothing on education was added until later.[15]

At that point, if not earlier, Washington began preparing his final manuscript of the address, further marking the work as his own. In writing out the address in his own hand, Washington made numerous stylistic changes and alterations to suit his manner. He preferred, for instance, that government have "vigor" rather than "force and strength" and thought that the people should "discourage and restrain" rather than "discountenance and repress" the spirit of party. Under extraordinary circumstances, Washington trusted "temporary" instead of "occasional" alliances. He also edited a number of Hamilton's phrases, making them more concise and terse. Instead of Hamilton's phrase "Against the Mischief's of Foreign Influence all the Jealousy of a free people ought to be continually exerted," Washington wrote "Against the insidious wiles of foreign influence . . . the jealousy of a free people ought to be *constantly* awake." Instead of "Permanent alliance, intimate connection with any part of the foreign world is to be avoided," Washington penned the famous phrase "'Tis our true policy to steer clear of permanent alliances with any portion of the foreign world." Washington probably remembered a line he had read in Thomas Paine's *Common Sense*: "It is the true interest of America, to steer clear of European contentions, which she can never do, while by her dependence on Britain, she is made the make-weight in the scale of British politics."[16]

In the process Washington added a number of important phrases and sentences. He formed a new paragraph on the unity of government, taking part from Hamilton's second draft and adding a call for a "cordial, habitual & immovable attachment" to union and the deprecation of attempts to alienate any portion or "enfeeble the sacred ties which now link together the various parts." At the end of the section on union he added the phrase: "In this sense it is, that your union ought to be considered as a main prop of your liberty, and that the love of the one ought to endear to you the preservation of the other." Washington also wrote the short paragraph on education, one of the most succinct in the document, and inserted it after the paragraph on morality.[17]

Washington made several changes to Hamilton's passage on religion and morality. He modified the phrase "nor ought we to flatter ourselves that morality can be separated from religion" to read "let us with caution indulge the supposition that morality can be maintained without religion." Where Hamilton had written that one could not "in prudence suppose" that national morality could be maintained without religious principles, Washington wrote more forcefully that "reason & experience both forbid" the same conclusion. He also dropped the next sentence, probably objecting to its specificity: "Does it not require the aid of a generally received and divinely authoritative Religion?" In the next paragraph Washington left out the last sentence, even though it was similar to a phrase he used in his First Inaugural: "The uncommon means which of late have been directed to this fatal end seem to make it in a particular manner the duty of the Retiring Chief of a Nation to warn his country against tasting of the poisonous draught."[18]

Toward the end, Washington made changes and additions to the section on the government's neutrality policy and added three paragraphs explaining his understanding of the right and obligation of the United States to maintain a position of neutrality. Here he attached the statement that it had been his motive to gain time to establish the government and build the strength necessary for the nation to command its fortunes.[19]

Finally, Washington went back and struck out the phrases and paragraphs he either did not believe important or considered redundant. He dropped a long paragraph on the "less dangerous" aspects of political parties and most of a paragraph arguing that the primary inlets of tyranny in a large republic were conflicts of popular faction. At one point Hamilton had written that "your Government as at present constituted is far more likely to prove too feeble than too powerful." Washington crossed it out and wrote instead that it was "little else than a name, where the Government is too feeble to withstand the enterprises of faction, to confine each member of the Society within the limits prescribed by the laws & to maintain all in the secure & tranquil enjoyment of the rights of person & property." Washington deleted a paragraph on industry and frugality as insufficiently important. Lastly, he crossed out Hamilton's concluding paragraph (which Washington thought had "the appearance of self distrust and mere vanity") and wrote one keying off a phrase from Madison's draft.[20]

It was this manuscript, in Washington's handwriting, that Washington showed to his cabinet and then had delivered to David Claypoole, the owner and editor of *Claypoole's American Daily Advertiser.* Four proofs of the Address were made, three of which were examined by the President, "who made but few alterations from the original, except in the punctuation, in which he was very minute." When Claypoole returned the original manuscript to the President and expressed regret at parting with it, Washington graciously allowed him to keep his only copy of the document.[21]

Mr. Hamilton's Role

Speculation about Alexander Hamilton's contributions to the Farewell Address has existed for some time. The French, who saw the Address as an attack on French diplomacy by a pro-British administration, immediately assumed that Hamilton was behind the statement. In addition to "the lies it contains, the insolent tone that governs it, the immorality which characterizes it," according to the French diplomatic representative, the Farewell Address displayed "the doctrine of the former Secretary of the Treasury, Hamilton, and the principles of loyalty that have always directed the Philadelphia Government." After Hamilton's death in 1804, when the executor of his estate found a draft of the Address in Hamilton's handwriting, this question became a matter of some public controversy. Mrs. Hamilton, who maintained that her husband was the original author of the Farewell Address, successfully sued to have the draft returned, and it was eventually deposited with the Library of Congress and finally published in 1859 as part of the Hamilton Papers. To make matters worse, John Jay claimed to have influenced the Address as well—an assertion that turned out to be exaggerated.[22]

This situation has led some contemporary scholars to conclude that the mind behind the Address—and thus its true author—was not George Washington but rather Alexander Hamilton. Felix Gilbert argued in his 1961 work on the Farewell Address that the most important section of the Address reflected Hamilton's distinctive ideas on foreign policy, ideas that show an original contribution by Hamilton that changed the document and gave it real weight. Joseph Charles, in his 1956 book on the origins of political parties in America, argued that the discussion of foreign policy on the eve of the presidential election of 1796 was "political propaganda" written "in the terms which Hamilton put into Washington's mouth." Washington was little more than a symbol of national unity who had, in the hands of Hamilton, become a potent political weapon. He was "the tool of a party without apparently being aware of it." The Address was "basically a statement of the partisan political philosophy of Alexander Hamilton" according to Alexander DeConde, author of a 1958 book on early American foreign policy. To assume otherwise would be to "endow Washington with powers reserved for the gods of Olympus."[23]

Earlier scholarship on the matter came to a different conclusion. The first study on the formation of the Address, by Horace Binney in 1859, concluded that Washington was the true author: "The fundamental and radical thoughts were [Washington's], and were to remain his, even in a new draught. The Address was to disclose his principles and admonitions, of which he gave a full outline, in sentiments sufficiently delineated by him to characterize and identify them." Washington left everything else—order, amplification, justification, additions—to Hamilton "under the names of 'form' and 'shape,' by which Washington distinguished the external appearance of composition, from the general and fundamental truths." Victor Hugo Paltsits, who wrote in 1935 what is considered the definitive study of the preparation of the Address, concluded similarly: "In the last analysis, Washington was his own editor; and what he published to the world as a Farewell Address, was in its final form in content what he had chosen to make it by process of adoption and adaptation. By this procedure every idea became his own without equivocation." Samuel Flagg Bemis assayed that while "the shimmering foliage dancing and shining in the sunlight" was Hamilton's, the "trunk and branches of the sturdy tree" were the work of Washington. Thomas Jefferson, who was in part privy to the history of the Address, had a similar view. He recognized parts of the Address as having been prepared by James Madison, several others by Hamilton, and others by Washington himself: "These he probably put into the hands of Hamilton to form into a whole, and hence it may appear in Hamilton's hand-writing, as if it were all of his composition."[24]

From the beginning, Hamilton understood himself as acting on Washington's instructions, following the President's intentions, and serving his purpose. Hamilton never claimed authorship or intimated publicly that his ideas were the ones reflected in the Address. In order to render better Washington's thoughts and ideas, Hamilton turned to sources beyond the draft he had been provided, but even here the major influence was Washington. The two most important sources for the Farewell Address other than Washington's draft were the Circular Address of 1783 and the First Inaugural—both of which were familiar to Hamilton and were clearly referenced by Washington in his original draft. As Washington often sent copies of his major correspondence to his close advisors, it is also probable that Hamilton was privy to many of Washington's earlier letters and ruminations and was familiar with the President's thoughts and ideas on the subjects contained in the Address. That Hamilton had been an associate of and collaborator with Washington for nearly twenty years also increased his insight into the President's general beliefs and philosophy. Hamilton, of course, brought much talent and expertise to his task. To the list of sources can be added Hamilton's own previous writings, for instance, his cabinet memorandum of 15 September 1790 (his first discussion of foreign affairs while in Washington's cabinet), and his defense of the Jay Treaty written under the pseudonym Camillus in 1795. There were also similar arguments in *The Federalist Papers* that Hamilton had contributed in 1787 and 1788. (It is worth noting, however, that the passage in *The Federalist* that is most similar to one in the Farewell Address was written not by Hamilton but by John Jay.)[25]

These similarities prove less about the Farewell Address than about the views of the American statesmen of the time. The widespread discussion of similar ideas concerning foreign policy and national independence illustrates the fact that there were many common opinions circulating during the Founding era that were not the private property of either Washington or Hamilton. For example, the writings of the first two decades of independence are full of similar statements about America's policy toward Europe. As early as 1776, Thomas Paine's *Common Sense* made an argument for national independence based on a separation from European politics and the avoidance of foreign political alliances, emphasizing a policy of free trade and extensive commercial relations. In 1783 James Madison introduced and the Continental Congress approved a resolution asserting that "the true interest of these states requires that they should be as little as possible entangled in the politics and controversies of the European nations."[26] Many of the ideas of the Address germinated throughout Washington's correspondence extending back to the American Revolution. That Hamilton elaborated on these points establishes no more than the fact that Hamilton, Washington, and much of the Founding generation were of a like mind when it came to a subject as widely discussed as foreign policy, despite the intense partisanship that emerged during the 1790s.

Washington's Legacy

Washington must have been pleased with the final product when it appeared in the *American Daily Advertiser* on 19 September 1796. The Farewell Address was by far the lengthiest writing of his life, serious, dignified, forward-looking and far-reaching. It was an appropriate capstone to his extensive writings and long public career, the culmination of his political thought and four decades of practical experiences. As such, the Address should be approached seriously and attentively and read as Washington's last legacy and final commentary on the American Founding.

The Farewell Address opens in a gradual but deliberate manner. Its purpose, as well as the determination of the author, is clear from the beginning. The next election of "a citizen" to administer the executive branch of government was not far distant, and Washington solemnly declared that he would not be among those "out of whom the choice is to be made." Without directly mentioning the presidency or his role as the nation's first and only chief executive, Washington announced that the American people must now choose another citizen to hold this "important trust."[27]

By declining to be a candidate for a third presidential term, Washington raised the question of his own political succession. The young American nation had never operated without George Washington as its president, and his withdrawal from the scene immediately set loose an open competition to determine his political heir. "It will serve as a signal," Fisher Ames told Oliver Wolcott upon first reading the Address, "like dropping a hat, for the party racers to start, and I expect a great deal of noise, whipping, and spurring."[28] Washington was the first and last president to be elected unanimously. His departure also marked the first time that an executive freely stepped down to allow the free election of a successor. After the Revolutionary War, General Washington surrendered his commission to Congress and retired from military life at a moment when he could have become—as some hoped—an American monarch. A little over a decade later Washington was voluntarily stepping down from the highest office in the new nation, at a time when he easily could have remained—a prospect many assumed would be the case—for life. So powerful was Washington's decision to serve only two terms that it lasted as an unenforced precedent until Franklin Roosevelt's wartime third term in 1940. Although he was eventually succeeded by his own Vice President, John Adams, it was Washington's voluntary retirement from office and support of the constitutional process for choosing another president that laid the groundwork for the election of Thomas Jefferson, and the peaceful ascendancy of a rival political party, in 1800. Had Washington remained president until his death in 1799, the election of Jefferson—and the possibility of turning over the government to an enemy political party, perhaps for the duration of Jefferson's life—might well have led to civil war and the collapse of the new republic.

Despite the significance of the moment—perhaps because of it—the Address begins in the modest language of republicanism. The opening of the Address was an explanation and defense of Washington's decision to retire and remove himself from public service. In the drafting process Washington had noted that he wanted to express his thoughts directly to the people in "plain and modest terms" and "an honest; unaffected; simple garb," and the final product reflects this intention. The model is his own First Inaugural of 1789, to which he refers the reader in this part of the

Farewell Address. There he spoke with great humility about assuming the office of president and the challenging circumstances under which he began that "arduous task." The same modest tone and humble manner are evident here as well. From the beginning of his presidency Washington had been aware of the "inferiority" of his qualifications and had discharged his responsibilities as best "a very fallible judgment was capable." Now, at the age of sixty-four, the "weight of years" made the "shade of retirement" as necessary as it was otherwise welcome. The phrasing suggests the imagery of one of Washington's favorite biblical passages (Micah 4:4), which he often rendered looking forward to his own retirement: "A few months more will put an end to my political existence," Washington cheerfully wrote in late 1796, "and place me in the shades of Mount Vernon under my vine and fig tree."[29]

Washington's modesty, however, was less self-criticism and true humility than homage to a higher sense of duty, for the opening of the Farewell emphasizes even more Washington's deferential sense—deference to his country, to republicanism, and to honor. With no constitutional requirements or precedents to guide him in his decision, he turned to the dictates of moral and political obligation. The decision to retire, Washington explained, was made with a strict regard to the requirements of "a dutiful citizen" and reflected neither a diminution of zeal nor a deficiency of gratitude on Washington's part. Indeed, he considered his two terms as president to have been nothing less than "a sacrifice of inclination to the opinion of duty." When Washington wanted to retire at the end of his first term, he told his readers, he had prepared a similar address to declare this intent, but "mature reflection on the then perplexed and critical posture of our Affairs with foreign Nations" as well as the unanimous advice of his advisors led him to abandon the idea. Now, the state of the nation's internal and external affairs rendered the "pursuit of inclination" no longer incompatible with the "sentiment of duty, or propriety."[30]

Washington completed the defense of his decision not to seek reelection by noting that while "choice and prudence" invited him to retire, he believed that "patriotism does not forbid it." Throughout his life, patriotic duty provided a strong call for Washington to serve his country. But patriotism meant not only loyalty to country but also opposition to tyranny and support for republican government. Washington had wondered in 1787 whether his nonattendance at the Constitutional Convention would be seen as a dereliction of his duty to the cause of republicanism. But attend he did: he believed, and argued in his First Inaugural, that the model of republican government was deeply and perhaps finally staked on the American experiment. "The establishment of our new Government seemed to be the last great experiment for promoting human happiness by reasonable compact in civil Society," Washington wrote soon after becoming President, aware of his unique role in the process. "In our progress towards political happiness my station is new," he observed, "and, if I may use the expression, I walk on untrodden ground."[31] By 1796 Washington was satisfied that he had fulfilled this patriotic duty and considered himself free to abide by his own choice and the recommendations of prudence.

In the Farewell Address, Washington also thanked his country for allowing him the opportunity to perform his duty and prove his attachment to his country. He expressed his gratitude not only for the honors that the nation had conferred upon him but also for the opportunity it had given him for acting honorably—"for the opportunities I have thence enjoyed of manifesting my inviolable attachment, by services faithful and persevering." If any benefits resulted from these actions, Washington noted in republican manner, it should always be remembered as "an instructive example in our annals" that popular support was the "essential prop" and a guarantee of his efforts.[32] The actions of the American people, which ultimately made Washington's deeds possible, brought them honor as well.

The lengthy explanation of Washington's decision to retire made up only a small part of the Address, yet set the tone and gravity of the whole. The opening carried such weight precisely because it explained more about the decision-maker, Washington, than about his actual decision. The effect of placing Washington at center stage from the very beginning, which may strike some as self-serving, was pivotal to the Address's larger purpose. It is a rule of classic rhetoric, first put forth by Aristotle, that the opening of a speech serves the purpose of establishing the speaker's *bona fides* for the audience, providing a proof of the speaker's character. Likewise, the opening of the Farewell Address was a proof of Washington's character, emphasizing two virtues in particular—modesty and duty—as evidence of his republicanism. By reminding the reader of his exemplary character and republican credentials, Washington was calling forth his own prestige and moral authority as persuasive evidence for the arguments that were to follow.

Washington concluded the introductory section with a succinct statement, a prelude of the general themes of the Address. He did so, significantly, in the form of a recitation of the unceasing vows to heaven that he would take with him to his grave. Washington's final prayer was that divine beneficence toward America would continue, that "Union and brotherly affection [would] be perpetual," that the Constitution would be "sacredly maintained," that the government would be administered with wisdom and virtue, and that the many blessings enjoyed by America would inspire "every nation which is yet a stranger" to it.[33] These five points were not only the main themes and lessons of the Farewell Address but also those of Washington's public life; they encompass all the great themes of his statesmanship. The central point—that the Constitution be sacredly maintained—was the highest political teaching of the Farewell Address.

Sentiments and Reflections

If announcing his decision to retire had been Washington's sole intention, he could easily and understandably have ended his statement at this point: "Here, perhaps, I ought to stop." A consideration of the people's well-being, however, combined with an apprehension of potential dangers to that well-being, urged Washington to proceed. Instead of a short announcement of his intentions and possibly a succinct statement of his views, Washington chose to use the occasion to offer some specific thoughts and recommendations for the "solemn contemplation" and "frequent review" of the American people. These were not the immature ideas of a moment but the result of "much reflection" and considerable observation, and they appeared to Washington to be "all important" to the future happiness of all Americans.[34] In presenting his sentiments in such a way, Washington not only made the address into a valedictory—he had called it such in his correspondence with Madison—but also transformed it into a political testament. The monarchs and statesmen of Europe sometimes used political testaments to leave to posterity their views of the purpose of state or the strategic concerns of the nation. The difference is that Washington's is a republican testament, reflecting both the challenges and grandeur of popular government.

Washington began by reminding his readers that he had expressed some sentiments on "a former and not dissimilar occasion," thereby pointing to his earlier valedictory, the Circular Address of 1783. In both argument and structure, the Circular Address was the model for the Farewell Address. The former announced his military retirement at the end of the Revolutionary War and laid out his sentiments about the future prosperity of the American people. Washington, we recall, recommended four policies in the Circular Address that he believed to be essential to the well-being and existence of the country: an indissoluble union of the states; a sacred regard to public justice; a proper peace establishment; and a pacific and friendly disposition among the American people that would break down local prejudices, induce concessions for general prosperity, and encourage individual sacrifice for the sake of the common good. These policies made up the four pillars of America's national character and independence.[35] Washington was moved to make his sentiments known in 1783 because he feared that Americans would not seize the great moment before them and establish a nation. Thirteen years later, in 1796, the moment had been seized and the nation founded. Americans now had a Constitution to uphold and defend. The challenge was no longer the establishment of institutions but their maintenance and perpetuation, and Washington was concerned about the obstacles and potential threats ahead for the new nation. And as we shall see, the last pillar of the Circular Address, that there be a proper disposition among the American people—which in 1783 Washington left to "the good sense and serious consideration" of others—became in 1796 a central theme of the Farewell Address.

The main body of the Farewell Address, like the Circular, is composed of a long section recounting Washington's sentiments and advice on the subjects that he thought imperative to America's future. These sentiments can be grouped into six areas: first, a statement of the necessity and importance of national union; second, a defense of the Constitution and the rule of law; third, discussion of his strong reservations about political parties; fourth, a lengthy consideration of the proper habits and dispositions of the people; fifth, his warnings against foreign influence in domestic affairs; and sixth, some reflections on international relations proper, covering foreign alliances, commercial policy, and neutrality. At first glance, this broad array of topics seems more haphazard listing than organized design, yet the order and argument make sense as a whole. Washington's general theme was the preservation of the Union as the core of American nationhood. The movement of the Address built a case for the steps needed to perpetuate the Union—the most important being a well-formed constitution and the proper dispositions on the part of the people. These dispositions extended as well into foreign policy, where the theme was national independence. His advice was to maintain the Union, the Constitution, and the habits of good citizenship, and to observe good faith and justice towards all nations. His warnings were to distrust the passions of political parties, be wary of foreign influence, avoid an entangling foreign policy, and be mindful of policies that might undermine the Union, the Constitution, or the good dispositions of the people. The thread that held all these thoughts together was self-government, for the question Washington's advice was intended to answer was whether the American people were capable of ruling themselves.

A Sacred Union

Before the Revolution, Washington described "an innate spirit of freedom" that had brought him to conclude that the measures of the British

Parliament were "repugnant to every principle of natural justice." It is no surprise that in the Circular Address of 1783 Washington noted that this innate sense of human liberty was the basis of the four pillars—union, public justice, national defense, and proper disposition—that supported America's national character and independence. A decade later, in the Farewell Address, liberty remained the base, fixed in the sinews of the American character: "Interwoven as is the love of liberty with every ligament of your hearts, no recommendation of mine is necessary to fortify or confirm the attachment." (Abraham Lincoln wrote in a similar vein much later, in 1861: "Without the Constitution and the Union, we could not have attained the result; but even these, are not the primary cause of our prosperity. There is something back of these, entwining itself more clearly about the human heart. That something, is the principle of 'Liberty to all.' "[36]) Washington did not need to inculcate the love of liberty, for it was already near and dear to every American.

Union, however, was a relatively new and still relatively fragile concept in the hearts and minds of the American people. Although their unity of government had "become justly dear," the idea of Union was still in the process of becoming a part of the national character. While no recommendations were necessary to convince Americans of the cause of liberty, it was necessary to fortify and confirm an attachment to the Union. The American people, Washington believed, should accustom themselves to thinking and speaking of the Union as the "palladium" not only of their political safety but also of their prosperity and happiness. They should watch over its preservation with "jealous anxiety." Pains would be taken by some to weaken these truths in the popular mind because, as the centerpiece of America's "political fortress," the Union would be the point against which internal and external enemies would concentrate their attacks.

In order to defend against these attacks and further strengthen the Union in the hearts and minds of the people, Washington presented three arguments in favor of Union. The first argument was that the Union supported the safety and happiness of the people—the ends of government as set forth in the Declaration of Independence. Union was "the support of your tranquillity at home; your peace abroad; of your safety; of your prosperity; [and] of that very Liberty which you so highly prize." It was the Union that allowed the states to act together as an independent nation, provided for their common defense, promoted expanded commercial and economic activity, and by doing so maintained their liberty. None of these blessings would be possible without a political Union of the states. A central theme of the Circular Address of 1783 had been that Union was necessary to secure liberty and prevent anarchy and confusion. Using similar language, the Farewell Address argued that Union was "a main Pillar in the

Edifice of your real independence." But by 1796 Washington's public understanding of Union had expanded to encompass, in addition to security and freedom, a sense of nationhood. Just as real independence meant more than separation and autonomy, so Union was something more than a unity of government: it "constituted Americans as one people."

The second argument for Union was that of sympathy. As common citizens either by birth or choice, Americans' sympathies would naturally be directed toward their common country: "The name AMERICAN, which belongs to you, in your national capacity, must always exalt the just pride of Patriotism, more than any appellation derived from local discriminations. With slight shades of difference, you have the same Religion, Manners, Habits and political Principles." Having fought successfully together in the Revolution and having established their liberties by joint councils and joint efforts, they now had every reason to consider themselves citizens of one nation. A very similar argument is found in *Federalist* No. 2, where John Jay noted that the American people were "descended from the same ancestors, speaking the same language, professing the same religion, attached to the same principles of government, very similar in their manners and customs, and who, by their joint counsels, arms, and efforts, fighting side by side throughout a long and bloody war, have nobly established their liberty and independence."[37]

Washington knew, however, that patriotic sympathy was not a dependable motivation; he had cautioned against an overreliance on it during the Revolution. At the time, Washington believed that patriotism was a necessary but insufficient basis upon which to build an army for a long and bloody war, although great achievements might be accomplished under its influence. "We must take the passions of Man as Nature has given them," Washington observed from Valley Forge in 1778, "and those principles as a guide which are generally the rule of Action." This did not mean that Washington denigrated more noble sentiments: "I do not mean to exclude altogether the Idea of Patriotism. I know it exists, and I know it has done much in the present Contest." But such patriotism "must be aided by a prospect of Interest or some reward. For a time, it may, of itself push Men to Action; to bear much, to encounter difficulties; but it will not endure unassisted by Interest." For Washington, the Union was the vehicle by which a national interest could best be developed and realized. He noted that the inducements of sympathy—religion, manners, habits, and principles—strongly recommended the Union. But these considerations, however powerful, "are greatly outweighed by those which apply more immediately to your Interest. Here every portion of our country finds the most commanding motives for carefully guarding and preserving the Union of the whole.''[38]

Washington's final argument for Union in the Farewell Address was based on the idea of a common interest—persuading the people that they could best achieve the material requirements of independence by being united rather than divided. The two primary benefits of this unity were prosperity and security. A formal Union, unlike the confederation government, offered the economic advantages of a commercial republic. Trade and an unrestrained commercial intercourse between North, South, East, and West, protected by the equal laws of a common government, made for "an indissoluble community of Interest as *one Nation*."[39] Americans also had an interest in the greater strength, resources, and security that would result from national political unity and "the united mass of means and efforts." As a result, foreign nations would less frequently interrupt the peace of the continent. A Union of the states—by exempting Americans from the conflicts and wars that would likely occur between thirteen rival nations—would also relieve the need for large military establishments "which under any form of Government are inauspicious to liberty, and which are to be regarded as particularly hostile to Republican Liberty."

Apparent differences of interest could be reconciled and made complementary inside a well-administered Union. In the Address, Washington cited the recently ratified Pinckney and Jay Treaties on this score to demonstrate specifically to the West that the general government and other sections would not practice a foreign policy that would abandon the West's interests in favor of their own. Washington did not present this policy as an example of sacrifice or magnanimity, but rather of self-interest, rightly understood, on the part of all. Washington thus offered a preliminary definition of the national interest: foreign (and domestic) policies that benefit all particular sections and interests or that at least do not benefit one section to the disadvantage of another. Washington believed that "temperate measures and good dispositions will produce such a system of national policy, as shall be mutually advantageous to all parts of the American Republic." Early in the life of the new Constitution he had written to Gouverneur Morris that "the Farmer, Merchant, and the Mechanic have seen several interests attended to, and from thence they unite in placing confidence in their representatives, as well as those in whose hands the execution of the laws is placed."[40]

That Washington singled out the West in the Farewell Address for this example is revealing. Washington's plan of attaching the West to the Atlantic states by means of extending the inland navigation of the river system is well known: "I wish sincerely that every door to that Country may be set wide open that the commercial intercourse with it may be rendered as free and as easy as possible." In correspondence during the 1780s, Washington had argued that such intercourse was more of a political than a commercial question: "This in my judgement is the best, if not the only, cement that can bind those people to us for any length of time." Without this cement, Washington could "easily conceive they will have different views, separate interests and other connexions." It was imperative that the West be shown that it was "easier and cheaper for them to bring the produce of their labour to our markets, instead of going to the Spaniards southerly, or the British northerly." If Westerners made such foreign connections out of commercial need, "they will be quite a distinct people; and ultimately be very troublesome neighbors to us. In themselves considered merely a hardy race, this may happen; how much so, if linked with either of these powers in politics and commerce." Washington had no doubt that Britain and Spain (and France), if given an opening, would pursue a policy of containing and dividing America by supporting the emergence of separate political communities.[41]

Washington believed that without the West, a self-governing American empire was impossible. Nor was this simply a question of material necessity. Washington, in common with the Republicans, held something of a frontier thesis—the belief that settlement of the West would underpin public virtue. In the same way that its remoteness from other nations precludes America from being drawn into foreign quarrels, Washington had explained in his discarded First Inaugural,

> . . . so the extent of territory and gradual settlement will enable us to maintain something like a war of posts, against invasion of luxury, dissipation, and corruption. For after the larger cities and old establishments on the borders of the Atlantic, shall, in the progress of time, have fallen prey to those Invaders; the Western States will probably long retain their primaeval simplicity of manners and incorruptible love of liberty. May we not reasonably expect that, by those manners and this patriotism, uncommon prosperity will be entailed on the civil institutions of the American world?[42]

In the Farewell Address Washington insisted that these considerations—safety and happiness, sympathy, and interest—spoke persuasively to every "reflecting and virtuous mind." The arguments that these considerations made should convince all Americans that Union was "a primary object of Patriotic desire." It was both reasonable and good, then, for Americans to concentrate their warmest political affections on the Union. It was the agreement of these often-conflicting motivations that made

Union so overwhelmingly attractive and worthy of choice. Indeed, the many principled and practical advantages of Union gave sufficient reason to immediately "distrust the patriotism" of all those who "may endeavor to weaken its bands."[43]

Washington's view of Union, to repeat, was not a mere agreement of security or convenience. Not only did he urge the people to discourage any hint of abandoning the Union and to disapprove any attempts to alienate its geographic sections, but he also warned of those who sought to "enfeeble the sacred ties which now link together the various parts." What was it that made the ties of Union sacred? Washington argued that if the people would assess the immense value of national Union not only to their collective but also to their individual happiness, they would inevitably come to "cherish a cordial, habitual and immoveable attachment to it." It was his hope that Union, as with the love of liberty generally, would become interwoven with every ligament of the American heart. For this to happen, the ties that linked the various parts—the foremost tie being the Union, the formal tie being the Constitution—must come to be cherished as *sacred* and must be *sacredly* maintained. Long before Lincoln, Washington was calling for a political religion. Until all Americans came to love the Union as much as liberty itself, commercial and security interests should be more than adequate to cement the relationship. Over time, Washington noted, "the love of the one ought to endear to you the preservation of the other."[44] But while interest is the cement of the Union, Washington taught that interest alone did not assure political harmony.

The Constitution

The cornerstone of this sacred Union, according to the Farewell Address, was the uniting of the states under one government: "To the efficacy and permanency of Your Union, a Government for the whole is indispensable." However, not just any government of the states would be adequate to bring about a Union in the sense of it that Washington conceived. "In a word," Washington had written in 1783, "the Constitution of Congress must be competent to the general purposes of Government; and of such a nature as to bind us together. Otherwise, we may well be compared to a rope of Sand."[45] Political alliances between the states, Washington argued in the Farewell Address, were not an adequate substitute for political union; they were subject to the infractions and interruptions that always plague such agreements. And the previous loose confederation of the states—despite being called "Articles of Confederation and Perpetual Union"—

had already been tried and proven inadequate to the purposes of nationhood. Fortunately, this faulty endeavor to establish a government had been "improved upon" by a plan calculated to create such a national union and better administer public affairs. Unlike the earlier attempt, the new Constitution was sufficiently energetic to meet the requirements of good government yet completely free and limited in its scope. As such, it staked "a just claim" to the confidence and support of all Americans.

Washington was responding, in part, to the traditional argument that good government, difficult even on a small scale, was not possible in a large, extended republic. He consistently denied that liberty was inherently a local phenomenon, a claim advanced by the anti-Federalist opponents of the Constitution (and, implicitly, by some Republican critics of his administration), who argued that better government and greater happiness would result from a loose confederation where the states retained virtually all powers over domestic affairs. According to Washington, republican liberty was not only safe but would prosper in the larger rather than the smaller, in the whole rather than in the parts. This was also a reflection of Washington's long-standing distrust of local or particular attachments, which could lay claim to the affections of the people as well as the loyalty of the natural leaders of the community. For Washington, America could not truly command its own fate unless it abandoned or subordinated local or incomplete attachments for something greater. As Washington frequently insisted, the local views of each state, and the separate interests, must yield "to a more enlarged scale of politics," or the country would be "weak, inefficient and disgraceful." The national interest was something higher than the particular interests, and particular interests could best and only be realized in the context of a larger nation. As Washington had written to Lafayette in 1783, the "honour, power, and true Interest of this Country must be measured on a Continental Scale."[46]

As with any other human institution, Washington pointed out, time and habit were needed "to fix the true character" of the government. "To form a new Government, requires infinite care, and unbounded attention," Washington wrote at the time of the Revolution, "for if the foundation is badly laid the superstructure must be bad, too much time therefore, cannot be bestowed in weighing and digesting matters well." Experience was the surest standard of determining the true tendency of the government and would ultimately decide whether a republican government would embrace so large a sphere as that contemplated in the new Constitution. In light of the many powerful and obvious motives to Union, though, Washington was confident that the experiment would be successful.[47]

The new Constitution, Washington noted in the Farewell Address, was also based on and upheld the idea of the rule of law. In its creation, the new federal government was "the offspring of our own choice uninfluenced and unawed, adopted upon full investigation and mature deliberation." In its operation, it was "completely free in its principles, in the distribution of its powers, uniting security with energy, and containing within itself a provision for its own amendment." As a product of this wisdom and deliberation, the Constitution was, as *The Federalist* said, the result of reflection and choice rather than accident and force.[48] Washington was concerned about those tendencies that weakened the rule of law and undermined the duties of citizenship, for that which served to block the execution of the laws with the intent of disrupting the deliberation and action of the duly constituted authorities also disrupted the underlying principles of popular government. These obstructions fostered faction and allowed a small minority to block the will of the majority. In the long run, disrespect for the rule of law would allow "cunning, ambitious and unprincipled men" to subvert the people and take the reins of government. Thus, Washington warned in the Farewell Address not only of "irregular oppositions" to legitimate authority but also of "the spirit of innovation" that desired to bring about change in order to circumvent the principles of the Constitution.

Washington often warned of the "Democratic Societies" that were appearing in America, originally to support the cause of the French Revolution. These groups, instigated in Washington's view by the French (and in particular by Citizen Genet), sought to circumvent the administration's neutrality policies and involve the nation in the wars of the French Revolution. Behind their "popular and fascinating guises" Washington saw the "most diabolical attempt to destroy the best fabric of human government and happiness" known to the world. By designating themselves as permanent judges of legitimately made laws and taking the law into their own hands, these self-created societies undermined the Constitution and the basis of popular government. Washington viewed the Whiskey Rebellion of 1794 as "the first formidable fruit" of these societies. A group of Pennsylvania farmers refused to pay taxes on distilled liquor, and Washington, determined to execute the lawful policies of the government, called forth the militia to suppress the rebellion. In his Message to Congress about the insurrection, Washington spoke of the embittered men who sought to control the will of others "by the guidance of their passions" in order to produce riots and violence against the will of the majority. When it was over, Washington invited the rebels to "return to the demeanor of faithful citizens" and praised the general citizenry that had remained loyal for maintaining "the authority of the laws against licentious invasions."[49]

According to Washington, Genet's purpose was to draw a line between the people and their government, after he found that the officers of the latter would not yield to the hostile measures in which he wanted to embroil the country. Washington argued that the Democratic Societies challenged the basic logic of constitutionalism, which was a reverence for the law. No law had yet been made that hit the taste exactly of every man or every part of the community—but men could not cut and carve out what they would and would not obey, leaving only force to execute the law. The Constitution deserved public confidence and support: it had been chosen deliberately by the people, it united security with liberty, and it contained within itself the provision for its own amendment. For Washington, this meant respect for its authority, compliance with the laws, and acquiescence in its measures, as a matter of duty as enjoined by the fundamental maxims of liberty.

The underlying basis of the American legal system, according to Washington, was the right of the people to make and alter their government. Likewise, according to the Declaration of Independence, governments derived their just powers from the consent of the governed; it was the right of the governed to form, alter, or abolish their Constitution so as to best effect their safety and happiness. The new Constitution, as Washington noted in the Farewell Address, was formed on the basis of this principle. Because of its grounding in the consent of the governed, the Constitution was "sacredly obligatory upon all" until it was formally changed "by an explicit and authentic act of the whole People." One is reminded of Jefferson's injunction to "bear in mind this sacred principle, that though the will of the majority is in all cases to prevail, that will to be rightful must be reasonable." What made the obligation to obey the law sacred, then, was not the law's force or ability to compel obedience as much as its basis in just principles of government. Indeed, it was the "very idea of the power and the right of the People to establish Government," Washington wrote, that "presupposes the duty of every Individual to obey the established Government."[50]

In an extensive republic, government must have as much vigor as is consistent with the security of liberty. Government must be able to resist the enterprises of faction, prevent the minority from preventing majority rule, and be able to enforce the law. To be legitimate, however, that government must secure the rights of persons and property. The "surest Guardian" of liberty, for Washington, was not a small and weak government but a strong government of adequate powers that were both strictly limited and properly distributed and balanced.

Party and Faction

One major problem of faction, Washington went on to note in the Farewell Address, was found in geographical discriminations and sectionalism within the Union. Washington was concerned that a strong preference for one's home state or local section of the country would become prejudicial and destructive of the common interest and national character. In particular, he feared that designing men would misrepresent the opinions of other sections of the country as an expedient to their own political power. This would cause local jealousies and passions to become central even though they might not naturally be as divisive. "You cannot shield yourselves too much against the jealousies and heart burnings which spring from these misrepresentations," Washington warned. A perception of insurmountable local interests and views, far from uniting the country, tended to render "Alien to each other those who ought to be bound together by fraternal affection."

This discussion in the Address foreshadowed the conflict between Union and sectionalism in the mid-nineteenth century over the question of slavery, a practice Washington strongly, but not directly, opposed. Although Washington owned slaves, his actions—for instance, restructuring his farm so as not to depend on slave labor, emancipating his slaves in his will, and providing for their care after his death—and his writings left little doubt that he opposed the peculiar institution.[51] It is notable that Washington did not bring up the question of slavery in the Farewell Address's discussion of sectionalism. He did not, for example, recommend that others follow his personal example in laying the groundwork for eventual emancipation. Washington undoubtedly believed that an explicit public discussion would work against such a peaceful and gradual solution, by inflaming the sectional and political passions, and thereby undermining the creation of the Union and constitutional government that were necessary to the safety and happiness of the American people. Once Union and Constitution had been secured and public opinion soundly based, future statesmen might enjoy the latitude to deal with the great contradiction of a slave-holding republic.

In the Farewell Address, Washington's initial solution to the generic problem of sectionalism was that of encouraging a national interest: such distinctions would be solved by building trust among the various sections, disproving their suspicions and prejudices, and establishing the advantages that the sections would gain through common actions such as commerce and foreign relations. It was in this context that Washington noted the value of the Jay and Pinckney Treaties and in general referred back to his earlier arguments for individual sectional interests in the Union.[52] Taking "a more comprehensive view," Washington proceeded to warn of "the baneful effects of the Spirit of Party"—one of the two most famous recommendations of the Farewell Address. (The other recommendation, concerning foreign alliances, came later.) This was not surprising, for the question of party, and the more notorious problem of faction, was the dominant question of Washington's presidency and a prominent concern throughout his career. Indeed, the development of political parties is often seen as a defining phenomenon of the Washington administration, with Washington caught between Jefferson and the Republicans on the one hand, and Hamilton and the Federalists on the other.

From Washington's perspective, parties were only a small part of the struggle of the Founding. To the extent that political parties did not threaten this larger project, they were to be tolerated as stemming from a natural difference of opinions. When parties got in the way of nation-building, they were a serious annoyance but something that intelligent patriots should be able to overcome. When party disputes came to threaten the government and undercut the principles on which the government was based, Washington believed that parties were to be condemned and combated. Parties were especially dangerous when the partisans accused each other of seeking to change the form of the government and considered each other to be grave enemies. A volatile debate of this nature would appeal to the passions rather than the reason of the people and was not conducive to the stable and peaceful conditions needed for the flourishing of republican government. Given his view from outside the party controversy raging at the time, Washington naturally chose to warn the people about the spirit of party and the dangers of factionalism.

Washington's consideration of party in the Farewell Address began by noting that the roots of the spirit of party were to be found in the "strongest passions" of the human mind and thus were inseparable from "our nature" as men. While it was to be regretted, this meant that the spirit of party could not be removed from human activity and hence was to be found, to some extent or other, in every form of government. (The same argument is found famously in *Federalist* No. 10, where James Madison writes that "the latent causes of faction" are "sown in the nature of man.") Washington was well aware that in some monarchies party might be a useful check on the administration of government and thus serve the cause of liberty. Nevertheless, it was "a spirit not to be encouraged" in popular governments.[53]

Washington's reason for opposing party spirit was a matter of prudence. As there was never a lack of party feeling, there was always enough for every possible beneficial purpose. The real threat that party spirit presented, then, was not its existence but "the constant danger of excess." Washington saw party spirit as a force that stirred up individual passions and overpowered man's reason, thus bringing out the worst aspects of popular government. It was in a regime based on popular opinion, not coincidentally, that party spirit tended to be seen "in its greatest rankness," making it the "worst enemy" of free government. In its worst form the spirit of party distracted the government, agitated the community, fomented riots and insurrections, and opened the door to foreign influence and corruption. It was at this point that party spirit became factional and, in Washington's view, far more dangerous than mere disagreements over policy or personality. The successive dominion of one faction over another was itself "a frightful despotism," and the disorders that resulted encouraged the tendency toward tyranny and dictatorship. The myriad problems of party spirit, Washington concluded, made it both "the interest and duty of a wise People to discourage and restrain it."

On numerous occasions during the Revolution, Washington lamented that party disputes and personal quarrels had become the order of the day with the political leadership. Congress was then "rent by party" and concerned with business of a trifling nature instead of the critical matters of great national moment. In mid–1779 Washington, perhaps thinking of his own political role, observed that it would be worthy of "the ambition of a patriot Statesman" to "endeavor to pacify party differences," restore vigor to the government, and build confidence in the people.[54]

After the Revolution, in the 1780s, Washington thought that local prejudices and jealousies stood in the way of building a national character, unifying the country, and establishing a well-ordered constitution. What was needed was a national sense of disinterestedness and a common good that transcended the petty opinions of local and state politicians. At the time, he did not consider opposition to these goals to be the result of "party" opinion but of demagogues and faction. Shays's Rebellion was an extreme example of this: "There are surely men of consequence and abilities behind the curtain who move the puppets; the designs of whom may be deep and dangerous." During the debate over the proposed Constitution, Washington worried that the anti-Federalists were trying to alarm and stir up the passions of the people, rather than appeal to their reason and judgment. Nevertheless, he thought that the ratification debate was highly beneficial: it put a new light on the science of government and led to a better understanding of the rights of man. If the intentions of the Constitution were only properly explained to the public, Washington maintained, it would prove satisfactory to all. During the first elections, although he warned of anti-Federalist machinations and intrigue, he was pleased with the favorable pro-Federalist (that is, pro-Constitution) outcome and did not consider these electoral divisions to be based on party distinctions.[55]

Although Washington recognized (and often lamented) the establishment of political parties and more and more during his presidency sided with the policies of one rather than the other, Washington never considered himself a partisan. He maintained that political problems could be solved by the wise cooperation of gentlemen. "I was no party man myself," he told Jefferson in 1796, "and the first wish of my heart was, if parties existed, to reconcile them." He preferred to follow principle rather than the orthodoxy of party or the tenets of men. Indeed, shortly before his death, he warned his own supporters of their disinclination to follow principle: "If *Men*, not *Principles*, can influence the choice on the part of the Federalists, what but fluctuations are to be expected?" Washington believed that if the Federalists gave up their claim to the principles of the Founding, their cause would soon be at an end.[56]

In the Farewell Address, Washington associated the republican principles of the Revolution and the Constitution with the policies of his administration, all of which were intended to establish a nation based on those principles. Those who radically opposed the administration's basic policies, therefore, were just as surely opposing the government and the republican project. Before he retired he told Timothy Pickering that he would not bring someone into his administration whose political tenets were "adverse to the measures which the *general* government" was pursuing. To do so would be "a sort of political Suicide" not as much for Washington's administration or a political party but for the general government itself. In 1798, Washington told Lafayette that a party was "determined (as all their Conduct evinces) by Clogging its Wheels indirectly to change the nature of it, and to subvert the Constitution" while the friends of the government, who wanted to preserve peace and neutrality so as to preserve the new nation, were accused of monarchism and aristocratic tendencies. With the passage of the Virginia and Kentucky Resolutions that same year, Washington regretted that individual states were now leading the partisan opposition to the government, pursuing measures that would eventually either dissolve the Union or lead to coercion. Washington feared that the nation was "hastening to an awful crisis."[57]

When party politics had begun to emerge in the early 1790s, Washington maintained that there were two types of characters opposing his administration: the good characters who were opposed to the government's policies—like Jefferson and Madison—and those bad and diabolical characters who not only opposed administration policy but also sought to undermine the people's confidence in the government itself—like Philip Freneau and Benjamin Bache, editor of the opposition paper *Aurora*. It was the latter, and not the former, whom Washington considered the real source of the partisanship that was dividing popular opinion. As a result, it was they who presented the threat to constitutional order. By seeking to undermine a popular government, legitimately approved by the people, these characters were encouraging factionalism. Their arguments were intended to confuse those "men of cool and dispassionate minds" who ought to be alarmed by and seek to moderate such outrageous rhetoric. Washington maintained that Jefferson and Hamilton were republicans *and* federalists— the very point Jefferson would make in his Inaugural Address of 1801. Based on their fundamental agreement to advance the republican cause under the new Constitution, Washington thought they should be able to work together despite their many policy differences. When Jefferson defended himself in correspondence with Washington, but still accused Hamilton of a design to subvert the Constitution, Washington could only add his hope that "the cup wch. has been presented, may not be snatched from our lips by a discordance of *action* when I am persuaded that there is no discordance in your *views*."[58]

In drawing a distinction between "the friends and foes of order and good government," Washington lamented that while the latter worked at distilling their "poison," the former depended too often on the convictions of the people without encouraging the means of establishing those convictions.[59] The implication was that any legitimate party should seek first and foremost to maintain and inculcate the core principles of the nation, rather than to generate platforms and slogans. If that were the case, Washington figured, formal political parties would not be necessary.

The Farewell Address presented Washington's solution to the party problem. In *Federalist* No. 10, Madison argued that there were only two ways to remove the causes of faction: either "destroying the liberty which is essential to its existence" or "giving to every citizen the same opinions, the same passions, and the same interests." The first was worse than the disease because while liberty was necessary for political freedom, it was also "to faction what air is to fire." Without liberty, faction "instantly expires"; with too much it becomes "a destructive agent." In the Farewell Address, Washington concurred that, as the deepest roots of party spirit were found in "our nature," it was a "fire not to be quenched." Instead, party spirit demanded "a uniform vigilance to prevent its bursting into a flame, lest instead of warming it should consume."[60]

The implication was that party spirit must be moderated and properly channeled. Madison, again in *Federalist* No. 10, concluded that the causes of faction could not be removed and that relief lay in controlling their effects. Although Madison was well aware of the need to shape, and rely upon, public opinion, and despite the fact that *Federalist* No. 10 was by no means his (or *The Federalist's*) final word on the subject, Madison's solution in *Federalist* No. 10 was to extend the sphere of government so as to include a variety of parties and interests. Washington, however, was still interested in controlling, or at least moderating, the causes of party spirit and faction. An effort ought to be made to mitigate and assuage it, he argued, not by law or coercion but by "the force of public opinion."[61] His solution was not to increase the diversity of interests so much as to shape a common opinion that would transcend the petty and self-interested differences that divided men. Washington's conception of how a common opinion would be shaped had four distinct elements, each of which he proceeded to discuss in the Farewell Address: civic responsibility; moral and religious obligation; education; and justice toward foreign nations. These elements, coupled with the mitigating influence of good government, would serve to restrain the dangerous tendencies of free government by moderating the natural passions that, among other things, encouraged party animosities. A common opinion would also build a common understanding about government, a sacred regard for the Union, and a common American character.

Civic Responsibility

The Farewell Address, then, taught that the creation of a Union with a national purpose and a national character demanded not only a good government but also the cultivation of the proper habits and dispositions on the part of both the rulers and the ruled. "The blessed Religion revealed in the word of God will remain an eternal and awful monument to prove that the best Institutions may be abused by human depravity," Washington had written in the draft of his First Inaugural. Political institutions could always be brought down to the "vilest of purposes" by either the lustful appetite for power of those who administer the government or the laziness and corruption of those who are represented by the government. When these passions overcame the constitutional barrier, thus violating "the unalienable rights of humanity," it would be another proof that no mere contract among men is perpetual or sacrosanct. No matter how well constructed or scrupulously ratified, Washington argued, "no Wall of words, . . . no mound of parchment can be so formed as to stand against the sweeping torrent of boundless ambition on the one side, aided by the sapping current of corrupted morals on the other."[62]

The problem under the regime of the Articles of Confederation and the dominance of state governments had been that jealous and petty politics invited and encouraged a jealous and petty spirit in the people. By nourishing petty politics, speculation, and special interests, and in general aiding narrow political passions, bad government generated licentious appetites and corrupted morals. In at least two ways, Washington argued in the Farewell Address, the new Constitution actually encouraged moderation and good habits of government. First, the separation of powers and the system of checks and balances thwarted governmental despotism and encouraged responsibility in public representatives. A responsible government, in turn, bolstered responsible people. Second, the legitimate constitutional amendment process allowed democratic reform at the same time that it elevated the document above the popular passions of the moment, thereby encouraging deliberation and patience in the people.

Washington also hoped that good opinions in the people, and good government, would have a complementary effect on politics. On the one hand, the "habits of thinking" in a free people would "inspire caution" in their representatives and thereby confine them to their constitutional responsibilities and prevent a spirit of encroachment in government: "A just estimate of that love of power, and proneness to abuse it, which predominates in the human heart is sufficient to satisfy us of the truth of this position." On the other hand, the people would learn from the law-making process to curb their own passions for immediate political change and abide by the legitimate legal process. The demands of good public policy would cause the people to be moderate and circumspect. In order to avoid the accumulation of debt and support the legitimate operations of the government, Americans would learn to cherish public credit and pay their due taxes. This discussion in the Farewell Address echoed the public justice argument made in the Circular Address. Washington also made in this context an argument for a strong national defense: timely preparations were less costly than emergency expenditures, making it in the national interest constantly to be vigilant.[63]

For Washington, a necessary precursor to the encouragement of civic responsibility and the moderation of public passion, though, was the moderation of private passion through the encouragement of private morality. Republican government was only possible if the public and private virtues needed for civil society and self-government remained strong and effective. "As there is a degree of depravity in mankind which requires a certain degree of circumspection and distrust, so there are other qualities in human nature which justify a certain portion of esteem and confidence," Madison wrote in *Federalist* No. 55. "Republican government presupposes the existence of these qualities in a higher degree than any other form."[64] In his

First Inaugural Washington had pointed out the connection, repeated in the Farewell Address, between private morality and public happiness. This led him to turn to two widely recognized sources of private and public moral obligation: religion and education.

Moral and Religious Obligations

Like most of the leading Founders, Washington believed that religion provided an essential element in popular education and the formation of moral citizens. The "advantages of a finished education," Washington wrote to his step-grandson, were both a "highly cultivated mind, and a proper sense of your duties to God and man." Washington knew that churches and religious denominations cultivated individuals of good character and were in a particularly useful position for encouraging not only private morality but also civic virtue. In his first presidential Thanksgiving Proclamation, Washington called for a day of public thanksgiving and prayer to acknowledge "the many signal favors of Almighty God." These included "the civil and religious liberty with which we are blessed, and the means we have of acquiring and diffusing useful knowledge."[65] In assuring religious liberty, Washington hoped that religious education in America would flourish and become one of those means.

In the Farewell Address, we note, Washington presented Union as a main pillar of American independence, a fact to be recognized by "every reflecting and virtuous mind." The "great Pillars of human happiness" and the "firmest props of the duties of Men and citizens," though, inhered in religion and morality. "Of all the disposition and habits which lead to political prosperity," Washington wrote, "Religion and morality are indispensable supports." That is, religion and morality were understood to be the firmest props of duty, the indispensable supports of the dispositions and habits that lead to political prosperity, and the great pillars of human happiness. Since respect for duty and good habits was needed for good government, religion and morality served as indirect supports of good government by teaching men their moral obligations and creating the conditions for decent politics. Neither the religious nor the political man, Washington proceeded to point out, could ignore this fact. "The mere Politician, equally with the pious man ought to respect and to cherish them," he wrote. A sense of individual religious obligation, Washington noted, was needed to support the oaths necessary in courts of law. Religion, he argued, was necessary for the maintenance of public justice. And no matter what might be conceded to the "influence of refined education on minds of peculiar structure"—a reference to the atheistic tendencies of some forms of Enlightenment education—"reason and experience both forbid us to expect that National morality can prevail in exclusion of religious principle."

While there might be particular cases where morality did not depend on religion, Washington thought that this was not the case for the morality of the nation. In most cases, religion was needed to give weight to morality: "And let us with caution indulge the supposition, that morality can be maintained without religion." It was "substantially true," Washington concluded in the Farewell Address, that "virtue or morality is a necessary spring of popular government." This rule—as with his warning against the extremes of party passions—extended to "every species of free Government." No "sincere friend" of free government could ignore attempts to weaken the "foundation of the fabric."[66]

It has often been noted that Washington's tendency was to speak publicly in the general terms of "providence" rather than in more explicitly religious language. This has led some to conclude that Washington's view of religion was merely instrumental and utilitarian. But the context of Washington's statements, as with those of many of the other Founders, must not be overlooked: they were setting out to create a nation where civil and religious freedom flourished, and this was to be accomplished, among other things, through the separation of church and state. Washington, for his part, nevertheless always saw morality and religion as potential sources of unity rather than strife. They were, to repeat, "great Pillars of human happiness."

Soon after he became President, Washington received congratulatory messages from many individuals and groups, including various churches and religious assemblies. In response, Washington wrote an important series of letters, one to each denomination, thanking them for their sentiments and encouraging their attachment to the new nation. These letters shed additional light on Washington's observations about religion and morality in the Farewell Address. The prospects of national prosperity should excite all good men, Washington told a group of Roman Catholics: "America, under the smiles of a Divine Providence, the protection of a good government, and the cultivation of manners, morals, and piety, cannot fail of attaining an uncommon degree of eminence, in literature, commerce, agriculture, improvements at home and respectability abroad." Those who conducted themselves according to these characteristics, regardless of denomination or beliefs, deserved the protection and support of the government. While he wanted to make sure that religious citizens were patriotic citizens, Washington also wanted them to infuse the general citizenry with their virtues and characteristics. He told a group of Presbyterians that the "prevalence of piety, philanthropy, honesty, industry, and oeconomy" was "particularly necessary" for the happiness of the new nation and encouraged them to emulate these virtues through the "innocence of their lives and the beneficence of their actions." In this way, Washington hoped that America would provide an example of "an enlarged and liberal policy" concerning "liberty of conscience and the immunities of citizenship." Washington's best elaboration of the necessary connection between the fundamental rights of conscience and the duties of citizenship is in his striking letter to the Hebrew Congregation of Newport, Rhode Island:

> It is now no more that toleration is spoken of as if it were the indulgence of one class of people that another enjoyed the exercise of their inherent natural rights, for, happily, the Government of the United States, which gives to bigotry no sanction, to persecution no assistance, requires only that they who live under its protection should *demean themselves as good citizens* in giving it on all occasions their effectual support.[67]

Education

In the midst of the drafting of the Farewell Address, we recall, Washington at one point wrote Hamilton to say that, after further considering the contents of the address, he regretted that the important subject of education had been omitted. After pointing out that education served to advance not only knowledge but also the political task of uniting disparate individuals, Washington directed Hamilton to his (Washington's) letter to the Virginia governor, and the resolves of the Virginia legislature responding to the same, as sources for his thought on the subject. Hamilton recommended that a fuller statement on education be reserved until Washington's upcoming Message to Congress but said that he would add a general comment on education to the main draft. Although Hamilton told Washington that he had included a short paragraph on the subject, nothing on education was added.[68] Washington then himself wrote the statement on education, one of the most succinct of the Address: "Promote, then, as an object of primary importance, institutions for the general diffusion of knowledge. In proportion as the structure of a government gives force to public opinion, it is essential that public opinion should be enlightened." The briefness of this statement, however, is by no means indicative of the relative importance Washington placed on the question of education.

As Hamilton had suggested, Washington returned to this proposal in the Eighth Annual Message, where he explained that the reasons for establishing a national university were to provide for a republican education:

> Amongst the motives to such an Institution, the assimilation of the principles, opinions and manners of our Country men, by the common education of a portion of our Youth from every quarter, well deserves attention. The more homogeneous our Citizens can be made in these particulars, the greater will be our prospect of permanent Union; and a primary object of such a National Institution should be, the education of our Youth in the science of Government. In a Republic, what species of knowledge can be equally important? and what duty, more pressing on its Legislature, than to patronize a plan for communicating it to those, who are to be the future guardians of the liberties of the Country?[69]

In fact, Washington had long been a strong supporter of education, an aspect of his life that is often overlooked. While his view of education was primarily practical, it cannot be said that Washington was either unaware or unappreciative of more speculative knowledge and the scholarly life. He believed, for instance, that mathematical investigations trained the mind and were "peculiarly worthy of rational beings." It was here that "the rational faculties find a firm foundation to rest upon." Such investigations also encouraged higher theoretical knowledge: "From the high ground of mathematical and philosophical demonstration, we are insensibly led to far nobler speculations and sublimer meditations." In the end, however, Washington's conception was foremost that of a solid and ethical general education. The "best means of forming a manly, virtuous and happy people, will be found in the right education of youth," Washington wrote in 1784. "Without this foundation, every other means, in my opinion, must fail." Education and knowledge were to be encouraged for the purpose of "qualifying the rising generation for patrons of good government, virtue, and happiness."[70]

Washington believed that formal schooling was especially important and supported numerous public institutions of learning. In 1785 he gave all of his shares in inland waterway companies to the establishment of two charity schools for the education and support of poor and indigent children, in particular those who were the children of fallen soldiers. Later that year he supplied the endowment for a charity school in Alexandria, Virginia, that would provide an education in reading, writing, and arithmetic for poorer and less privileged citizens. Washington was equally dedicated to higher education and used his influence to support various colleges, at one point becoming the Chancellor of William and Mary College.[71]

Washington's most important contribution in this area was an attempt to create a national university in which the arts, sciences, and belles lettres would be taught, providing the liberal education "necessary to qualify our citizens for the exigencies of public, as well as private life." One of Washington's intentions was to overcome the desire of many young students to go abroad for their education, where they might imbibe "principles and habits not friendly to republican government." By bringing the best students, who Washington hoped would become future national leaders, together in an academic setting in the United States, a university would serve to break the prejudices and unreasonable jealousies "which prevent or weaken friendships and impair the harmony of the Union." It was also hoped that common education would unify the people in the same way that the Revolution had done for the previous generation. "What, but the mixing of people from different parts of the United States during the War rubbed off these impressions?" Washington asked. With the end of the war and the renewed growth of local prejudices, Washington saw a national university as the primary means to provide "the intimate intercourse of characters early in life" necessary to encourage support for Union.[72]

To secure the blessing of providence for America required the "cool and deliberate exertion" of the "patriotism, firmness and wisdom" of those making the laws, Washington wrote in his First Message to Congress in January 1790. Yet in that brief address, Washington made no specific policy recommendations outside those outlined in Article I, section 8, of the Constitution. The one recommendation that he did make was a call for the general promotion of knowledge, "the surest basis of public happiness." Knowledge, good under all governments, was essential in a free government. It reminded those in power that the ends of government were found in "the enlightened confidence of the people." More importantly, it taught the citizens to know and defend the rights that the government was formed to protect, to distinguish between oppression and lawful authority, and "to discriminate the spirit of liberty from that of licentiousness—cherishing the first, avoiding the last."[73] With this type of knowledge, the people would have the political and moral education necessary for republican government.

Justice Toward Foreign Nations

It followed from the discussion in the Farewell Address of the proper habits and dispositions that the United States should "observe good faith and justice towds. all Nations." As there was a connection between private morality and public happiness in a people, so there was a connection be-

tween the virtue and happiness of a nation. As there were proper dispositions and habits of people, so too with nations. This conduct was enjoined
by both religion and morality as well as good policy. The main reason, in
addition to cultivating friendly relations with other nations, was that the
honor of the nation required such conduct. Washington wrote in the Address that "it will be worthy of a free, enlightened, and at no distant period,
a great Nation, to give to mankind the magnanimous and too novel example of a People always guided by an exalted justice and benevolence."
Besides, proper conduct toward other nations would serve to elevate and
distinguish the national character. "The experiment," Washington wrote,
"is recommended by every sentiment which ennobles human Nature."[74]

Good faith and justice in foreign affairs demanded not only freedom
of action but also independent thinking. True independence depended on
not only the absence of physical restraint and control but also the flourishing of an autonomous and free character. If just and amicable relations
with other nations were to be cultivated, any "inveterate antipathies" or
"passionate attachments" on the part of the people must first be overcome.
Washington told Americans in the Farewell Address that they must be free
from their hatreds and allegiances to foreign nations if they were to become
partisans of their own nation and the larger cause of human freedom that it
represented. Preconceived positions restricted policy options and prevented
the nation from responsibly choosing its own course and seeking justice for
itself and others. When these attachments dominated the public mind, they
not only led the nation away from its duty and interest but made the supposedly free nation "in some degree a slave" to the other. Governments
based on consent often followed the "national propensity" to adopt
"through passion what reason would reject." The habitual hatred of particular nations encouraged insult and injury, and this often led to unnecessary
conflicts and wars. Foreign attachments, on the other hand, encouraged
public support and national concessions on issues where no common interest existed. They also brought the nation imprudently into the particular
quarrels and disputes of the other. Passionate attachments to foreign nations
had the added problem of giving to "ambitious, corrupted, or deluded
citizens" an easy opportunity to betray their country without malice or
popular disapproval. Those who resisted favoritism—the "real patriots"
like Washington—were the ones who became "suspected and odious"
while the "tools and dupes" often gained the approval and support of the
people.[75]

Washington favored harmony and liberal intercourse with all nations.
This was a position recommended by "policy, humanity and interest."
Washington had followed these principles in declaring the United States'

neutrality toward the European war in April 1793. This position could be inferred, he argued, from the obligations of justice and humanity to maintain peace and amity toward all nations. The United States not only had a right but was also bound by duty and interest to take such a position. "The duty of holding a Neutral conduct may be inferred, without any thing more, from the obligation which justice and humanity impose on every Nation, in cases in which it is free to act, to maintain inviolate the relations of Peace and amity towards other Nations." Washington, in turn, chose to maintain the policy with "moderation, perseverence and firmness." He argued that the United States should not forego the advantages of the peculiar political and geographic situation it providentially found itself in. It was his final recommendation—indeed, the theme of his whole understanding of foreign and defense policy—that the nation pursue a long-term course of placing itself in a position to defy external threats, defend its own neutrality, and, eventually, choose peace or war as its own "interest guided by our justice shall Counsel." "My ardent desire is, and my aim has been," Washington explained to Patrick Henry in 1795,

> to comply strictly with *all* our engagements, foreign and domestic; but to keep the U States free from *political* connexions with *every* other country. To see that they *may be* independent of *all*, and under the influence of *none*. In a word, I want an *American* character, that the powers of Europe may be convinced we act for *ourselves* and not for *others*; this in my judgment, is the only way to be respected abroad and happy at home and not by becoming the partizans of Great Britain or France, create dissensions, disturb the public tranquillity, and destroy, perhaps for ever the cement wch. binds the Union.[76]

Citizenship

The tone of the Farewell Address's conclusion was that of humility and modesty, as if Washington was lowering the reader's expectations. Although he noted that he was "unconscious of intentional error," he recognized that it was possible that he had "committed many errors" in the course of his presidency. "Whatever they may be," he noted, "I fervently beseech the Almighty to avert or mitigate the evils to which they may tend." Washington asked for the nation's indulgence and hoped that "the faults of incompetent abilities" would be "consigned to oblivion, as myself must soon be to the Mansion of rest."[77] Having learned at the beginning of the Address that he was retiring from public life, the reader is now reminded that Washington will not live forever.

Washington was reluctant to assume that his counsels would have the effect he intended: "I dare not hope they will make the strong and lasting impression, I could wish." Perhaps he feared that this would not be the first time that his advice fell on deaf ears; the Circular Address of 1783, he had noted on a previous occasion, had largely been ignored until it was almost too late to heed its advice.[78] Given the significance that Washington must have known would be accorded his closing thoughts under the circumstances of his retirement, this comment seems to be an intentional understatement—much like Lincoln's remark that his words at Gettysburg would be little noted nor long remembered. By the end of the Farewell Address, the reader, whether he agreed with the sentiment or not, must surely have felt the full moral authority of Washington's words.

Washington was well aware of the high aim he had in mind. He hoped that his advice might lead Americans to "controul the usual current of the passions" and "prevent our Nation from running the course which has hitherto marked the Destiny of Nations." The impression that Washington wished to engrave on his nation was not one of policy but one of character—a much more difficult task. He endeavored to affect the usual current and course of human affairs. His advice sought to inculcate maturity and moderation in both domestic and international affairs. If they chose to follow his advice, the American people would have to learn to control not only their public but also their private proclivities to follow their desires instead of their reason. And if this were too much to ask, Washington held out the prospect that his sentiments might still be productive of some partial benefits. He hoped that his advice might "now and then" be remembered so as to "moderate the fury of party spirit, to warn against the mischiefs of foreign Intriegue, [and] to guard against the Impostures of pretended patriotism." If his words did not moderate the people, at least they might serve to moderate their leaders and representatives.[79]

The political teaching of Washington's statesmanship, including the Farewell Address, was that of moderation. In his *Life of Washington,* John Marshall wrote that Washington always respected "the real and deliberate sentiments of the people, [as] their gusts of passion passed over, without ruffling the smooth surface of his mind," yet at the same time "had the magnanimity to pursue [the nation's] real interests, in opposition to its temporary prejudices." Washington argued in the Farewell Address that political passions must be moderated by good government and a sound common opinion based on proper dispositions and habits, and that local sentiments must be replaced by a sacred attachment to the Union and the Constitution. This was the sum total of the national character. It is in this sense that the general argument of the Farewell Address is essentially the same as Abraham Lincoln's much-quoted 1838 Lyceum Address. There Lincoln argued that the political passions of the American Revolution were no longer sufficient and were, perhaps, dangerous for maintaining republican political institutions. Instead, he called for "new pillars in the temple of liberty" to be hewn from the materials of unimpassioned reason. "Let those materials be molded into general intelligence, sound morality, and, in particular, a reverence for the Constitution and laws," Lincoln argued. All this he presented in the name of Washington: "that we improved to the last, that we remained free to the last, that we revered his name to the last, that during his long sleep we permitted no hostile foot to pass over or desecrate his resting-place, shall be that which to learn the last trump shall awaken our Washington."[80]

The final themes of the Farewell Address were citizenship and friendship. Washington anticipated his own retirement, he noted, with "pleasing expectation." After forty-five years of public service, Washington surely deserved the peace and quiet of private life. He hoped to enjoy for himself the blessings of the more perfect Union that he had worked so long and hard to form. Yet the "ever favourite object" of Washington's heart, which he believed to be "the happy reward" of the Founders' "mutual cares, labours and dangers," was not a life of individual solitude. Instead, Washington spoke as a republican citizen looking forward to sharing the rights and responsibilities of his political community: "I anticipate with pleasing expectation that retreat, in which I promise myself to realize, without alloy, the sweet enjoyment of partaking, in the midst of my fellow Citizens, the benign influence of good Laws under free Government." While free government was necessary for good laws, what sweetened the enjoyment of liberty and justice for Washington was the participation and fellowship of citizens sharing in the common project of self-government, of ruling and being ruled. Washington wrote in the spring of 1797 that

> No wish in my retirement can exceed that of seeing our Country happy; and I can entertain no doubt of its being so, if all of us act the part of good Citizens; contributing our best endeavors to maintain the Constitution, support the laws, and guard our Independence against all assaults from whatever quarter they may come. Clouds may and doubtless often will in the vicissitudes of events, hover over our political concerns, but a steady adherence to these principles will not only dispel them but render our prospects the brighter by such temporary obscurities.[81]

It is no coincidence that the Farewell Address was framed by references to citizenship and friendship. Washington began by referring to himself as a "dutiful citizen" and concluded by speaking of "my fellow Citizens" and to "you, my Countrymen." Early in the Farewell Address, Washington presented his sentiments as the "disinterested warnings of a parting friend," while toward the end he made reference to "these counsels of an old and affectionate friend."[82] These two ideas, citizenship and friendship, were literally the beginning and the end of Washington's collected wisdom for the nation.

Easily overlooked, but of great significance, is the salutation Washington used for the Farewell Address. When he prepared his draft in 1796, before sending it to Hamilton for revision, Washington added at the top of the first page: "Friends and Fellow Citizens." This was, in part, a recognition of an international audience; by the use of this phrase Washington meant to include those who were not his fellow Americans but were the citizens of foreign nations. This point was further emphasized by the location from which the address was issued: not Mount Vernon, or New York, but the United States. Washington was addressing his advice to all the friends of republicanism and, by extension, the opinions of mankind. The final say as to whether he had been faithful in discharging his duties, he noted, would be left "to You and to the world."[83] This inclusion appealed to the natural ground of peaceful and just relations among all human beings, whatever conventional divisions might separate and distinguish them.

Another way of looking at the phrase, reflecting Washington's understanding of his domestic audience, becomes apparent when it is considered in the political context of the complete Address. In 1789, when Washington left Virginia to become President of the United States, he addressed the mayor and citizens of Alexandria as "Gentlemen." His First Inaugural was delivered to his "Fellow-citizens of the Senate and the House of Representatives," as were all eight of his annual messages. The Second Inaugural was addressed to his "Fellow-citizens." Significantly, only the Farewell Address was directed to his "Friends and fellow Citizens." And as if to underline who his friends and fellow citizens were, the headline before the salutation noted that the Address was "To the People of the United States." In the progression of Washington's public rhetoric, the bonds of civility were replaced by political bonds and then strengthened by the private ties of friendship. "True friendship is a plant of slow growth," Washington observed in 1783, "and must undergo and withstand the shock of adversity before it is entitled to the appelation."[84] The deep love of liberty, enlightened patriotism, and common dispositions displayed by the American people over the course of the American Revolution not only had made them fellow countrymen but also had created a deeper attachment.

At the beginning of the Farewell Address, it should be noted in this context, it was one of Washington's vows to heaven that not just Union but "Union and brotherly affection be perpetual." This was reminiscent of Washington's description of his Revolutionary War soldiers as having become a "patriotic band of Brothers." This should be seen in contrast to his warning, in the Farewell Address, of a growing perception of insurmountable local interests and views that tended to render "alien to each other those who ought to be bound together by fraternal affection." In the end, although commercial and security interests would cement the relationship, true political harmony and the love of Union—the essence of the American character—would only exist if Americans were tied together by the bonds of friendship. This reflected Aristotle's classic observation that it is friendship above all else that seems to hold political communities together. Once again Washington's words presaged the words of Lincoln, this time in Lincoln's First Inaugural Address:

> We are not enemies, but friends. We must not be enemies. Though passion may have strained, it must not break our bonds of affection. The mystic chords of memory, stretching from every battlefield and patriot grave to every living heart and hearthstone all over this broad land, will yet swell the chorus of Union, when again touched, as surely they will be, by the better angels of our nature.[85]

With the Farewell Address, not only had Americans become friends and fellow citizens, but also Washington had joined their ranks. In the consummate proof of his dedication to republican government, the extraordinary Washington was stepping down from the pinnacle of political power to participate in government as an ordinary citizen. What seemed to be a radical lowering of Washington's status, however, was actually an elevation of the standard: he was not bringing himself to the common level but raising the people to the level of his own character. In his eulogy of Washington, Bishop John Carroll observed as much: "Whilst he lived, we seemed to stand on loftier ground, for breathing the same air, inhabiting the same country, and enjoying the same constitution and laws, as the sublime and magnanimous Washington. He was invested with a glory, that shed a lustre on all around him." Washington's own sense of duty and sacred obligation—to which could be added the "fervent love" of country that he described in the Farewell Address—now became the model for all Americans. Just as Washington hoped that the love of liberty would be transformed into a love of Union, so he hoped that the love and respect that Americans had for him would be transformed into love and respect for each other and their country.[86]

Independence, the establishment of the Constitution, Union—all were necessary and important steps, but steps nonetheless, in the formation of civic friendship. That Washington could say in 1796 that Americans had become friends and fellow citizens—despite the geographical differences, party divisions, and foreign policy dangers at the time—suggested that the Founding, meaning the *creation* of the regime, was in his mind complete. The challenge was to ensure its health and endurance. This required vigilance in sacredly maintaining the Union and the Constitution and sustaining, and deepening, the brotherly affections of the people. This was to be done by guarding and encouraging the dispositions and habits most conducive to republican government. Only in this way would the happiness of the people, under the auspices of liberty and independence, be made complete.

4

OUR INTEREST,
GUIDED BY OUR JUSTICE

$\mathcal{G}$eorge Washington's Farewell Address represented the culmination of his great public task: to define and elevate the American character by shaping a common opinion, a common view of citizenship, that would transcend the petty and self-interested differences that otherwise divided the people and sections of America. The creation of this common opinion was essential if the great American experiment was to be realized—that is, for Americans to prove that men were good enough to govern themselves and thereby to vindicate the rights of mankind as well as their own. The Farewell Address should therefore be viewed not only, and perhaps not primarily, as being about foreign policy. Washington, in this respect, evinced the classical understanding of politics, which recognized the centrality of internal political questions, as against external problems (that is, problems of survival).

That said, Washington fully appreciated that America's relationship with the rest of the world would necessarily play a major role in determining the success of the great experiment. Washington called attention to this when he stated in the Address that he would have retired in 1792, "but mature reflection on the then perplexed and critical posture of our Affairs with foreign Nations, and the unanimous advice of persons entitled to my confidence, impelled me to abandon that idea."[1] The sections in the Address on foreign affairs had been added since the original draft in 1792, and as a consequence we are allowed to see Washington's full reflections on international as well as domestic policy and on the close relationship between the two. In addition, Washington had to take into account the opinions of a candid world; thus, the president wrote to Hamilton that he wanted the Farewell Address to be calculated "to meet the eye of discerning readers (foreigners particularly, whose curiosity I have little doubt will lead them to inspect it attentively and to pronounce their opinions on the performance)."[2]

Washington's reflections had been focused by the nation's experience during the war between Britain and France that had begun in 1793, a war that had amply demonstrated the continued dangers to American security from that quarter, as well as the vulnerability of American politics to outside influence and pressure. The European war had sharpened the factional conflict in America that Washington had begun to sense in his first presidential term; in fact, the "unanimous advice of persons entitled to my confidence" against retirement in 1792 had been on the grounds that Washington's continued presence in office was necessary to keep these factions in check. But the pressures of foreign affairs had still proven enormously, almost fatally, divisive. As Washington wrote to Jefferson in 1796, "until the last year or two, I had no conception that Parties would, or even could go, to the length I have been witness to." Jefferson had earlier written to James Monroe: "The war has kindled & brought forth the two parties with an ardour that our own interests merely, could never excite."[3]

For Washington, the rise of factionalism based on disagreements over foreign affairs threatened to ruin the American character. Initially, Washington had been optimistic that factional conflict over American foreign policy would prove manageable. In 1793, Secretary of the Treasury Hamilton and Secretary of State Jefferson had worked under Washington's guidance, effectively if unhappily, to craft a neutrality policy that kept the country out of the war, yet retained American honor. As the historians Stanley Elkins and Eric McKitrick have written:

> Washington was the only one present whose viewpoint was in no way complicated by partisan concerns. He was confronted with two distinct lines of argument, each advocated with ingenuity and intelligence. The distance between them, however, was sufficiently close as to enable his own judgment to operate at a level of selective precision, and the end-product reflected it.[4]

The resulting Neutrality Proclamation of April 1793, supplemented by the Neutrality Act of 1794, would become a central and undisputed pillar of American foreign policy for nearly a century and a half. As Professor Bradford Perkins has noted:

> Within a few years the prudence of this form of neutrality seemed clear even to those who initially questioned it. In 1800 the act, originally temporary, was made permanent. In 1817, over the objections by friends of the colonial rebellions in Latin America, the prohibitions were extended to wars of revolution. In 1818 a final piece of legislation codified the system. . . . Except in detail, however, the code of neutrality was not

changed, and the position laid down in 1793 and 1794 remained in place until World War I and beyond.[5]

But Washington's success was not fully evident at the time, in the midst of increasingly intense partisan battles. Washington well understood the differences between his secretaries of treasury and state—he had earlier referred to his administration as a "coalition"—but at the time, he believed those differences to be reconcilable. The uneasy coalition broke down, however, after Jefferson's resignation at the end of 1793. Washington could not entice any other leading Republican (Madison would have been his first choice) to replace him. Jefferson's eventual successor as secretary of state, Edmund Randolph, tried to follow Washington's lead in seeking a middle ground between the two parties, but he lacked Washington's prestige or capability and eventually fell victim to Federalist accusations of being corrupted by the French. But Washington could not have failed to note that Randolph received no real support upon his resignation from leading Republicans, either. And after a highly unsatisfactory experience with James Monroe, a Republican who had been named minister to France, Washington concluded that he could no longer appoint to office someone who did not fully support his administration. Essentially, government from the center, a political coalition, was no longer possible, at least as long as the European war raged. Washington, it is fair to say, now headed a Federalist administration when he pondered the question of retirement in 1796.[6]

Is the Farewell Address then simply a Federalist manifesto, especially in foreign policy? Suspicion on this score deepens once Hamilton's involvement in its drafting is known. Even if Hamilton was not the author of the Address, as we demonstrated in the previous chapter, the fact that Washington turned to Hamilton for assistance—rather than, say, to Madison, who aided Washington in the 1792 drafting process—may say much about the president's state of mind. This partisanship seems confirmed by the contemporary reaction of some Republicans, who thought the Address a thinly veiled attack on Republicanism and on France, and an effort to influence the upcoming election in favor of the Federalists. Certainly by this time Washington unquestionably had deep suspicions of the methods and motives of those who called themselves Republicans, including Jefferson. But Washington was still guided by his conviction that "I was no party man myself, and the first wish of my heart was, if parties did exist, to reconcile them."[7]

In foreign policy terms, the striking fact about the Address is not what was new and original, but what was familiar and common to all Americans,

Republican as well as Federalist. Taken out of their immediate context, many of Washington's arguments could easily have been expressed by a Republican. The basic sentiment of the Farewell Address was restated most memorably in Jefferson's First Inaugural of 1801: "peace, commerce, and honest friendship with all nations, entangling alliances with none."[8] The fact that the expression "entangling alliances" is often mistakenly attributed to Washington and the Farewell Address is an indication of how well Washington captured the common ground about foreign policy that existed among Americans, above the ordinary level of political debate. In Washington's view, this common ground had been forgotten, distorted, or used for bad purposes in the heat of the battle over the direction of American foreign policy. The Address sought to reestablish standards by which Americans could dispassionately judge men's actions and thereby weigh their true intentions.

In this context, Washington did not intend the Farewell Address merely to be a defense of his apparent shift towards Federalism. Rather, it was to provide in speech what he could no longer do in day-to-day politics: to articulate the grounds on which all Americans genuinely interested in the national welfare could be rallied. The Farewell Address was intended to be a guide to the true and enduring middle ground of American politics. This is not to say that Washington sought consensus for consensus' sake or that he was willing to accept the lowest common denominator between the competing factions. Instead, he proposed to appeal to the highest possible grounds of agreement. We are reminded of his attitude toward the Constitutional Convention, when he called on his collaborators to "adopt no temporizing expedients, but probe the defects of the [Articles of Confederation] to the bottom, and provide radical cures."[9] This was Washington's approach to public affairs and to the building of the American character: while fully appreciating the difficulties, prejudices, and self-interested qualities of American life, he sought to elevate that life by pointing towards something higher.

Commanding Its Own Fortunes

What was that highest possible ground? Washington wrote Lafayette in 1789 that he thought he saw "a *path*, as clear and as direct as a ray of light, which leads to the attainment" of the "permanent felicity of the American commonwealth." That path, Washington told us in the Farewell Address, was designed "to gain time for our country to settle and mature its recent institutions, and to progress, without interruption, to that degree of strength and consistency, which is necessary to *give it, humanly speaking, command of its own fortunes.*"[10]

Washington here set out the central, definitive objective of American foreign policy—the highest possible common denominator that all Americans of good will and character could support. Washington's objective—to give America command of its own fortunes—was interpreted by the great diplomatic historian, Samuel Flagg Bemis, to be one of strategic independence, or freedom of action, for the United States in international affairs.[11] It was surely that. But it was also something more. Washington's expression, "command of its own fortunes," called to mind the image of a gentleman able to manage his own affairs well, who had mastered his own passions and who could make his own way in the world. This, of course, was a fair description of Washington himself. Further, his qualification of America's goal—"humanly speaking"—served as a reminder that fortune might under the best of circumstances be commanded, but never conquered. There were limits on human wisdom, power, and virtue that prudence and humility could never ignore. Washington self-consciously distinguished America's path from the modern Machiavellian project of subjecting chance or nature to human will.

Another way to understand command of one's own fortunes is to recall the classical goal for a political community—self-sufficiency.[12] Self-sufficiency does not refer exclusively to material things, although the possession of those things is necessary to leading a complete and fulfilling life. Instead, it refers to those conditions sufficient for a sense of common moral purpose and well-being, of harmony, that needs no outside support or guidance for its existence or perpetuation. The classics taught that a citizen, even a gentleman like Washington, could not be self-sufficient. But a self-sufficient America could freely choose its own leaders, establish its own laws, and follow its own conscience, so as to be able to reach its full and complete potential as a republican political community. In the Farewell Address, Washington referred to this situation as one of "real independence." If successful, the United States would be truly sovereign: to use Jefferson's expression, America, and Americans, could then exercise their natural independence free from everything but the moral law that bound all mankind.[13]

It is important to note that Washington and the Founders' understanding of "command of its own fortunes" was not in all respects identical with the classical understanding of self-sufficiency. Most notably in terms of foreign policy, the American project as defined by Washington was that of self-government on an continental scale, rather than the ancient ideal of the small communities of ancient Greece. This expansiveness was not

merely territorial in character: the American notions of justice and humanity were cosmopolitan and outward-looking. Further, America would be a
commercial republic, not a military one, in contrast to Rome. As Alexander Hamilton wrote: "Neither the manners nor the genius of Rome are
suited to the republic or the age we live in. All her maxims and habits were
military, her government was constituted for war. Ours is unfit for it, and
our situation still less than our constitution, invites us to emulate the conduct of Rome, or to attempt a display of unprofitable heroism." Washington and the Founders proposed to do what Rome could not: establish an
empire of liberty.[14]

The key to self-sufficiency for Washington was to create the political
grounds—a public and private character—that would successfully reconcile, or comprehend, justice with utility, duty with interest, the general
good with particular advantage. This comprehension represented the essential grounds for citizenship and, ultimately, for the possibility of friendship
and happiness in a modern, self-sufficient political community. Upon
Rhode Island's ratification of the Constitution in 1790, Washington wrote
that "the bond of Union is now complete, and we once more consider
ourselves as one family . . . we should all remember that we are members
of that community upon whose general success depends our particular and
individual welfare."[15] The comprehension of interest and justice was
equally essential for dealing with other nations and peoples through a republican foreign policy.

We recall in this respect Washington's First Inaugural: "there is no
truth more thoroughly established, than that there exists in the economy
and force of nature, an indissoluble union between virtue and happiness;
between duty and advantage; between the genuine maxims of an honest
and magnanimous policy, and the solid rewards of public prosperity and
felicity." Such comprehension of justice and utility, of duty and interest,
and of the general and particular welfare, is especially demanding and difficult in foreign affairs. International relations are arguably the realm of necessity—above all, of survival, of self-preservation—that overrides, or at
least narrows, the pursuit of the nobler ends of the regime. As Hamilton
wrote in the *Federalist*: "Safety from external danger is the most powerful
director of national conduct. Even the ardent love of liberty will, after a
time, give way to its dictates."[16] If necessity reigns supreme, as the European diplomatic tradition held, then justice certainly is not possible in international relations. This is the logic of reason of state: no nation, including
America, can make justice a central component of its foreign policy. Alter-
natively, if justice is impossible in international relations, perhaps America
should withdraw from the world to retain the possibility of justice at home.

Or, a just America arguably can only be involved in the world if it makes that world just, by enforcing its notion of justice on others.

Washington, as we shall see, implicitly rejected in the Farewell Address each of these alternatives to reconcile, or separate, justice and interest in American foreign policy—what can respectively be called power politics; isolationism; and crusading internationalism. Each contained an element of truth and therefore would have to be taken seriously by Washington, in part because each position toward justice and interest had its advocates in American politics. But each was deficient in and of itself. Washington tried to take the best of each to create the grounds of a truly American foreign policy, able to command its own fortunes. Washington believed that it was possible to have a foreign policy neither driven by necessity nor ignoring it—a policy of pursuing what Washington termed *"our interest, guided by our justice."*[17]

Further, Washington insisted that addressing both terms—interest and justice—was essential to the proper formation of the American character. To neglect to pursue legitimate American commercial and strategic interests in the world would be unwise. The United States needed wealth and security to undergird the national character. Neglect of these would lead the European powers to take advantage of America; it would divide and weaken the body politic, as some domestic groups benefitted and others suffered. But to behave badly toward other nations and peoples, in the immoderate pursuit of these interests, would debase the American character. By the same token, allowing others to behave badly toward the United States would degrade that character in different ways.

If the United States successfully pursued these national interests of security and prosperity, Washington, like many of his contemporaries, believed that America would become a great nation. But Washington's definition of greatness attempted to distinguish "between happiness and splendour." America, as he put it in 1788, would become "a great, *respectable*, and commercial Nation, if we shall continue United and faithful to ourselves." Washington wrote in his discarded First Inaugural Address that the American people "may doubtless enjoy all the great blessings of the social State; and yet the United States may not for a long time to come make a brilliant figure as a nation, among the nations of the earth." But even once America had become a brilliant figure, if the people should properly be "actuated by principles of true magnanimity, they will not suffer their ambition to be awakened."

> They should guard against ambition as their greatest enemy. We should not, in imitation of some nations which have been celebrated for a false

kind of patriotism, wish to aggrandize our own Republic at the expense of the freedom and happiness of the rest of mankind. The prospect that Americans will not act upon so narrow a scale affords the most comfortable reflections to a benevolent mind.[18]

At a certain point, of course, such noble sentiments would have to be translated into policy. There must be a prudent application of the imperative of commanding the American fortune, through a policy of self-interest guided by justice. As we shall see in the Farewell Address, for Washington this meant adopting a policy of strict American neutrality toward the wars among the European powers and defending that policy against its enemies at home and abroad. Although the neutrality policy was geared toward shielding the emerging American regime from the pressures then being created by foreign wars, that policy also contained within it Washington's longer-term recommendation: "Observe good faith and justice towds. all Nations. Cultivate peace and harmony with all."[19]

Union and Interest

Washington's injunction in the Farewell Address, for America to command its own fortunes, required, to a first order, taking care of the nation's material interests. All political communities need to defend themselves and to acquire things that they need but do not possess, whether through commerce or conquest. At the same time, individuals within the community will inevitably pursue their own security and well-being. (Madison defined interest "in the popular sense" as "the immediate augmentation of property and wealth.") Washington fully recognized the self-interested dimensions of private, public, and international affairs, and the need to incorporate interest into calculations of policy. Self-sacrifice was the exceptional rather than the ordinary motivator of action among men and nations.[20]

Washington did not deny the possibility of patriotism or of disinterested behavior, but he understood the need to augment and reinforce virtue with the prospect of advantage. For Washington, the Union was to be the vehicle by which the national interest with respect to foreign powers, as well as the interests of individuals and sections, could best be realized. As we noted in the previous chapter, the Farewell Address defended Union on the grounds of both sympathy and interest. The people were to be reminded, or persuaded, that they could best achieve the material requirements necessary to command their own fortunes by being united rather than divided. On the point of security, the greater strength and greater resources provided by the Union meant "proportionately greater security against external danger, a less frequent interruption of their Peace by foreign nations." As to prosperity, Washington recounted in the Farewell Address the complementary resources and enterprises of the various sections (North, South, East, and West), which among other items provided the whole with important advantages in foreign commerce.[21]

Washington believed that a league or alliance of American states or regions for the purposes of defense and foreign policy was insufficient. No necessary harmony of interest among the sections would override other opposing political forces working against a common defense and foreign policy. If sympathy alone would not serve to keep Americans at peace, then neither would the supposed attractions of interest. Specifically, Washington was convinced that the dynamics of international politics would take over: there would be rivalries among the sections, and they would engage in frequent wars and broils. As Hamilton had written in *The Federalist*: "it has from long observation of the progress of society become a sort of axiom in politics that vicinity, or nearness of situation, constitutes nations natural enemies." These inherent rivalries would be stimulated and embittered by opposite foreign alliances, attachments, and intrigues. In Washington's words from his Circular Address of 1783, America would then become "the sport of European politics, which may play one State against another to prevent their growing importance, and to serve their own interested purposes." As Washington noted in a letter the same year, this was so "altho' we might have no *great* inclination to jar among ourselves." Washington thereby suggested, perhaps contrary to Hamilton, that harmony among several American confederacies might indeed be possible if the necessities of foreign affairs did not intervene.[22]

But those necessities would intervene: and so while insisting that interest was the cement of the Union, Washington taught that interest alone does not assure political harmony. Cement might be necessary to hold a wall or building together, but the structure would not stand if it were poorly or inappropriately designed—if the architect had not done his job well. Apparent differences of interest among sections, then, could be reconciled and made complementary only inside a well-constructed and administered Union. Further, Washington deliberately encouraged interdependence among the sections, so as to bring about the popular recognition of truly national interests and thereby support the emergence of a common public opinion. One of Washington's favorite maxims was that the people must *feel* before they would *see*. Washington's experience during the Revolution was that those states that were removed from the immediate threat of British invasion or attack were naturally reluctant to meet their obligations to the Congress and the army. To overcome this tendency after the

Revolution, Washington proposed to so link the prosperity and defense of the various sections that they would *feel* simultaneously any threat to their economic well-being or security and thereby *see* the necessity of a common solution to their problems. Put more positively, the people would feel and thereby see common opportunities to better themselves. For Washington, the dramatic turnaround of public opinion on the Jay Treaty—which treaty Washington deliberately linked in the Farewell Address to the popular Pinckney Treaty with Spain—resulted from the manifestly increased prosperity and security enjoyed by all sections and interests.[23]

Washington supported this point about public opinion in the Farewell Address by further arguing that the rivalries among the sections, unless moderated and reconciled by the existence of a well-administered Union, would lead to the creation among them "of those overgrown Military establishments, which under any form of Government are inauspicious to liberty, and which are to be regarded as particularly hostile to Republican Liberty." Such a fear of standing armies had long been a rallying cry of opponents of Union and a strong central government, who claimed that such a system was bound to degenerate into rule by force. Washington, following the logic of *The Federalist Papers*, tried to demonstrate instead that the real danger of military despotism resided in allowing the logic of international relations to intrude into the affairs of America and not in creating an effective central government and strong Union. The jealousies created by the distinct interests and uneven economic growth that would inevitably divide the separate confederacies would add fuel to this intra-American military competition.[24]

In this way, Washington quietly introduced the question of political health, not just self-interest, into his defense of Union and an extended republic. We recall Madison's definition of interest, in the "popular sense," as being that of "the immediate augmentation of property and wealth." But Madison distinguished this from a second meaning of interest: one "synonymous with ultimate happiness," and as such "qualified with every moral ingredient." Washington's desire to open the American character to this second, higher concept of interest led him to a fuller discussion in the Farewell Address of the gravest challenge to the political health of the American character—that of faction, especially as it had become intertwined with foreign affairs.[25]

Faction and Foreign Policy

The gravest threat to the political health of the American regime, according to the Farewell Address, was identical to one of the most dangerous threats to all republics. "History and experience," Washington told his readers, "prove that foreign influence is one of the most baneful foes of Republican Government." But to threaten the political health and good character of the American republic, foreign influence required a means of entrance. Domestic faction—the absence of a sense of political community, the domination of particular interests adverse to the common good— "opens the door to foreign influence and corruption, which finds facilitated access to the government itself through the channels of party passion." Having gained entrance, foreign influence would be afforded many opportunities "to tamper with domestic factions, to practice the arts of seduction, to mislead public opinion, to influence or awe the public councils!" Washington reminded his fellow citizens that "thus the policy and the will of one country are subjected to the policy and will of another. . . . Such an attachment of a small or weak toward a great and powerful nation dooms the former to be the satellite of the latter."[26]

To put the United States in such a condition of foreign dependence, stemming from foreign influence on American politics, was for Washington the negation, or antithesis, of commanding one's own fortunes. In addition to the obvious consequences of allowing the nation's foreign policy to be dictated by outside powers, this meant more fundamentally the subjugation of America to a nonrepublican regime and hence the inevitable transformation of the American Constitution and character. The two competing political factions, Federalist and Republican, each claimed that the other was attempting to remake the Constitution in the image of a foreign political system—the monarchical British or the radical atheistic French system. But the real danger to the American regime, according to Washington, stemmed not from a deliberate conspiracy among some Americans to import foreign political principles, but rather from the immoderation of the factional conflict itself. To be sure, by 1796 Washington had come to believe that a pro-French conspiracy did in fact exist. But the remedy of the Farewell Address was to recommend an even-handed response rather than a pro-British attitude.

The corruption of the American character that Washington feared would be manifested initially by "permanent, inveterate antipathies against particular Nations and passionate attachments for others." The indulgence of habitual hatred or habitual fondness towards other nations would render America "in some degree a slave. It is a slave to its animosity or to its affection, either of which is sufficient to lead it astray from its duty and interest." For Washington, to bring up this image of slavery in the Farewell Address recalled the avowed purpose of the Revolution: to resist the incipient tyranny of the British imperial system over the American colonies. As

Washington had written in 1774, if Americans submitted to these British impositions and failed to assert their rights, then "custom and use shall make us tame and abject slaves, as the blacks we rule over in such an arbitrary way." American independence was still at risk in the 1790s: the essential spiritedness necessary to defend American liberty would be dulled and misdirected by foreign attachments because of the passions spent in defending some and opposing other nations. It would then become impossible for Americans to understand correctly the duty (justice) and interest (utility) that constituted the proper aim of liberty, much less reconcile them.[27]

In the Farewell Address, Washington provided examples of how the American character could be weakened and made highly susceptible to the political diseases of factionalism by slavish relations with foreign powers—all the while sacrificing its essential interests. Antipathy towards a particular nation would lead to a national character that was more readily disposed "to offer insult and injury, to lay hold of slight causes and umbrage, and to be haughty and intractable, when accidental or trifling occasions of dispute occur." This excessive sensitivity would result in "frequent collisions, obstinate, envenomed and bloody contests"—just as excessively proud gentlemen could be provoked unnecessarily into accepting duels. Public opinion that was prompted by such ill will and resentment could drive the government into war, "contrary to the best calculations of policy"; public officials would adopt "through passion what reason would reject." The nation thereby would become "subservient to projects of hostility instigated by pride, ambitions, and sinister and pernicious motives."[28]

Many contemporaries of Washington, as well as later scholarship, interpreted this admonition as being directed specifically against excessive hatred of Great Britain (just as the warning against excessive attachments was understood as applying to France). There is no question that Washington believed this to be true in the circumstances at hand. And Hamilton, who penned the precise language at this point in the Farewell Address, had earlier accused Jefferson and Madison of having "a womanish attachment to France and a womanish resentment against Great Britain."[29]

But the fact that Washington did not specifically identify Britain in the Farewell Address as the potential object of excessive American hatred (or France as the object of excessive regard) should not be ignored. In his notable book on the foundations of American foreign policy, Felix Gilbert usefully compared Washington's Farewell Address with the political testaments commonly delivered by European monarchs, most famously by Frederick the Great of Prussia. But in the latter testimonial, Frederick named names—that is, he identified specific countries and thereby indicated Prussia's natural allies and enemies. Washington's reticence on this score reflected his belief that no such natural connections and enmities should exist for America and that artificial connections should not be manufactured as a way of influencing American domestic politics.[30]

As Washington wrote to Patrick Henry in 1795: "My ardent desire is, and my aim has been . . . to comply strictly with *all* our engagemnts. foreign and domestic; but to keep the UStates free from *political* connexions with *every* other Country. To see that they *may be* independent of *all*, and under the influence of *none*. In a word, I want an *American* character, that the powers of Europe may be convinced we act for *ourselves* and not for *others*." This, in Washington's judgment, was "the only way to be respected abroad and happy at home"—whereas "by becoming the partizans of Great Britain or France," Americans would "create dissensions, disturb the public tranquility, and destroy, perhaps for ever the cement wch. binds the Union." To William Heath, Washington wrote in similar fashion: it was essential that citizens should "advocate their own cause instead of that of any other Nation under the sun; that is instead of being Frenchmen or Englishmen, in Politics, they would be Americans." Americans must be "indignant at every attempt of either [Britain or France], or any other power to establish an influence in our Councils, or that should presume to sow the seeds of distrust or disunion among ourselves."[31]

In our judgment, Washington was sincerely trying to set down a general rule of conduct in the Farewell Address and not merely to attack the Republicans or the French. He signaled this by avoiding references to specific countries (or factions) so that later Americans not caught up in, or even aware of, the political battles of the mid-1790s could profit from his advice. But he also signaled his intention by distancing his advice from the existing circumstances even further: he did not refer specifically to America when he discussed the vices of permanent, inveterate antipathies and passionate attachments. Instead, Washington generalized the problem. He spoke of the behavior of "one Nation" in regard to another. Washington appreciated that disastrous effects of intemperate behavior towards others permeated international relations. As argued below, Washington's solution to this—an American foreign policy that cultivated "just and amicable feelings towards all"—also represented his broader recommendation to all mankind.[32]

Washington's insistence in the Farewell Address on even-handedness with respect to foreign powers must be qualified in some important respects. He was in fact quite concerned with the specific impact of an excessive hatred of Britain on American politics. Washington was determined that the American regime be defined in positive rather than negative terms.

The people's understandable hostility to the British, their former colonial master and recent adversary, must not become a defining feature of the American character or the basis of the nation's political cohesion. At best, anti-British phobia would result in a stunted or limited national character. Washington wrote to Benjamin Harrison shortly after the end of the war that the American opposition to Great Britain and the achievement of independence would be "to very little purpose, if we cannot conquer our own prejudices."[33]

Washington himself shared much of the popular dislike of Britain. He certainly was not pro-British. But he was careful in public not to display these views. This would have been the easy way for Washington to retain his popularity, but he believed that an overtly anti-British policy would be unsustainable and dangerous. Like Hamilton, and unlike Jefferson, Washington then assessed the power relationship between America and Britain as decisively favoring the latter—irrespective of the justice of America's complaints against London. Washington did not assume, as did Jefferson and Madison, that America possessed the means to coerce Britain through threats of commercial retaliation. Given this relative weakness, America would be driven to war or humiliation; and in the event of war with the British, the United States would inevitably be driven to seek to redress this imbalance—as it had done during the Revolution—through closer ties with France. In the political climate of the times, excessive hatred of Britain would invariably lead to the opposite vice.[34]

That vice would, of course, be a passionate attachment to Britain's rival, France. Again speaking generally in the Farewell Address, Washington warned his readers that such attachments "facilitate the illusion of an imaginary common interest, in cases where no real common interest exists." The enemies of one nation unnecessarily would become the enemies of another, and that nation could be led "into a participation of the wars and quarrels" of the other, "without adequate inducement or justification." Both interest and justice would thus be betrayed. The deluded nation could also be led to make concessions of privileges to its favorite that were denied to others, a policy that was doubly injurious: this surrendered what ought to have been retained, while "exciting jealousy, ill will, and a disposition to retaliate, in the parties from whom equal privileges are withheld." In specific terms, the United States would become, at best, nothing more than a permanent appendage to French policy and ambitions, as Portugal had become to Britain.[35]

According to the Farewell Address, the delusion of common interest, leading to unjust and unwise behavior, also provided an avenue for the corruption of the American character. "Ambitious, corrupted, or deluded citizens (who devote themselves to the favourite nation)" not only "betray, or sacrifice the interests of their own country," they may do so "without odium, sometimes even with popularity." The corrupted citizens would utilize and encourage popular passions that might exist on behalf of the favored nation to appear to display "a virtuous sense of obligation," "a commendable deference for public opinion, or a laudable zeal for public good." Equally as distressing, this would lead to the unpopularity of "Real Patriots"—men not passionately devoted to the cause of others.[36] Washington's 1796 letter to Jefferson made clear his personal identification with this problem.

> I believe until lately, that it was not within the bonds of probability, hardly within those of possibility, that while I was using my utmost exertions to establish a national character of our own, independent, as far as our obligations, and justice would permit, of every nation of the earth; and wished, by steering a steady course, to preserve this Country from the horrors of a desolating war, that I should be accused of being the enemy of one Nation, and subject to the influence of another; and to prove it, that every act of my administration would be tortured, and the grossest, and most insidious mis-representations of them be made (by giving only one side of a subject, and that too in exaggerated and indecent terms as could scarcely be applied to a Nero; a notorious defaulter; or even to a common pick pocket).[37]

We can dismiss these complaints as those of a proud and overly sensitive man who could not stand public criticism. And to some extent Washington surely was sensitive. But let us recall the kind of invective that Washington did face. This came from Thomas Paine, by then a passionate advocate of the French cause, in a letter to Washington that was released to the press as Washington contemplated his retirement: "And to you, sir, treacherous in private friendship (for so you have been to me, and that in the day of danger) and a hypocrite in public life, the world will be puzzled to decide, whether you are an apostate or an imposter; whether you have abandoned good principles, or whether you ever had any."[38]

Notably, Washington did not personalize his complaints about the treatment of "Real Patriots" in the Farewell Address. (His initial draft of 1796 did contain some language to the effect that Washington himself had been abused unfairly by "some Gazettes," but between Hamilton and Washington, this was edited out of the final version.) Instead, Washington attempted to speak not just for himself, but for all those of talent, ability, and integrity, whom the republic would need to recruit for public service in the future. When invective reigned, when such was "the turbulence of human passions in party disputes; when victory, more than truth, is the

palm contended for," Washington believed the poet to be correct in saying
" 'that the Post of honor is a private station.' " At the end of his life, Washington could afford to take this attitude, but if younger men of good character took this attitude in the future, the American experiment would be
condemned to failure.[39]

In the Farewell Address, Washington approved of constant wakefulness
against "the insidious wiles of foreign influence." But the natural spiritedness or jealousy of the people—their passion for their own liberty—must
be impartial with respect to allegations of foreign influence. Excessive suspicion of possible treasonous behavior on behalf of one country "causes
those whom they actuate to see danger only on one side, and serve to veil
and even second the arts and influence on the other." This would only
encourage foreign governments to assume that there were fundamental
domestic divisions—when none in fact existed—and to base their policies
toward the United States on that erroneous basis.[40] As Washington wrote
to Gouverneur Morris in 1792:

> From the complexion of some of our News-papers Foreigners would be
> led to believe that inveterate political dissensions existed among us, and
> that we are on the very verge of disunion; but the fact is otherwise;
> the great body of the people now feel the advantages of the General
> Government, and would not, I am persuaded, do any thing that should
> destroy it; but these kind of representations is an evil wch. must be placed
> in opposition to the infinite benefits resulting from a free Press; and I am
> sure you need not be told that in this Country a personal difference in
> political sentiments is often made to take the garb of general dissensions.[41]

By the time of the Farewell Address, Washington may not have been
as sanguine on this score. In Washington's mind, many of those who
seemed partial to the French were really pursuing their own domestic political advantage. Washington wrote to Richard Henry Lee in 1793 that "it is
not the cause of France, nor I believe, of Liberty, which they regard; for, if
they could involve this country in war (no matter with whom) and disgrace, they would be among the first and loudest to complain about the
expense and impolicy of the measure." Washington was reported to have
told William Blount, who had offered to show the President letters from
Paris proving the hostile intentions of the French government, that "I am
informed and beleive [*sic*] your information to be true, but if War comes,
it originated here, not there. The people of this Country it would seem,
will never be satisfied until they become a department of France: It shall be
my business to prevent it."[42]

By encouraging Europeans to assume that pro-French (and pro-British) factions really did exist in America, Washington insisted, opponents of his administration were erroneously leading both France and Britain to see American foreign policy actions solely as the result of domestic politics, rather than as a reflection of America's true interests. For instance, Washington, although being "not favorable" to the Jay Treaty, did not see it as being directed against the French or at bringing America into an alliance with Britain. A limited accommodation with Britain was a matter of necessity under the circumstances, if it could be achieved without irreparable harm to American honor and interests. But Washington feared that the treaty would be wrongly interpreted by Paris as a hostile act, not because of the intrinsic merits of the agreement but because that agreement was being publicly misrepresented by opponents of the government (including the American minister to Paris, James Monroe) as anti-French. This opposition faction was inventing a British conspiracy in America, where one did not in fact exist. But Washington feared that their arguments would become a self-fulfilling prophecy if the adverse French reaction to the Jay Treaty pushed America into Britain's arms.[43]

To take this point further: if we take at face value Washington's even-handed language in the Farewell Address about the dangers of passionate attachments and hatreds, rather than merely assume that he was criticizing the Republicans and the French, another message, directed at Federalist partisans, can also be distinguished. That message to Federalists was a warning against overreacting to fears of Republicanism and the French Revolution and becoming passionately attached to Great Britain. For this reason, as we will argue below, Washington's public statements about the French Revolution were few, moderate, and generally supportive, despite his private misgivings. Republican extremism must not serve to drive others into equally extreme positions—for example, into a pro-British foreign policy, or acceptance of British political forms, or an eagerness to go to war with France. It is too much to say that Washington foresaw the eventual fate of Federalism, condemned to minority status and then extinction as it turned itself to localism and separatism, as exemplified by the Hartford Convention in 1814. But the logic was there to see in the Farewell Address. A few months after the Farewell Address appeared, Jefferson would write in the same spirit: "Our countrymen have divided themselves by such strong affections, to the French & the English, that nothing will secure us internally but a divorce from both nations; and this must be the object of every American." Albert Gallatin, Republican leader in the House of Representatives, agreed in 1798 that "to detach ourselves from any connection with European politics, will tend to reconcile parties," so that "our own united efforts may then prove not altogether unsuccessful in promoting the happiness of America, and conciliating the affections of every part of the Union."[44]

Washington's warning in the Farewell Address against excessive attachments and antipathies towards other nations reflected his larger understanding of an underlying cause of factionalism in politics: "men are very apt to run to extremes." The task of Washington's statesmanship, particularly after 1793, was to fight the tendency towards extremism in foreign and domestic policy (the two being practically inseparable). Washington rejected the adoption of extremist policies of his own to combat extremism of another sort, so as to create conditions whereby political moderation was possible. To bring about such moderation, Washington was prepared to lean against the prevailing extreme if necessary, even at the risk of unpopularity. Washington concluded that the circumstances of the moment required him to reach an accommodation with the British, as long as American honor was not sacrificed in the process. To be sure, this meant that the French must still be treated justly—"so far as we have already formed engagements let them be fulfilled," in the words of the Farewell Address. But Washington's advice ran against the pro-French tendency of large segments of public opinion, which regarded any accommodation of the British as being inherently anti-French. Washington relied on his prestige, on the public's assurance that his object was neither alliance with Britain nor adoption of British forms of government, to win the day. But Washington understood that "enlightened statesmen will not always be at the helm"—and that in any case, even enlightened statesmen in the future might lack the public credibility that he enjoyed to carry out such an unpopular policy.[45]

In the Farewell Address, Washington therefore argued for the adoption of a certain type of foreign policy that would best insulate America from the type of foreign connections that would add fuel to the fire of factional politics—that would wrongly encourage "men to run to extremes." This is the "Great rule of conduct for us, in regard to foreign nations . . . in extending our commercial relations with them [to have] as little *political* conduct as possible. . . . 'Tis our true policy to steer clear of permanent Alliances, with any portion of the foreign world." The distinction between commercial and political relations was an important one, and we shall return to it below. For the moment, we note that Washington based his argument for political separation on interest: he sought to persuade his countrymen that they had no natural connection with the interests of Europe. "Europe has a set of primary interests, which have to us none, or a very remote relation." European interests were the source of "frequent controversies, the causes of which are essentially foreign to our concerns." It was therefore unwise—that is, against American interests—"to implicate ourselves, by artificial ties, in the ordinary vicissitudes of her politics, or the ordinary combinations and collisions of her friendships, or enmities." By so interweaving its destiny with any part of Europe, the United States would "entangle our peace and prosperity in the toils of European Ambition, Rivalship, Interest, Humour or Caprice." Why would America want to forego the advantages of such a unique situation, enjoyed by no other country in the Western world—"why quit our own to stand upon foreign ground?" Washington's goal of freedom of action was designed to allow the United States to pursue a policy of interest guided by justice. As he wrote in his first draft of the Address: "if there be no engagements on our part, we shall be unembarrassed, and at liberty at all times, to act from circumstances, according to the dictates of Justice—sound policy—and our essential Interests."[46]

Washington had described to Jefferson in 1788 the essential distinction between the European and American systems that he wished to see established: "In whatever manner the Nations of Europe shall endeavor to keep up their prowess in war and their balance of power in peace, it will be our policy to cultivate tranquility at home and abroad; and extend our agriculture and commerce as far as possible." If the United States could "keep disengaged from the labyrinth of European politics and Wars" it could adopt a policy to "administer to their [European] wants," through commerce, "without being engaged in their quarrels." (Or, as Jefferson put it, "our object is to feed and theirs is to fight.") Washington had reflected to Gouverneur Morris in 1791 that he trusted that the "local situation" of America would allow the United States to "never lose sight of our own interest and happiness as to become, unnecessarily, a party in their [European] political disputes." This favorable relationship for America was one "which otherwise, could not, perhaps, be preserved by human wisdom." Wisdom, then, dictated using the accident of geographical distance between America and Europe to confirm their essential political distance, which distance might otherwise be overcome by the force of interests or passions.[47]

In his Fifth Annual Message to Congress in 1793, Washington had remarked that "there is a rank due to the United States, among nations, which will be withheld, if not absolutely lost, by the reputation of weakness." A proper and favorable reputation with foreign nations—a rank due to the United States—was an integral part of the American character. The European wars of the 1790s offered the United States the chance to redeem itself in the eyes of the Europeans, who had hitherto viewed America either in the distresses of the Revolution or in the weakness of the Confederation. The Europeans' troubles, Washington noted, would allow the United

States "to remove the prejudices imbibed against us" and thereby "open a new view of things" and "burst upon them, as it were with redoubled advantages." Good government at home was essential to this reputation; it was necessary because of general doubts in Europe about the ability of a republican government to survive, as well as specific doubts about the American character. But respect abroad ultimately required self-respect at home.[48]

Of specific concern to Washington in the Farewell Address was the danger that Americans would turn to outsiders to make decisions that should be reserved to a self-respecting people of good character. During the Revolution, in Washington's view, Americans had turned increasingly to the French for aid because they could not themselves muster the political unity to generate the necessary financial and military resources to win independence on their own. At the end of the war, divisions within the Continental Congress prevented the issuance of a set of instructions to the American delegation that would deal with the British about peace. Instead, the delegates were essentially told to let the French decide. This was the easy way out, but Americans would inevitably pay a high price for their lack of true independence. For this reason, Washington did "not like to add to the number of national obligations. I would wish as much as possible to avoid giving a foreign power new claims of merit for services performed to the United States, and ask no assistance that is not indispensable."[49]

The Farewell Address, then, provided the vision of a truly successful American foreign policy: "Our detached and distant situation invites and enables us to pursue a different course. If we remain one People, under an efficient government, the period is not far off, when we may defy material injury from external annoyance; when we may take such an attitude as will cause the neutrality we may at any time resolve upon to be scrupulously respected; when belligerent nations, under the impossibility of making acquisitions upon us, will not lightly hazard the giving us provocation; when we may choose peace or war, as our interest, guided by our justice shall Counsel." Washington had earlier phrased this object to Gouverneur Morris: "if this country is preserved in tranquility twenty years longer, it may bid defiance, in a just cause, to any power whatever, such, in that time, will be its population, wealth, and resource." In the meantime, according to the Farewell Address, security against foreign aggression could be maintained by "keeping ourselves on a respectably defensive posture," and "trusting to temporary alliances for extraordinary emergencies."[50]

Washington's brief invocation in the Farewell Address of the need to maintain a "respectably defensive posture" is interesting precisely because of its brevity. Washington's other public pronouncements, including the

Circular Address of 1783 and his Eighth Annual Message (delivered to Congress not long after the Farewell Address) contained far more elaborate and prominent discussions of the importance of a proper defense establishment. There was above all Washington's famous and repeated use of the Roman maxim: "To be prepared for war, is one of the most effectual means of promoting peace." The safety of the United States, "under divine protection, ought to rest on the basis of systematic and solid arrangements; exposed as little as possible to the hazards of fortuitous circumstances." As detailed in Washington's annual messages to Congress, those arrangements were to include the creation of a well-organized militia; development of a moderate naval force sufficient to vindicate American commerce from insult or aggression; the promotion of such manufactures that would render the United States independent of others for essential military supplies; the provision of military stores, arsenals, and dock yards; and the establishment of a military academy. Washington was anxious that the country "leave nothing to the uncertainty of procuring a warlike apparatus at the moment of public danger."[51]

The silence of the Farewell Address on these particulars of national defense perhaps in part signaled Washington's willingness to accommodate Republican opinion on this topic. The Republicans had opposed, or at least were indifferent to, much of this Federalist agenda for the creation of a modest but effective military establishment. According to these critics, such an establishment—characterized above all by the dreaded standing army—was an integral part of the Federalist plan of monarchical corruption. Washington did not wish to challenge this view in the Address, because at bottom he thought that national security depended above all not on armies and navies but on remaining "United and faithful to ourselves"—as well as practicing "good faith and justice towds. all Nations." As Jefferson would remark in his First Inaugural: "I believe this . . . [is] the strongest government on earth. I believe it is the only one where every man, at the call of the laws, would fly to the standard of the law, and would meet invasions of public order as his own personal concern." That was also an underlying message of the Farewell Address; if Washington succeeded in reinforcing this opinion, he assumed that the particulars of a military establishment could be decided in the ordinary course of politics.[52]

Washington did feel compelled in the Farewell Address explicitly to raise and defend one key element of policy relative to the national defense, just prior to his recommendation to "observe good faith and justice towds. all Nations." That was his advice to "cherish public credit." This was not merely a financial recommendation; as Washington made clear elsewhere, due regard for public credit was at bottom an issue of public justice. But here again, Washington attempted to demonstrate the close relationship in his mind between domestic and foreign policy, and between duty and interest. (As he had written during the Revolution, "in modern wars the longest purse must chiefly determine the event.") Public credit could be preserved by using it as sparingly as possible, particularly by cultivating peace—debts being almost exclusively the result of having to pay for war. But at the same time, "timely disbursements to prepare for danger frequently prevent much greater disbursements to repel it." In times of peace, vigorous exertions should be made "to discharge the Debts which unavoidable wars may have occasioned, not ungenerously throwing upon posterity the burthens which we ourselves ought to bear." Washington left the execution of these maxims to "your Representatives" but pointed out that "it is necessary that public opinion should cooperate"—bluntly put, by paying taxes.[53]

Washington admitted that any tax was more or less inconvenient and unpleasant and that it was always difficult to select the proper object of taxation. But Washington here sought to demonstrate to the Republicans in particular that they could not have their cake and eat it, too. The United States could not pay off the government debt and avoid war, while using commercial means to coerce foreign powers—central elements of the emerging Jeffersonian persuasion—without providing appropriate means of revenue. Washington did not defend the controversial particulars of the Federalist persuasion on this point (that is, the need to keep open commerce with Britain to generate sufficient public revenue through import duties and access to British funds). Those particulars were less important than reminding "your Representatives" and "public opinion" what was truly at stake in maintaining the public credit.[54]

Good Faith and Justice

The argument in favor of the greater security and domestic tranquility provided by non-entanglement was not Washington's final word on the rationale for maintaining a political separation from the affairs of Europe. Political separation was for Washington the logical corollary of his other central recommendation in the Farewell Address for America's approach to the world: "Observe good faith and justice towds. all nations. Cultivate peace and harmony with all." European politics represented the realm of necessity, where American "choice" must be decisively circumscribed by superior "force." In the condition of relative American weakness, the United States could neither expect nor exact political justice from the stronger European states. America might cultivate peace in all good faith, but it was not yet within its means to harvest it. Separation from European politics would allow the United States to follow a more enlightened approach to the world. Characteristically, Washington linked this recommendation of good faith and justice with a recognition of American interests. "Religion and morality enjoin this conduct; and can it be that good policy does not equally enjoin it?" This formulation recalled Washington's earlier invocation of religion and morality in domestic affairs. He was in full agreement with Jefferson's often-quoted view that there was "but one code of morality for man whether acting singly or collectively." For Washington, "the attributes which can win the affection of its citizens, and command the respect of the world" were essentially the same: "the propitious smiles of Heaven can never be expected on a nation that disregards the eternal rules of order and right, which Heaven itself has ordained."[55]

For Washington, it was this standard of morality that should finally characterize America, abroad as well as at home. This was the higher aim, not the lower, that defined the American purpose in the world, the reason why America must command its own fortunes. Washington wrote in the Farewell Address: "Can it be, that Providence has not connected the permanent felicity of a Nation with its virtue? The experiment, at least, is recommended by every sentiment which ennobles human nature. Alas! is it rendered impossible by its vices?" At the beginning of the Address, Washington told his countrymen that the great American experiment—to bring about the happiness of the American people under the auspices of liberty—would acquire to them the glory of recommending it to the applause, the affection, and the adoption of every nation yet a stranger to it. This was the great elevating theme of the Founding: that Americans would demonstrate the viability of self-government not only for themselves, but for all mankind.[56]

As Washington stated in his First Inaugural Address in 1789, "the preservation of the sacred fire of liberty, and the destiny of the republican mode of government, are justly considered as *deeply*, and perhaps as *finally*, staked on the experiment entrusted to the hands of the American people." In his discarded First Inaugural, Washington spoke more elaborately on this point, in language reminiscent of the Declaration of Independence:

> Could it be imagined that so many peculiar advantages, of soil & climate, for agriculture & for navigation were lavished in vain—or that this Continent was not created and reserved so long undiscovered as a Theatre, for those glorious displays of Divine Munificence, the salutary consequences of which shall flow to another Hemisphere & extend through the interminable series of ages. Should not our Souls exult in the pros-

pect? . . . I rejoice in a belief that intellectual light will spring up in the
dark corners of the earth; that freedom of inquiry will produce liberality
of conduct; that mankind will reverse the absurd position that *the many
were, made for the few; and that they will not continue slaves in one part of the
globe, when they can become freemen in another.*[57]

Or as he stated publicly later that year:

It should be the highest ambition of every American to extend his views
beyond himself, and to bear in mind that his conduct will not only affect
himself, his country, and his immediate posterity; but that its influence
may be co-extensive with the world, and stamp political happiness or
misery on ages yet unborn.[58]

In explaining what America had to offer to ages yet unborn, Washington did not point to the ability to fight and win a war against an oppressive
colonial power, as America had against Britain. Rather, as he told the Pennsylvania Legislature, it was the highest American ambition "to convince
the world that the happiness of nations can be accomplished by pacific
revolutions in their political systems, without the destructive intervention
of the sword." The process of peacefully creating, ratifying, and imple-
menting a democratic constitution through democratic means—of demonstrating that reflection and choice, not accident and force, could govern
men—was the conduct that would ultimately give America influence co-
extensive with the world. As James Wilson had remarked, "the United
States now exhibit to the world, the first instance, as far as we can learn, of
a nation, unattacked by external force, unconvulsed by domestic insurrections, assembling voluntarily, deliberating fully, and deciding calmly, concerning that system of government, under which they would wish that
they and their posterity should live."[59]

In the Farewell Address, Washington introduced the equivalent American ambition for greatness in foreign policy: "It will be worthy of a free,
enlightened, and, at no distant period, a great Nation, to give mankind the
too novel example of a People always guided by an exalted justice and
benevolence."[60] In the course of time, Washington told his readers, whatever temporary advantages that might be lost by following such a foreign
policy would be richly repaid. If Washington's vision were realized, the
practice of other nations, eventually following America's example in foreign as well as domestic affairs, would lead to a set of relations among states
that would better secure American interests (security and prosperity) than
would an America acting without regard to justice in an international system marked by narrowly self-interested behavior. America could better

command its own fortunes—serve its duty and realize its interests—in a peaceful and prosperous world than in a world torn by strife.

To be sure, Washington did not think that such a peaceful and prosperous world was around the corner, any more than he believed that self-government would soon become the norm elsewhere in the world. But America must do its part in leading by example in foreign as well as domestic affairs. This part of the great American experiment would further elevate and extend the American character, by giving a moral content to American interests with respect to other nations and peoples. Indeed, in persuading Americans of the need to practice a strict neutrality toward the war in Europe, Washington argued that the American character would not be made whole until both the foreign and domestic dimensions of policy were properly accounted for.

> To complete the American character, it remains for the United States to shew the world, that the reproach heretofore cast on republican Governments for their want of stability, is without foundation, when that government is the choice of an enlightened people: and I am fully persuaded, that every well-wisher to the happiness and prosperity of this Country will evince by his conduct, that we live in a government under laws; and that, while we preserve inviolate our national faith, we are desirous to live in amity with all mankind.[61]

For Washington, the American character was inextricably linked to the American mission "to shew the world" the worth of self-government, in foreign as well as domestic relations. At the same time, the American people's desire to live in amity with all mankind usefully moderated their determination to preserve inviolate their national faith. Without such moderation, Americans might be unwisely tempted to war with other nations by exaggerated attention to foreign slights—in that case, the American character would become dangerously illiberal. The prudent direction not only of interest, but of interest guided by justice, would thus serve to moderate American domestic politics as well as international relations—because "men are apt to run to extremes" if they attempt to pursue either interest or justice in isolation from the other. Americans should be an "enlightened and liberal people" who deserved the reputation of that character "by shewing themselves the true friends of mankind and making their Country not only an Asylum for the oppressed of every Nation, but a desirable residence for the virtuous and industrious of every Country."[62]

Of course, Washington's invocation of justice in the Farewell Address could be nothing more than a pious platitude, nothing more than the narrow expression of American self-interest. Obviously, no European nation in 1796 proclaimed its policies to be aiming at injustice; every nation, as Hamilton put it, had an interest "in not entirely forfeiting its reputation for honor and fidelity."[63] We are therefore entitled to inquire more closely into Washington's view of justice; or, more accurately, interest guided by justice. Our review points toward a consistent framework—a set of rules, closely tied to what the Founders regarded as the laws of nature and of nations—that aided Washington in determining the sort of justice that ought to guide American interests.

Us and Them

To begin with, in the Farewell Address, Washington distinguished "justice and good will" from altruism. A nation relying on the altruism of others would "pay with a portion of its Independence" for that conceit. Its putative friends would only seek to "demand equivalents for nominal favours" and yet reproach it "with ingratitude for not giving more." Washington insisted in the Address that "there can be no greater error than to expect, or calculate upon real favours from Nations." This was a long-held view of Washington. In 1778, Washington had already expressed concern that "hatred to England may carry some into an excess of Confidence in France; especially when motives of gratitude are thrown into the scale." It was for this precise reason that Washington sought to limit the French contribution to the American cause, so as to avoid creating such motives. Washington never wavered from the view that it was "the universal experience of mankind, that no nation is to be trusted farther than it is bound by its interest; and no prudent statesman or politician will venture to depart from it."[64]

From Washington's perspective, this stress on interest did not contradict the importance of justice in American foreign policy. Rather, he sought to persuade his countrymen that it was in their true interest to behave justly towards other peoples. Jefferson had formulated it this way in his Second Inaugural Address: "We are firmly convinced, and we act on that conviction, that with nations, as with individuals, our interests, soundly calculated, will ever be found inseparable from our moral duties."[65]

Still, the implicit distinction between altruism and justice in the Farewell Address seemed to represent a major reservation on Washington's part about the role of morality in international affairs. We would suggest that, for Washington, the apparent difference was in what one owed to one's own, as compared to that owed to others. Relations among nations—as among strangers—should properly be correct (that is, just), but they could not be based on the higher ground of what Washington called "disinterested friendship." According to Aristotle, justice is not needed among friends (although it is undoubtedly a precondition for friendship, and the truest form of justice has a friendly quality). Washington granted the possibility that individuals from one nation could be friends with individuals from another because they shared a common human nature that transcended political communities. Washington occasionally referred to himself as a "friend of humanity"—"a citizen of the world." But this was Washington speaking as a human being, not as the President of the United States, who, in his executive capacity, represented the United States to the other nations of the world. Command of America's own fortunes must first and foremost be sought on a national, not an international, basis. For the United States to exist as a cohesive political community, in which sacrifice and accommodation among friends and fellow citizens could take place, America must first make the fundamental, and proper, distinction between "us" and "them."[66]

We can see Washington's attempt to distinguish between "us" and "them" in his desire to create a national university, whose central object would be "the assimilation of the principles, opinions, and manners, of our countrymen, by the common education of a portion of our youth from every quarter . . . The more homogeneous our citizens can be made in these particulars, the greater will be our prospect of permanent union." Most importantly, Washington equated Americanism with republicanism. For this reason, Washington regretted that Americans went abroad for their education: "Altho' it would be injustice to many to pronounce the certainty of their imbibing maxims, not congenial with republicanism; it must nevertheless be admitted, that a serious danger is encountered, by sending abroad among other political systems those, who have not well learned the value of their own."[67]

Washington's imperative to establish an American, and a republican, homogeneity extended to his understanding of how foreign immigration should be treated. Washington thought that the right sort of character among European settlers should be sought—especially the "virtuous and persecuted of mankind," who would be attracted by "the spirit of the Religions and the genius of the political Institutions of this Country." Washington sought especially those of "moderate property" who were "determined to be sober, industrious, and virtuous members of society." In response to a proposal by John Adams that the University of Geneva faculty should be relocated in the United States, Washington had argued that a policy of settling them in a body "may be much questioned; for, by doing so, they retain the Language, habits and principles (good and bad) which they bring with them. Whereas by an intermixture with our people, they, or their descendants, get assimilated to our customs, measures and laws: in a word, soon become one people."[68]

This distinction between justice and disinterested friendship—between us and them—was Washington's essential reply to those who argued that the United States owed gratitude to the French for their support during the American Revolution. In the Farewell Address, Washington acknowledged America's obligation to France under the terms of the Alliance of 1778: "So far as we have already formed engagements, let them be fulfilled, with perfect good faith."[69] But he denied that this entitled France to any gratitude, as claimed by some Republicans. That is, Washington opposed any potential sacrifice of America's true interests on behalf of France, or on behalf of the cause of "liberty" as supposedly embodied in the French cause in the European wars.

Washington's sense of justice in international relations was precisely that of justice in public and private life—fulfilling one's obligations, especially in matters of commerce and trade. Referring in the Farewell Address to the existing engagements with France, Washington wrote that "I hold the maxim no less applicable to public than to private affairs, that honesty is always the best policy." For Washington, a policy of honesty still left reasonable scope for interpretation of those obligations and allowance for changed circumstances—including the established fidelity or infidelity of the other party. As Washington wrote to Hamilton in 1793, while the president and his cabinet struggled to formulate a policy of neutrality: "To take *fair* and *supportable* ground I conceive to be our best policy, and all that can be required of us by the Powers at War; leaving the rest to be managed according to circumstances and the advantages which may be derived from them."[70]

The problem that the United States faced in the midst of European wars and broils was the extraordinary difficulty of maintaining such a fair and supportable ground simultaneously in the eyes of all foreign powers. What seemed fair to one side (that is, Britain) would undoubtedly seem unfair to the other (France). As Washington indicated in the Farewell Address, the Neutrality Proclamation—what he called "the index to my Plan" of dealing with the war in Europe—was designed to find, and expand, such middle ground as then existed.[71] He had previously rejected Jefferson's proposals to threaten the adoption of a decidedly pro-French neutrality as a means of coercing Great Britain, as well as Hamilton's proposal to suspend or nullify the Treaty of Alliance with France. Over the longer term, Washington's policy of political separation from Europe represented his best effort to avoid such impossible choices in the future, to broaden the middle ground available to future statesmen. Because international relations, especially wars, were so driven by necessity as to make justice problematic at best, Washington sought to limit the occasions when America might find its sense of justice in conflict with the imperative of self-preservation.

In this sense, justice for Washington consisted of minding one's own business. As he wrote to a correspondent in 1795: "For in politics, as in religion my tenets are few and simple: the leading one of which, and indeed that which embraces most others, is to be honest and just ourselves, and exact it from others; meddling as little as possible in their affairs where our own is not involved. If this maxim was generally adopted wars would cease . . ."[72]

In addition, Washington could also look to the guidelines of usage and right reason, as represented by the law of nature and nations, to determine the boundaries of justice in foreign affairs. To be sure, the law of nations was often controversial and ill-defined, but it pointed toward certain principles and practices that conformed to a sense of natural justice. In the Farewell Address, the foremost of these principles was identified as "the obligation which justice and humanity impose on every Nation, in cases in which it is free to act, to maintain inviolate the relations of Peace and amity toward other nations." As Washington wrote in 1793: "the happiness and true interest of a people are best secured by observing such a line of conduct as will, while they discharge their political obligations, preserve to their Country peace with other Nations, and cultivate the good will of mankind towards them." In following a strict and just neutrality, Americans would "shew the world, that they have as much wisdom in preserving peace at this critical juncture, as they have heretofore displayed in defending their rights."[73]

For Washington, the qualification "in cases in which it is free to act" represented a positive injunction not merely to avoid war, but to develop a command of the national fortunes that would prevent the United States from being forced into war by the actions of others, or by its own weakness. As Hamilton wrote in the *Federalist*: "The rights of neutrality will only be respected when they are defended by adequate power. A nation, despicable by its weakness, forfeits even the privilege of being neutral." John Jay added that the American people ought to support steps that would "put and keep them in *such a situation* as, instead of *inviting* war, will tend to repress and discourage it."[74] We recall again Washington's articulation in the Farewell Address of the advantages of self-sufficiency:

If we remain one people, under an efficient government, the period is not far off when we may defy injury from external annoyance; when we may take such an attitude as will cause the neutrality we may at any time resolve upon to be scrupulously respected; when belligerent nations, under the impossibility of making acquisitions upon us, will not lightly hazard the giving us provocation; when we may choose peace or war, as our interest, guided by our justice shall Counsel.[75]

The dictates of justice in international affairs, as Washington understood them—meeting one's obligations honestly, non-interference in the affairs of others, peace—were essential arguments for the strength of the American government. This was the corollary to Washington's argument in the Farewell Address about the compatibility of republican government with energy in the domestic arena. Weak government led not to greater freedom but to injustice, both to the American people and to foreign nations. Washington had noted in 1788 that the United States would inevitably become involved in future European war, against the dictates of duty and utility, "unless there is energy enough in Government to restrain our people within proper bounds." To remain apart from such a war, the United States would need "an efficient general Government to regulate our Commercial concerns, give us a national respectability, and to connect the political views and interests of the several states under one head in such a manner as will effectively prevent them from forming separate, improper, or indeed any connection with the European powers which can involve them in their political disputes."[76]

In Washington's view, a reputation for being just—a reputation that reflected a just national character—mattered considerably in international affairs, as it did in ordinary human relationships. Washington believed firmly that the United States ought to behave in such a way as to establish this reputation. After the peace with Great Britain in 1783, for example, the United States had chafed under British failure to implement parts of that agreement, most notably to evacuate the northwest frontier posts. However, in Washington's view, the United States was equally or more at fault because, under the Articles of Confederation, it could not fully live up to its end of the bargain. "We seem to have forgotten, or never to have learnt, the policy of placing the enemy in the wrong. Had we observed good faith on our part, we might have told the tale to the world with a good grace; but complts. illy [*sic*] become those who are found to be the first aggressors." To exact justice, in Washington's view, the United States must first establish the prior moral grounds for its actions. If there was disagreement with another nation, America should "explain what may have been apprehended, and correct what may have been injurious to any nation; and, having thus acquired the right, to lose no time in inquiring the ability, to insist upon justice being done to ourselves."[77]

The diplomatic historian Samuel Flagg Bemis argued that the watchword of U.S. foreign policy during the Founding period was "America's advantage from Europe's distresses." The United States clearly accepted such benefits as were presented to it under the Washington administration, especially in the realm of a growing commercial prosperity. As Washington wrote to Thomas Jefferson: "whenever a contest happens among them, if we wisely and properly improve the advantages which nature has given us, we may be benefitted by their folly, provided we conduct ourselves with circumspection and under proper restrictions." But the Farewell Address does not directly advocate such a policy. A sense of "our interest, guided by our justice," suggested to Washington that the United States ought to be circumspect in trying to take undue advantage of European distresses brought about by the wars of the 1790s. Washington had reflected to Gouverneur Morris: "I believe it is among nations as with individuals, the party taking advantage of the distresses of another will lose infinitely more in the opinion of mankind and in subsequent events than he will gain by the stroke of a moment." And to a French correspondent, he had written earlier that "notwithstanding it might probably, in a commercial view, be greatly for the advantage of America that a war should raise on the other side of the Atlantic; yet I shall never so far divest myself of the feelings of a man, interested in the happiness of his fellow men, as to wish my country's prosperity might be built on the ruins of that of other nations."[78]

To be sure, Washington here spoke as a man, not as a national leader. But as a national leader, he was aware that this rule reflected not merely sentiment but also calculation. "There is no ground on which treaties can be formed that will be found permanent or satisfactory," Washington had written to Spanish Minister Diego de Gardoqui in 1786, "unless they have these [true and reciprocal] benefits for their basis." Treaties that lacked mutual benefits were not likely to be of long duration; as Washington reflected to Gouverneur Morris, "it is vain to hope for a continuance of them beyond the moment when one conceives itself to be overreached in a situation to break off the connection." The balance of relative power between the contracting parties would, sooner or later, exert or reexert itself. Washington was therefore not surprised that the British had failed to keep the 1783 Treaty of Peace; the American negotiators had probably gained more than the objective circumstances warranted, a conclusion that a new British government soon reached.[79]

Because the relative balance of power among nations was bound to change over time—just as governments would change—any political agreement ran the risk of being overtaken by events as the sense of "true and reciprocal benefits" altered. Justice could not stand the strain if it were constantly invoked to defend compliance with agreements that no longer reflected the interest of one or more parties. Washington wrote in his first draft of the Farewell Address: "Nations as well as individuals, act for their own benefit, and not for the benefit of others, unless both interests happen to be assimilated (and when that is the case there requires no contract to bind them together)." This helps us to understand Washington's desire in the final version of the Farewell Address, "to have with them as little political connection as possible," so that justice would not solely and constantly be defined in terms of the interest of the stronger. [80]

The historian Edmund Morgan has observed that Washington had a profound sense of the role of power in international relations. Morgan demonstrated this by quoting from the remarkable letter that Washington wrote in 1778 to Henry Laurens, president of the Continental Congress, stating the reasons why Washington opposed a joint American-French expedition to take Canada. Washington observed that the introduction of a large body of French troops into Canada "alarms all my feelings for the true and permanent interests of my country," because it would put the French into the possession of Quebec, where they were attached by "all the ties of blood, habits, manners, religion, and former connexion of government." Washington feared that it "would be too great a temptation, to be resisted by any power actuated by the common maxims of national policy" for the French to withdraw from Canada, for Paris not to realize the striking advantages that France would gain by remaining there, especially united with Spain against the British. The French would then, as a consequence, be "certainly superior, possessed of New Orleans, on our Right, Canada on our left and seconded by the numerous tribes of Indians on our Rear from one extremity to another." Such an outcome would reverse the results of the French and Indian War, but with America now separated from England and unable to establish its own independent security. This would tend to make France again the enemy of America, or at least give it the power "to give law to these states."[81]

This was, as Morgan argues, a tough-minded argument about power and interest in international relations. But Washington's implicit point, made clearer in the Farewell Address, was that it was within America's power to avoid creating such temptations. By winning its independence with as little foreign assistance as possible and then by establishing a well-administered Union that observed justice and good faith in international relations, the United States would have created circumstances where other nations would lack the incentive or opportunity to become America's enemy. The interests of the United States and other nations were not static or immutable; America, within the limits of what was humanly possible, could shape in a positive (as well as negative) fashion a world where amity among nations—or at least between the United States and the rest of the world—was possible.

Washington's argument raised the interesting question of to whom the United States owed justice. By the standards of the Declaration of Independence, all of mankind were "friends" in peace. But the governments of nations other than America were—at least prior to the French Revolution—illegitimate, to a greater or lesser degree. In addition to the kingdoms of Europe, there were also those who were considered barbarous peoples (for example, the Algerines) and savages (the American Indians). Washington insisted that in all cases, it was still possible to render justice as it was necessary to exact it. As he informed the Senate in 1789, "it is doubtless important that all treaties and compacts formed by the United States with other nations, whether civilized or not, should be made with caution and executed with fidelity." This was always a particular problem with the Indian nations, in substantial part because of the actions of the white frontier settlers who repeatedly encroached on Indian lands and who entertained the erroneous view "that it is not the same crime (or indeed no crime at all) in killing an Indian as in killing a white man." Such failures, if not rectified, would mean that "this Country will be constantly embroiled with, and appear faithless in the eyes not only of the Indians but the neighboring powers also."[82]

Commerce, Not Conquest

Washington's reflections in the Farewell Address on interest, guided by justice, indicated that commerce, not conquest, was the natural and preferred means of acquiring the necessities for national life that the United States did not possess within its territory. It was in the commercial realm— where America had an interest in prosperity—that justice could best be defined, rendered, and exacted. Washington told the readers of his Farewell Address that "harmony, liberal intercourse with all Nations are recommended by policy, humanity, and interest." Writing to Lafayette in the 1780s about his desire to improve commercial ties with France, Washington had observed that "nations are not influenced, as individuals may be, by disinterested friendships; but, when their interest is to live in amity, we have little reason to apprehend any rupture." But to foster this pacifying effect—to create an interest in living in amity—American commercial policy, according to the Farewell Address, "should hold an equal and impartial hand, neither seeking nor granting exclusive favours or preferences; consulting the natural course of things; diffusing and diversifying by gentle means the streams of Commerce, but forcing nothing." Washington had previously expressed the view that "I believe it to be true in commerce as in everything else, that nature, however she may be opposed for a while, will soon return to her regular course."[83]

Although he opposed the United States entering into new and binding political agreements, Washington supported commercial agreements with other willing nations. He wrote in the Farewell Address that these agreements would "give to trade a stable course," by defining the rights of American merchants and enabling the government to support them. Washington indicated that such commercial agreements could follow conventional rules of trade—"the best that present circumstances and mutual opinion will permit, but temporary, and liable to be from time to time abandoned or varied, as experience and circumstances shall dictate." It was at this specific point in the Farewell Address that Washington offered his injunction that, in seeking commercial agreements, the United States should not expect or calculate on disinterested favors from other nations.[84]

Washington's warning against "forcing" foreign commerce could be read as an attack on the Republican policy of commercial discrimination against Great Britain and a defense of the commercial aspects of the Jay Treaty. Washington's language in this paragraph of the Farewell Address is certainly similar to that of the Federalists who had opposed Madison's proposed discriminatory legislation against Britain in 1794. But it could also be read the other way. Washington had earlier supported some form of commercial discrimination, and with it the promotion of a stronger economic connection with France, on the grounds that Britain enjoyed certain "unnatural" advantages because of its long-standing connections with its former colonies. In 1789, when sent a bill that lacked discrimination provisions as proposed by Madison, Washington had agreed to sign the legislation only on assurance that the question would subsequently be reconsidered, because "the opposition of the Senate to the discrimination in the Tonnage Bill, was so adverse to my ideas of justice and policy." But either way, as we shall see, Washington was always reluctant to define America's commercial interests in such as way as to increase the likelihood of war.[85]

Washington, like many of the Founders, had a somewhat ambivalent attitude towards foreign commerce. Shortly after the Revolution, Washington remarked that it had long been a speculative question among philosophers and wise men whether foreign commerce was of any real advantage—"that is, whether the luxury, effeminacy, and corruptions which are introduced along with it; are counterbalanced by the convenience and wealth it brings with it." But for Washington, "the decision of this question is of very little importance to us; we have abundant reason to be convinced, that the spirit for Trade which pervades these States is not to be restrained." As he had written Jefferson in 1784, the best that could be done was to place commerce "in the most convenient channels, under proper regulation, freed *as much as possible,* from those vices which luxury, the consequence of wealth and power, naturally introduce." Placed in the proper channels, however, the American genius for commerce could be an enormous boon: "A people however, who are possessed of the spirit of commerce, who see, and who will pursue their advantage, may achieve almost anything."[86]

For this reason, Washington was more attracted to the development of domestic than foreign commerce, both because it was more within the nation's power to control and because it promised greater political as well as material advantages. Domestic commerce "is well calculated to multiply Sailors, exterminate prejudices, diffuse blessings, and increase the friendship of the inhabitants of one State for those of another"—a point made in the first portion of the Farewell Address. All this indicated to Washington the need for a program of internal improvements—facilitating means of transportation, opening canals and improving roads, and improving the regular post.[87] In the context of the 1790s, this also meant subordinating the pursuit of foreign commerce to the necessity to remain at peace. Hamilton's verdict on the Jay Treaty undoubtedly reflected that of the president:

> Well considered, the greatest interest of this Country in its external relations is that of peace. The more or less of commercial advantages which we may acquire by particular treaties are of far less moment. With peace, the force of circumstances will enable us to make our way sufficiently fast in Trade. War at this time would give a serious wound to our growth and prosperity. Can we escape it for ten or twelve years more, we may then meet it without much inquieture and may advance and support with energy and effect any just pretensions to commercial advantages than [that] we may enjoy.[88]

Washington undoubtedly agreed also with Hamilton's view that "the most important *desiderata* in our concerns with foreign powers are the possession of the Western posts and a participation in the navigation of the Mississippi." These had been secured by the Jay and Pinckney Treaties, to which Washington alluded in the Farewell Address. "More or fewer Commercial privileges are of vastly inferior moment."[89]

At the same time, Washington appreciated the importance of foreign commerce to various American sections and interests, and he subscribed—

with reservations—to the Enlightenment view that the development of commerce was one of the best available to ameliorate conflict among nations. As he wrote to Lafayette in 1786:

> I cannot avoid reflecting with pleasure on the probable influence that commerce may hereafter have on human manners and society in general. On these occasions I consider how mankind might be connected like one great family in fraternal ties. I indulge a fond, perhaps an enthusiastic idea, that as the world is evidently much less barbarous than it has been, its melioration must still be progressive; that nations are becoming more humanized in their policy, that the subjects of ambition and causes for hostility are daily diminishing, and in fine, that the period is not very remote, when the benefits of a liberal and free commerce will, pretty generally, succeed to the devastations and horrors of war.[90]

We emphasize that Washington held this view with reservations. In his letter to Lafayette, he introduced these sentiments as being from someone who was "a philanthropist by character, and (if I may be allowed to use the expression) as a Citizen of the great republic of humanity at large." Such implicit qualifications—that is, Washington was speaking only in an unofficial capacity—were also generally accompanied in Washington's writings by language to the effect that "at the moment, however, too many motives and occasions exist for interrupting the public tranquility." The lack of international and domestic tranquility was painfully evident in 1796, and Washington accordingly does not express such fond and enthusiastic language for the future of humanity in the Farewell Address itself. Yet the possibility of transforming international relations, and the proper and necessary role that the United States should play in that transformation, remained an inseparable part of Washington's thinking.[91]

Peace, Not War

The American character toward the world, then, was to be defined, within limits, by commercial pursuits; and Washington expressed hope, within limits, that commerce might serve to moderate international relations. The American character and the way in which America would ideally pursue justice would by extension be pacific. Americans would mind their own business (literally as well as figuratively) and thus give little just cause for others to take offense. In the Farewell Address—as in his earlier farewell, the Circular Address of 1783—Washington implicitly rejected the pursuit of war, and the military culture that went along with war, as a pillar of national unity. This was an interesting judgment for someone who as a young man sought to make his mark in the world through military glory and who as an older man made an international reputation as the leader of an army of revolution.

In a 1788 letter to a French correspondent, Washington wrote:

> For certainly it is more consonant to all the principles of reason and religion (natural and revealed) to replenish the earth with inhabitants, rather than to depopulate it by killing those already in existence, besides it is time for the age of the Knight-Erranty and mad-heroism to be at an end. Your young military men, who want to reap the harvest of laurels, don't care (I suppose) how many seeds of war are sown; but for the sake of humanity it is devoutly to be wished, that the manly employment of agriculture and the humanizing benefits of commerce, would supersede the waste of war and the rage of conquest; that the swords might be turned into plough-shares, the spears into pruning hooks, and, as the Scripture expresses it, "the nations shall learn war no more."[92]

And to another correspondent, about the same time:

> How pitiful, in the eye of reason and religion, is that false ambition which desolates the world with fire and sword for the purposes of conquest and fame; when compared to the milder virtues of making our neighbors and fellow men as happy as their frail conditions and perishable natures will permit them to be.[93]

When Americans contemplated the Farewell Address, Washington hoped that the European war would prove an object lesson about the value of maintaining peace for their own safety and happiness. He had written to Lafayette in 1791: "The contrast between the situation of the people of the United States, and those of Europe is too striking to be passed over, even by the most superficial observer, and may, I believe, be considered one of the great causes of leading the people here to reflect more attentively on their own prosperous state, and to examine more minutely, and consequently approve more fully of the government under which they live, than they otherwise would have done." By 1795, this message was even clearer, as Washington told the Senate:

> While many of the nations of Europe, with their American dependencies, have been involved in contests unusually bloody, exhausting, and calamitous, in which the evils of foreign war have been aggravated by domestic convulsion and insurrection; in which many of the arts most useful to society have been exposed to discouragement and decay; in which the scarcity of subsistence has embittered other sufferings, while even the anticipations of a return of the blessings of peace and repose are alloyed by the sense of heavy and accumulating burthens, which press

upon all the departments of industry, and threaten to clog the future springs of Government; our favored country, happy in striking contrast, has enjoyed general tranquility—a tranquility the more satisfactory, because maintained at the expense of no duty. Faithful to ourselves, we have violated no obligation to others. Our agriculture, commerce, and manufactures, prosper beyond former example; the molestations of our trade (to prevent a continuation of which, however, very pointed remonstrances have been made), being overbalanced by the aggregate benefits which it derives from a neutral position.[94]

That said, Washington did not entirely dismiss the potential role of martial virtues, in the form of the willingness to defend liberty with one's life, in the American character. As we noted earlier, the continental army for Washington had represented a major vehicle through which the American character was given its initial impetus. After the suppression of the Whiskey Rebellion in 1794, Washington had spoken proudly of the spectacle "displaying to the highest advantage of the value of republican government, to behold the most and the least wealthy of our citizens standing in the same ranks, as private soldiers, preeminently distinguished by being the army of the constitution; undeterred by a march of three hundred miles over rugged mountains, by the approach of an inclement season, or by any other discouragement." During the war scare with France after he had left office in 1797, Washington wrote frequently of his confidence that the American people would fly to their country's defense if necessary. But this confidence was based on the republican, not the martial, character of America—the love of one's own, rightly understood, not the love of war.[95]

Further, although Washington favored a pacific character for America, he did not advocate pacifism. At the time of the Farewell Address, peace among the Europeans certainly did not seem to be in the cards, and this meant that the United States might be compelled to fight for its honor and independence. But Washington, more than most men, appreciated the fact that the "issue" of war was "*never* certain, always expensive," even in the best of circumstances. Washington further appreciated that America's weight in such a war "could be but small; tho' the loss to ourselves would be certain." War tended to benefit only a relative few, and often the least deserving, "whilst it must be distressing and ruinous to the great mass of our Citizens." Similar sentiments had been expressed by James Madison: "War is, perhaps, the most to be dreaded, because it comprises and develops the germ of every other. War is the parent of armies; from these proceed debts and taxes; and armies, and debts, and taxes are the known instruments for bringing the many under the domination of the few." Washington differed from the Republicans to the extent that he believed that prudent and limited military precautions might prevent war without bringing on these consequences. But because Washington shared the Republican reluctance to risk the American character in war, he tended to think, as he wrote to Gouverneur Morris, "nothing short of self-respect, and that justice which is essential to a national character, ought to involve us in War." (Washington made this point in his first draft of the Farewell Address: "That we may be always prepared for war, but never unsheath the sword except in self-defence so long as Justice and our essential rights, and national respectability can be preserved without it.") Hamilton put it this way: under the circumstances then facing the country, peace was "of such a great and primary magnitude" that it ought not be given up "unless the relinquishment be clearly necessary to Preserve Our Honor on some Unequivocal Point, or to avoid the sacrifice of some Right or Interest of Material and Permanent Importance."[96]

Washington, because he recognized America's weakness as well as its wish to do justice, sought to define in the Farewell Address a foreign policy that would not unnaturally increase the likelihood of war. For Washington, political connections among nations—such as the French Treaty—were essentially about war or, more precisely, about the conditions under which various parties would engage in war to support the other. It required making distinctions between "us" and "them" on the basis of defining some nations a priori as "enemies." Promotion of commerce, as advocated in the Farewell Address, would not have this effect. Even-handed commercial relations would not only serve immediate American interests, but they held out hope for the day when more natural, just, and pacific ties among men and nations would take hold.

Washington had a clear idea about what such a natural and just international order would look like and how it would contribute to the safety and happiness of America. As he had written to Gouverneur Morris:

> I can however with truth aver that this Country is not guided by such narrow and mistaken policy as will lead it to wish the destruction of any nation, under an idea that our importance will be encreased in proportion as that of others is lessened. We should rejoice to see every nation enjoying all the advantages that nature and it's [sic] circumstances would admit, consistent with civil liberty, and the rights of other nations. Upon this ground the prosperity of this Country would unfold itself every day, and every day would find it growing in political importance.[97]

Civil liberty at home and common respect for the rights of other nations so that all might achieve what their natural advantages might admit constituted for Washington that essential basis on which decent interna-

tional relations could be conducted. The promotion of international commerce on the basis of true reciprocity, as defended in the Farewell Address,
was the first and basic foundation on which this process could begin.
(Washington had written in his discarded First Inaugural: "A sense of reciprocal benefits will serve to connect us with the rest of mankind in stricter
ties of amity."[98]) Within limits, true reciprocity was something that the
United States had in its power to pursue, for its own good and that of
others.

The French Revolution held out the possibility that another nation,
so conceived and so dedicated, might join America in this task for creating
a more just, peaceful, and prosperous international order. Washington had
written to the President of the French National Assembly in 1791:

> The impressions naturally produced by similarity of political sentiment
> [with France] are justly to be regarded as causes of national sympathy;
> calculated to confirm the amicable ties which may otherwise subsist be-
> tween nations. This reflection, independent of its more particular refer-
> ence, must dispose every benevolent mind to unite in the wish, that
> a general diffusion of true principles of liberty, assimilating as well as
> ameliorating the condition of Mankind and fostering the maxims of an
> ingenuous and virtuous policy, may tend to strengthen the fraternity of
> the human race, to assuage the jealousies and animosities of its various
> subdivisions, and to convince them more and more, that their true inter-
> est and felicity will best be promoted by mutual good will and universal
> harmony.[99]

We see again in this quotation the interrelated strands of Washington's
thinking about foreign affairs, as he would display most comprehensively
in the Farewell Address. The first strand is the foundation of interest; Washington speaks of national "sympathy" (not interest) that "confirms" (but is
not the origin of) the ties that may "otherwise" subsist between nations.
But what is first in order is not necessarily final: Washington points to the
"true interest and felicity" that may eventually strengthen the fraternity of
the human race through the promotion of good will and universal harmony.

The French Revolution

During his second term of office, Washington found himself confronted with perhaps the greatest test of his statesmanship: dealing simultaneously with the grave foreign policy crises associated with the general war
in Europe and the domestic crises brought about by the conjunction of

that war with divergent American attitudes toward the French Revolution. The Farewell Address reflected Washington's practical as well as principled understanding of the statecraft necessary to this task. The Farewell Address accordingly included his implicit judgment and critique of the French Revolution. We speculate that this was Washington's greatest test because he was faced with the need to place his greatest public asset—his reputation—at risk for what he regarded as the greater good of the American political character.

Washington's statecraft, defended most fully in the Farewell Address, included the aim of distinguishing the American character, and cause, from the character and cause of the French Revolution—without either abandoning the enlightened defense of liberty or forfeiting American independence once again to Britain. In a letter to James Monroe, Washington insisted that his "public and private conduct" with respect to France could be summed up simply:

> . . . that I have always wished well to the French revolution; that I have always given it as my decided opinion that no Nation had the right to intermeddle in the internal concerns of another; that every one had a right to form and adopt whatever government they had liked best to live under themselves and that if this country could, consistently with its engagements, maintain a strict neutrality and thereby preserve peace, it was bound to do so by motives of policy, interest, and every other consideration, that ought to actuate a people situated and circumstanced as we are; already deeply in debt, and in a convalescent state, from the struggle we have been engaged in ourselves. On these principles I have steadily and uniformly proceeded; bidding defiance to calumnies calculated to sow the seeds of distrust in the French nation, and to excite their belief of an influence, possessed by Great Britain in the councils of this Country; than which nothing is more unfounded and injurious; the object of its pacific conduct being truly delineated above.[100]

As we examine this policy more closely, we note that Washington characterized his public and private conduct as being consistent in the case of France. By contrast, Washington had expressed strong anti-British views "with an energy that could not be mistaken by *any one* present" in "private conversations" and in "meetings with confidential servants of the public." As Washington had explained to Henry Lee, "I have made my public conduct accord with the system [of neutrality]; and whilst so acting as a public character, consistency and propriety as a private man, forbid these intemperate expressions in favor of one Nation, or prejudice of another, wch. many have indulged themselves in, and I will venture to add, to the embarrassment of government, without producing any good to the Country."[101]

As we noted earlier, Washington was undoubtedly reluctant to express such sentiments publicly because he did not want to lend authority to those who would use hatred of Britain to shape and define the American character. This was an implicit teaching of the Farewell Address. But he also wanted to shape popular opinion in the direction of the proper attitude toward France and the French Revolution.

Washington while in office spoke favorably in public about the French Revolution (while of course condemning those who would sacrifice America's interest to those of other nations). Washington's policy began with a recognition of the deep popular affections for France held by the American people, which began as an understandable by-product of France's support for the American cause during the war with Great Britain. As he wrote to the French minister in 1788: "I am egregiously deceived if the people of this country are not in general extremely well affected to France. The prejudices against that Kingdom had been so rivetted by our English connection and English policy that it was some time before our people could entirely get the better of them. This, however, was thoroughly accomplished in the course of the War, and I may venture to say that a greater revolution never took place in the sentiments of one people respecting another." This sentiment naturally increased as a consequence of the French Revolution. Most Americans initially welcomed the French cause as part of the worldwide liberation of mankind that the American Revolution had begun. The French Revolution further seemed to confirm the importance that the Founding generation placed on America as the leader and exemplar of that worldwide liberation. This sentiment was by no means confined to Republicans. John Marshall, a devoted Federalist, later recalled: "We were all strongly attached to France—scarcely any man more strongly than myself. I sincerely believed human liberty to depend in a great measure on the success of the French Revolution."[102]

Washington also recognized the widespread public sentiment among both Republicans and Federalists to stay out of the European war. As Jefferson had written to Gouverneur Morris in April 1793: "No country was ever so thoroughly against war as ours. These dispositions pervade every description of its citizens." Washington shared whole-heartedly in these dispositions. American neutrality was recommended, as Washington had written Monroe while the Farewell Address was being composed, "by motives of policy, interest, and every other consideration." Unfortunately for Washington, public sentiment favored a pro-French neutrality, and the emerging Republican faction wanted to threaten a tilt toward France in order to coerce the British finally to implement the Treaty of Peace and to make commercial concessions. The Republicans argued, not without reason, that an impartial neutrality actually worked against France. Washington, on the contrary, believed that a legally strict neutrality, which remained faithful to the letter of the French Treaty, was both possible and necessary to preserve the peace.[103]

Washington's controversial insistence on what Jefferson later termed a "sneaking" or "English" neutrality was not itself the cause of the party division that soon emerged full-bore onto the American political scene. That division was ultimately caused by the radically different interpretations that Americans had come to place on the French Revolution. Alexis de Tocqueville later made the point that the French Revolution had no country; it united and divided men in spite of law, traditions, characters, and language. Enemies became fellow countrymen; brothers became adversaries—as Tocqueville put it, the French Revolution created an intellectual country that was common to all and to which all could claim citizenship.[104]

As a practical matter, Washington rejected American allegiance to this intellectual country. His policies resisted those who argued for joining a worldwide revolution under French auspices for liberty, fraternity, and equality. He also rejected the close connection that Jefferson made at the time between the fate of the French and American causes. Washington refused to accept Jefferson's argument in the undoubted belief that allegiance to the French trans-national cause would divide, not unite, the American political community, unless the executive was prepared to purge its opponents and undertake a Terror at home. Washington told Jefferson that "if any body wanted to change its [the government's] form into a monarchy it was only a few individuals, & that no man would set his face against it more than himself; but this was not what he was afraid of; his fears were from another quarter, that there was more danger of anarchy being introduced." But for Washington, if America was to resist falling into despotism or anarchy, it must do it on its own accord and not by the example of others. This was necessary for America to command its fortunes, as sought by the Farewell Address.[105]

Tocqueville compared the French Revolution to a religious, rather than a political revolution. The Founders had been at pains to avoid religious faction; as Washington noted in 1792, "Religious controversies are always productive of more acrimony and irreconcilable hatreds than those which spring from any other cause." Washington feared that passionate attachments to foreign nations and foreign political systems could come to approximate those of religion. In the words of Fisher Ames, "Jacobism had become here, as in France, a sect rather than a party, inspiring a fanaticism that was equally intolerant and contagious." Factions might be managed if they were confined to domestic affairs, but not if one or several factions linked America's moral well-being with those of a sectarian character abroad. The greatest embarrassments under which America labored, in Washington's view, "proceed from the counteraction of people among ourselves; who are more disposed to promote the views of another, than to establish a national character of their own."[106]

Washington had come to this conclusion about the French Revolution over time. In following Washington's evolving views, we can see that he implicitly constructed a series of tests that would determine for him the character of the French Revolution and how the United States should respond to it. His conduct, private and public, was designed to help public opinion use the same criteria to reach the same conclusion in concert with him. The Farewell Address reflected Washington's final evaluation of the events in France, and this pointed toward a different direction for Americans than that which was followed by various Parisian revolutionaries.

Like other Americans, Washington had once been optimistic about the influence that the American Revolution would have on the cause of liberty elsewhere. As he wrote in 1788 to Jefferson, then American minister to France, "Indeed the rights of Mankind, the privileges of the people, and the true principles of liberty, seem to have been more generally discussed and better understood throughout Europe since the American revolution than they were at any former period." This in Washington's correspondence with a Frenchman just prior to the Revolution: "I am very happy to find . . . that the American Revolution, or the peculiar light of the age seems to have opened the eyes of almost every nation in Europe, and a spirit of equal liberty appears fast to be gaining ground everywhere . . ." By 1791, Washington believed that "the example of France will undoubtedly have its effects on other Kingdoms. Poland, by the public papers, appears to have made large and unexpected strides towards liberty . . ."[107]

As for the prospects for liberty in France itself, Washington had predicted as early as 1788 that the spirit awakened in the French Kingdom, "if managed with extreme prudence, may produce a gradual and tacit Revolution much in favor of the subjects, by abolishing Lettres de Cachet and defining more accurately the power of government." He wrote Gouverneur Morris in October 1789: "The revolution which has been effected in France is of so wonderful a nature that the mind can hardly realize the fact. If it ends as our last accounts to the first of August predict that nation will be the most powerful and happy in Europe."[108]

But as Washington's qualification indicated—"if managed with extreme prudence"—he saw the signs of long-term trouble: "I fear though it has triumphantly gone through the first paroxysm, it is not the last it has to encounter before matters are finally settled. In a word the revolution is of too great magnitude to be effected in so short a space, and with the loss of so little blood." To succeed, "great temperance, firmness, and foresight are necessary . . . To forebear running from one extreme to another is not an easy matter and, should this be the case, rocks and shelves not visible at present may wreck the vessel." Washington approved of the "spirit for political improvements" that were "rapidly and extensively spreading" throughout Europe. But he regretted those who were "prematurely accelerating those improvements," who were "making more haste than good speed, in their innovations." Washington's "greatest fear" had been that the French nation "would not be sufficiently cool and moderate in making the arrangements for the security of liberty, of which it seems to be fully possessed."[109]

To be sure, Washington acknowledged that, from so great a distance, Americans had no right to offer an opinion to the French as to how to proceed. And Washington admitted to Lafayette that a "just medium cannot be expected to be found in a moment" because "the first vibrations always go to the extremes, and cool reason, which alone can establish a permanent and equal government, is as little to be expected in the tumults of popular commotion, as an attention to the liberties of the people is to be found in the dark Divan of a despotic tyrant." A successful revolution for ordered liberty required "so much prudence, so much perseverance, so much disinterestedness and so much patriotism" to be observed by a nation's leaders. These were the implicit tests of performance that Washington set for himself and his fellow citizens in deciding on the character of the French Revolution. The American Founders had exhibited such characteristics, and Washington concluded that the French Revolution would ultimately fail unless it was led by men of similar attributes and attitudes, and unless it was aimed at the formation of a moderate national character.[110]

Over time, Washington came to have grave doubts that the leaders of the French Revolution sought such an equilibrium between extremes. The disorder that Washington saw increasingly in France was not caused principally by its foreign enemies—opposition to which ought to unite the country—but by deliberate policies of those in the government, who were ready to tear each other to pieces. Washington believed that there was an iron rule of the political consequences of going to extremes: "there is a natural and necessary progression, from the extreme of anarchy to the extreme of Tyranny . . . arbitrary power is most easily established on the ruins of Liberty debased to licentiousness."[111] For French leaders to push toward one extreme rather than to seek a political mean—the sort of mean that Washington had articulated for America in the Farewell Address—indicated to him the certain and fatal outcome of the process for France.

Still, Washington understood that the American public—like himself—thrilled to see the banner of liberty unfurled. As he wrote to the French minister in 1796:

> Born, Sir, in a land of liberty; having early learned its value; having engaged in a perilous conflict to defend it; having, in a word, devoted the best years of my life to secure its permanent establishment in my own country; my anxious recollections, my sympathetic feelings, and my best wishes are irresistibly excited, whensoever in any country, I see an oppressed nation unfurl the banners of Freedom. But above all, the events of the French Revolution have produced the deepest solicitude, as well as the highest admiration. To call your nation brave, were to pronounce common praise.[112]

Washington considered this sentiment a necessary and healthy part of the American political character. But Washington wished to teach his fellow citizens that their passion for the universal cause of human liberty must not be unreflective. In the form of praising the cause of France to the French minister, Washington made explicit to the public the grounds on which Americans might evaluate the true merits of both the American and French Revolutions:

> I rejoice that the period of your toils and of your immense sacrifices, is approaching. I rejoice that the interesting revolutionary movements of so many years have issued in the formation of a constitution designed to give permanency to the great object for which you have contended. I rejoice that liberty, which you have so long embraced with enthusiasm, liberty, of which you have been the invincible defenders, now finds an asylum in the bosom of a regularly organized government; a government, which, being formed to secure the happiness of the French people, corresponds with the ardent wishes of my heart, while it gratifies the pride of every citizen of the United States, by its resemblance to their own.[113]

Washington explained elsewhere that the French Revolution would be a success when domestic tranquility was restored by a government respectfully energetic, founded on the broad basis of liberality and the rights of man. He was anxious that the rights of man would be well understood and permanently fixed through the avoidance of despotic oppression on the one hand; while licentiousness was not to be substituted for liberty, nor confusion for order, on the other. This reminds us of one of Washington's goals for America: "to convince the world that the happiness of nations can be accomplished by pacific revolutions in their political systems, without the destructive intervention of the sword."[114] The French had not followed the American example of pacific revolution—not only or primarily because of the inherent difficulties of such a revolution, but because of their own deliberate factionalism and extremism.

Still, Washington acknowledged that the French, and every other people, had a right to decide the form of their own government, through whatever process that might entail. His implicit criticism of their Revolution went to the means, not the end, of achieving liberty. Washington was accordingly determined to insulate the American character from the consequences of the French Revolution, to the extent that those consequences were not healthy to the American body politic. As he stated in 1793: "Sentiments sincerely friendly to the French Nation, and the most cordial wishes for their welfare, unite, I doubt not, all the Citizens of the United States; but it cannot be incompatible with these dispositions to give full weight to the great and commanding considerations which respect the immediate welfare of our Own Country." [115] Specifically, the United States must draw the line between what the French did for and to themselves— which was their own business—and French efforts to universalize the Revolution by meddling in the domestic affairs of others.

Toward an American National Character

To sum up: the Farewell Address was Washington's most complete articulation of his project to create a modern, self-sufficient American political community—in the form of a large commercial republic—able to command its own fortunes through a foreign policy that pursued the American interest, guided by justice.

The American political community and the national character depended on establishing in the mind of the people the proper relationship, and distinction, between America and other nations and peoples. Above all, the American character, its genius, was a republican character. America would be founded and sustained not merely on the basis of a particular people in a particular place, but on the common commitment of those people to achieving civil and religious liberty under the rule of law. Washington fully understood the necessary importance of interest in cementing this Union. He sought to define a national interest that transcended local interests and prejudices. The national interest reflected the common benefit—in terms of self-defense and prosperity—that all Americans would realize from being participants in a large, commercial nation able to hold its own in an often hostile world. But Washington also thought that it was only on such a scale that the higher purpose, or true national interest, of America could be realized. That higher purpose was to demonstrate to all mankind the feasibility of self-government. It was also to demonstrate that justice was the proper and sustainable grounds for relations among nations and peoples. The honor of striving for domestic and international justice would ennoble and give greater purpose to the American character. In the same vein, the sympathetic feelings and best wishes of America would be irresistibly excited whenever an oppressed nation unfurled the banners of freedom. Further, the United States would be a refuge for the sober, industrious, and virtuous of the world, and for those persecuted. By sympathy and by appropriate action, Americans would thereby show themselves to be true friends of humanity. America could not play that role if it were too closed, too interested, too parochial, or if it behaved badly towards other nations and peoples.

But the experience of the French Revolution, combined with the lessons of the European wars, also pointed to the danger of America being too open to the world, of being insufficiently interested in American things. Specifically, Washington feared the effects of excessively identifying the American cause with that of other nations. He emphatically opposed those who would try to use the pressure of outside events, of foreign interests and ideas, to "purify" domestic politics, or to alter the American regime. Cosmopolitanism had to be limited. There had to be a particular American character, one that essentially distinguished America from Europe. Washington attempted to make this distinction by showing that America had different material interests than those of the European combatants. But he also emphasized the difference between the republican government of America and the monarchies and despotisms of the Old World; and the distinction between republican liberty, on the one hand, and anarchy and license, on the other. Washington was prepared to use the follies of Europe as a negative lesson to his fellow citizens, to strengthen their attachment to what was rightly their own.

For Washington, a safe and healthy America must therefore be both open to the world and detached from it, in the proper proportion. That proportion would undoubtedly change over time. It would certainly change once the United States had settled and matured its institutions, when it had achieved the degree of strength and consistency that would have given it, humanly speaking, command of its own fortunes. It might conceivably change when the banners of freedom had truly been planted on others' soil and when these republics met the same test of liberty, good government, and respect for the rights of other nations and peoples that were to inform the American character.

Throughout their history, Americans have placed greater or lesser emphasis on Washington's particular terms for a truly American foreign policy:

the promotion and defense of the nation's interests; sympathy for the cause of human liberty as an elevating and ennobling feature of those interests; and respect for the just rights of other peoples and nations, which respect suggested the need for a certain detachment from the ordinary nature of international politics, most especially when it came to engagement in war. At times, statesmen and scholars have viewed these terms as being discrete and mutually exclusive, whereas Washington insisted on the complementarity, or comprehension, of interest, liberty, and justice in a rightly constructed regime and foreign policy.

5

WASHINGTON AND THE
AMERICAN POLITICAL TRADITION

Thomas Jefferson, in an effort to persuade Washington not to retire from office in 1792, wrote to the president that "I knew we were to try some day to walk alone; and if the essay should be made while you should be alive & looking on, we should derive confidence from that circumstance, & resource if it failed."[1] When Washington decided to retire four years later, he reflected on the need to help provide his countrymen with the confidence and resources they needed to continue their journey, even after his death. Plutarch had written about the lives of the noble Grecians and Romans because the actions of good men implant in others, especially the young, an eager rivalry and a keen desire to imitate them. Washington's life was surely worthy of imitation. But he could not count on some future Plutarch to display his public and private character in such a compelling fashion. Also, Washington's situation as the Father of His Country was unique and not capable of being fully imitated. He therefore had to find other means to influence the American character after his death.

Washington understood that public opinion was everything in a popular government, and that the ability to affect that opinion was even more important than passing laws; it made the passage and enforcement of laws possible. Scholars have long noted that Washington's first retirement from public life in 1783—his voluntary renunciation of power—not only signalled Washington's reverence for republican and constitutional government, but it also had the effect of increasing his popular stature and reputation. He attained greater, not less, influence over public opinion in this fashion. But Washington did not allow this critical moment to pass in silence. He composed his famous Circular to the States, which explained his actions and which took advantage of the opportunity to articulate what was now required to complete the national character. A republican government, founded and ultimately sustained by reflection and choice, required reasoned explanations as much or more than noble deeds.

Washington's sense of when, and when not, to speak was critical to his ability to shape public deliberations, just as was his sense of when to give up power. (Some, like Hamilton, never quite learned when to shut up.) Washington's silence during the Constitutional Convention is most noteworthy in this respect. Washington also remained silent on many important questions of policy during his presidential administration, not only to the public but sometimes even to his closest advisers. Washington's reserve was deliberate. Tactically, it preserved his immediate options. But in a larger sense, it meant that when he spoke, people listened. The Farewell Address, of course, was to be the ultimate sermon that brought to bear Washington's full authority. It was designed to influence the reflection and choice of the American people, perhaps for generations to come.

Throughout American history, a few such pronouncements, or doctrines, have taken on a particular gravity and have essentially defined the course of acceptable political debate. The practice of republicanism, we would argue, depends in part on such political "centers of gravity" that necessarily go beyond (or behind) constitutionalism and provide fundamental guidance to governors and the governed. The Declaration of Independence, with its self-evident truths, was the first and foremost such sheet-anchor of American republicanism. Washington's call in the Farewell Address for Union at home and independence abroad was for years perhaps the next most influential. By 1829, Andrew Jackson's Secretary of State, Martin Van Buren, could write that the tenets of the Farewell Address had become "cardinal traits of the foreign policy of this government." These tenets had taken on an "obligatory character" which was now regarded "with a degree of reverence and submission but little, if anything, short of that which is entertained for the Constitution itself."[2] The same was essentially true for Washington's teaching about unity of government.

But times change, as does the range of choice open to those who would preserve, transform, or destroy the American regime. Washington's teachings, which became so ingrained in the American political tradition, naturally represented a source of strength to some and a barrier to others in the ongoing battle to mold public opinion. The proper interpretation of the Farewell Address became a critical part of the crises that led to the Civil War, and of America's response to the great World Wars (hot and cold) of this century.

Early Views of the Farewell Address

For a time, however, it appeared that the Farewell Address would never achieve its intended purpose of articulating a common ground to which all Americans of good will could repair. Not surprisingly, Washington's "disinterested warnings" were well received by politicians and publications associated with Federalism. Rufus King, in London, wrote to John Quincy Adams that "the topics he has discussed are very interesting to our Happiness and I think the performance will add to his reputation." Young Adams wrote to a correspondent that "I am sure that you will concur in the opinion that it is one of the most interesting papers as a public document, and in every respect worthy of one whose life has been one continued benefaction to his country."[3]

Many Republicans, by contrast, initially criticized the Address as a campaign document and for its alleged anti–French doctrine. Shortly after its publication, James Madison wrote to James Monroe that "the valedictory address of the president . . . shews that he [is] compleatly in the snares of the British faction; and in pursuance of their views is laboring *totis viribus*, [to] rear every obstruction as well as to remove every facility to an improvement of our commercial relations with France." Madison affected surprise on this score; he was aware that strong efforts had been made to "convey to his [Washington's] mind a rancor against that country [France] and suspicions of all who are thought to sympathise with its revolution and who support their policy of extending our commerce and in general of standing well with it." But he was surprised that Washington had been "wrought up to the tone that could dictate or rather adopt some parts of the performance in spite of the forbidding considerations both personal and public which ought not to have been forgotten." Madison indicated suspicions about the authorship of the Address: "I say personal with particular reference to the inconsistency between the language used on this and on other occasions."[4]

For his part, having been stung by his recall from his post as American minister to France, Monroe was even less charitable.

> It is to be regretted that Mr. Washingtons [*sic*] testament arrived before Mr. Pinckney [Monroe's replacement], for it confirmed previous unfriendly impressions. Most of the monarchs of the earth practice ingratitude in their transactions with other powers: they all however hold a different doctrine but Mr. W has the merit of transcending, not the great men of the antient republik[s], but the little monarchs of the present day, in preaching it as a public virtue. Where these men will pl[u]nge our affrs. God only knows, but such a collection of vain, superficial, blunderers, to say no worse of them, were never I think before placed at the head of any respectable State.[5]

Within a few years, however, the Farewell Address's advice began to take on much greater currency across the political spectrum, especially in terms of foreign policy. As John Quincy Adams wrote: "Can France possibly believe that Mr. Jefferson, or any other man, would dare to start away from that system which Washington has thus sanctioned, not only by his example, but by his retirement?" By 1797, Jefferson himself had reached the conclusion that "our countrymen have divided themselves by such strong affections, to the French & the English, that nothing will secure us internally but a divorce from both nations." In criticizing Federalist measures that seemed to anticipate or provoke war with France, the Republicans began explicitly to use the Farewell Address on their behalf—even before the apotheosis of Washington after his death. In 1798, New York Republican George Clinton cited the Farewell Address to appeal to Jefferson's ideal that America should follow the example of China, eschewing all foreign connections.[6]

The most significant dimension of the rise in the public stature of the Farewell Address was the explicit embrace of Washington by the Republicans following Thomas Jefferson's election in 1800. Jefferson sought to claim his fellow Virginian as a comrade in his battles against the supposedly monarchical faction in American politics and to deny Washington's prestige to that faction (the Federalists). Jefferson wrote of Washington: "He was true to the republican charge confided to him; & has solemnly and repeatedly protested to me, in our private conversations, that he would lose the last drop of his blood in support of it; and he did this the oftener, and with more earnestness, because he knew my suspicions of Hamilton's designs against it." In his First Inaugural Address, Jefferson referred to "our first and greatest revolutionary character, whose preeminent services entitled him to the first place in his country's love and destined him for the fairest page in the volume of faithful history." "I am convinced," Jefferson wrote in 1814, "that [Washington] is more deeply seated in the love and gratitude of the republicans, than in the Pharisaical homage of the federalist monarchists."[7]

In 1825, Jefferson, as a member of the Board of Visitors at the University of Virginia, corresponded with James Madison about developing a set of prescribed texts in government for the university's school of law. As Madison put it, it was essential that the "true doctrines of liberty" be inculcated in those who were to sustain and administer the system. The final list consisted of the writings of John Locke and Algernon Sidney, the Declaration of Independence, *The Federalist Papers*, Washington's Farewell Address, and the Virginia Resolutions of 1799. The Farewell Address (along with Washington's First Inaugural, later dropped) had been suggested by Madison, to provide balance—"they may help down what might less readily be swallowed." Madison remarked upon the "sound sentiments" of both of

Washington's writings, commenting that they "convey political lessons of particular value" and "contain nothing that is not good; unless it be the laudatory reference in the Address to the Treaty of 1795 with Great Britain." Madison's exception of the Jay Treaty was by no means a small one: it went to the heart of the difference between Republican foreign policy and that espoused by Washington and the Federalists. But Madison evidently believed that this large difference in policy could now be safely subsumed in general agreement with the framework of political discourse established by Washington. The Farewell Address was well on its way to a special status in American politics.[8]

The Farewell Address and the Crisis of Union

As the founding generation began to pass from the scene and as new challenges to American unity appeared in the nineteenth century, those portions of the Farewell Address dealing with Union became an especially important device by which nationalists sought to rally support for Union and the federal government. For instance, to counter resistance in New England to the policies of the Madison administration in 1812, James Monroe, in a series of newspaper editorials, quoted those passages of the Farewell Address that touched on the duty of the people to obey federal laws and condemned factional opposition to the government's policies.[9]

But the most prominent use of Washington and the Farewell Address for national purposes came during the sectional crises from 1820 to 1860. Daniel Webster, widely regarded as the greatest orator of this period, in particular used the Farewell Address in an effort to forge a truly national American identity. Because of Washington's strong defense of Union over sectionalism, Webster viewed him as the embodiment of American patriotism. His celebrated reply to South Carolina Senator Robert Hayne in 1830 invoked the Washingtonian theme of "Liberty and Union, now and for ever, one and inseparable."[10]

In one of his most famous orations, Webster spoke on the "Character of Washington" at the centennial of Washington's birth in 1832. Overshadowing this celebration, and indeed all of American politics at the time, was the ongoing struggle over South Carolina's attempt to insist on the constitutional right of a state to nullify federal laws. It was therefore important for Webster to stress the fact that Washington's birthday had led to "the voluntary outpouring of the public feeling, made to-day, from the North to the South, and from the East to the West," which proved that the public celebrations of the virtues of the Father of His Country were "both just and natural." In studying Washington's character, Webster pointed his audience toward his principles of administration, which were "to be found in the Constitution itself, in the great measures recommended and approved by him, in his speeches to Congress, and in that most interesting paper, his Farewell Address to the People of the United States."[11]

Webster was particularly struck by the fact that "its political maxims are invaluable; its exhortations to love of country and to brotherly affections among citizens, touching; and the solemnity with which it urges the observance of moral duties, and impresses the power of religious obligation, gives to it the highest character of truly disinterested, sincere, parental advice." Webster in particular praised Washington for the one sentiment "so deeply felt, so constantly uppermost, that no proper occasion escaped without its utterance . . . the Union was the great object of his thoughts."

> He regarded the union of these States less as one of our blessings, than as the great treasure-house which contained them all. Here, in his judgment, was the great magazine of all our means of prosperity; here, as he thought, and as every American still thinks, are deposited our animating prospects, all our solid hopes for future greatness. He has taught us to maintain this union, not by seeking to enlarge the powers of the government, on the one hand, nor by surrendering them, on the other; but by an administration of them at once firm and moderate, pursuing objects truly national, and carried on in a spirit of justice and equity.

Dismemberment of the Union, Webster stated, would strike at the very ability of the people "to resist or overcome misfortunes, to sustain us against the ordinary accidents of human affairs, and to promote, by active efforts, every public interest."

In seeking to place Washington and the Farewell Address into their proper context, Webster reflected that "a century from the birth of Washington has changed the world. The country of Washington has been the theatre on which a great part of that change has been wrought, and Washington himself a principal agent by which it has been accomplished." According to Webster, what marked the age of Washington, even more than the advances of science, art, and commerce, was "the spirit of human freedom, the new elevation of individual man, in his moral, social, and political character." Society had assumed a new character: "It has raised itself from *beneath* governments to a participation *in* governments; it has mixed moral and political objects with the daily pursuits of individual men; and, with a freedom and strength before altogether unknown, it has applied to these objects the whole power of human understanding." Washington, having been entrusted with the supreme command of the Revolution, had the "extraordinary fortune" to be placed at the head of the first government in which an attempt was made on a large scale to rear the fabric of the social order on the basis of a written constitution and of a pure representative principle. A government was to be established, without a throne, without an aristocracy, without castes, orders, or privileges; and this government, instead of being a democracy, existing and acting within the walls of a single city, was to be extended over a vast country, of different climates, interests, and habits, and of various communions of our common Christian faith.

For Webster, this was the American experiment, "so full of interest to us and to our posterity for ever, so full of interest, indeed, to the world in its present generation and in all its generations to come," which was "suffered to commence under the guidance of Washington." The whole world was interested in this experiment "to see whether society could, by the strength and peace of this principle, maintain its own peace and good government, carry forward its own great interests, and conduct itself to political renown and glory." Webster concluded:

> Our great, our high duty is to show, in our own example, that this spirit is a spirit of health as well as a spirit of power; that its benignity is as great as its strength; that its efficiency to secure individual rights, social relations, and moral order, is equal to the irresistible force with which it prostrates principalities and powers. The world, at this moment, is regarding us with something of a fearful admiration. Its deep and awful anxiety is to learn whether free states may be stable, as well as free; whether popular power may be trusted, as well as feared; in short, whether wise, regular, and virtuous self-government is a vision for the contemplation of theorists, or a truth established, illustrated, and brought into practice in the country of Washington.

By the mid-1850s, the patriotic nationalism of Washington became controversial and problematic. Not surprisingly, both sides claimed Washington for their side: the North embraced an ardent advocate of Union and opponent of sectionalism, the South claimed a strong defender of liberty and an enemy of tyranny. Ironically, the debate over the status and meaning of Washington heated up in 1850 when Henry Clay—sponsor of the Great Compromise—introduced a motion in the Senate to purchase the original manuscript of the Farewell Address. In his speech, Senator Clay asserted that the document should be re-read "amid the discordance and ungrateful sounds of disunion and discord which assail our ears in every part of this country and in both halls of Congress." Clay then went on to note Washington's warning "to beware of sectional division, to beware of demagogues, to beware of the consequences of indulging a spirit of disunion." Webster seconded the motion while Mississippi Senator Jefferson Davis, the future president of the Confederacy, objected on the grounds that there were numerous copies of the document already in circulation and that another was not needed.[12]

In response to calls for the preservation of the Union, the South advocated a redefinition of Union based on the rights of individual states. There would be American characters, not an American character. The great architect of the states' rights position was Senator John C. Calhoun of South Carolina, who argued that the nation was built on a compact of co-equal parts, each part retaining its sovereignty. In his final speech to the Senate, Calhoun responded to Clay and others and gave his assessment of Washington's example, by shifting the terms of the debate to accommodate his constitutional view. Washington, in this light, became a model for those who advocated disunion for the sake of liberty. Washington, Calhoun asserted, was after all "one of us—a slaveholder and a planter." Washington's fame rested on not just avoiding, but repelling wrong; there was nothing in Washington's example that supported submission to injustice. "Nor can we find any thing in his history to deter us from seceding from the Union, should it fail to fulfill the objects for which it was instituted, by being permanently and hopelessly converted into the means of oppressing instead of protecting us." Just the opposite, Calhoun found much to encourage the secessionists, "should we be forced to the extremity of deciding between submission and disunion." Calhoun noted that before the union under the Constitution, Washington had been loyal to the union under the British crown. When that union became oppressive he did not fail to draw his sword and lead the move for independence, "the great and crowning glory of his life."[13]

The legacy of Washington entered into the famous Lincoln-Douglas senatorial debates in 1858, when both candidates made reference to Washington and the teachings of the Farewell Address. Their debate, which centered immediately on the problem of slavery in the territories, was in fact a dispute over the future of the American character. Douglas and Lincoln were equally devoted to Washington's cause, that of Union and the Constitution, but they had distinct, and ultimately incompatible, views as to the animating force that would preserve America as a nation.

Senator Stephen Douglas, advocating popular sovereignty, noted that Washington and the other Founders had accepted the division of the nation into free and slave states from the very beginning, and that Washington always deferred to the authority of local laws and domestic institutions.

> Washington did not believe, nor did his compatriots, that the local laws and domestic institutions that were well adapted to the Green Mountains

of Vermont were suited to the rice plantations of South Carolina; they did not believe at that day that in a Republic so broad and expanded as this, containing such a variety of climate, soil and interest, that uniformity in the local laws and domestic institutions was either desirable or possible. They believed then as our experience has proved to us now, that each locality, having different interests, a different climate and different surroundings, required different local laws, local policy and local institutions, adapted to the wants of that locality. Thus our Government was formed on the principle of diversity in the local institutions and laws, and not on that of uniformity.[14]

For Washington and the Founders, then, Union did not mean uniformity. Douglas claimed that each state of the Union had the right "to do as it pleases, without meddling with its neighbors." The great mission of the Democratic party was "to unite the fraternal feeling of the whole country, restore peace and quiet, by teaching each state to mind its own business, and regulate its domestic affairs, and all to unite in carrying out the Constitution as our fathers made it, and thus to preserve the Union and make it perpetual for all time to come." There was no sectional strife in Washington's army: "They were all brethren of a common confederacy; they fought under a common flag that they might bestow on their posterity a common destiny, and to this end they poured out their blood in common streams, and shared, in some instances, a common grave." Sectional strife, as Douglas presented it, was the product of those like Lincoln who had created a new party, based on abolitionist principles, which (unlike the parties of old) had appeal only in one section of the nation.[15]

Abraham Lincoln offered a fundamentally different interpretation of American nationhood and the American national character. He argued that the preservation of the Union depended on halting the spread of slavery and placing the peculiar institution on the road of ultimate extinction—just as Washington himself had intended. In the debates, Lincoln challenged Douglas to show any evidence that Washington had considered negroes to be unequal to the white man or excluded from the principles of humanity set out in the Declaration of Independence. Lincoln's fullest defense of his position on the intentions of the Founders appeared in his February 1860 speech at the Cooper Union in New York: "Some of you delight to flaunt in our faces the warning against sectional parties given by Washington in his Farewell Address," Lincoln remarked. Nevertheless, it was Washington as president who had approved and signed the act to enforce the Ordinance of 1787, which included a prohibition of slavery in the Northwest Territory. Lincoln also noted Washington's letter to Lafayette on the subject, in which Washington wrote that "I have long considered it [negro slavery] a most serious evil, both socially and politically, and I should rejoice in any feasible scheme to rid our States of such a burden." Lincoln continued:

> Bearing this in mind, and seeing that sectionalism has since arisen upon this same subject, is that warning a weapon in your hands against us, or in our hands against you? Could Washington himself speak, would he cast blame of that sectionalism upon us, who sustain his policy, or upon you, who repudiate it? We respect that warning of Washington, and we commend it to you, together with his example pointing to the right application of it.

Lincoln concluded the Cooper Union address by warning against the "sophistical contrivances" being used to divert those who opposed slavery and supported the Union. Chief among those devices, Lincoln believed, were "invocations to Washington, imploring men to unsay what Washington said and undo what Washington did." These contrivances amounted to "groping for some middle ground between the right and the wrong, vain as the search for a man who should be neither a living man nor a dead man—such as a policy of 'don't care' on a question about which all true men do care."[16]

During his journey to Washington in 1861, before his inauguration, Lincoln addressed the New Jersey State Senate at Trenton. Lincoln recalled the battle there during the Revolutionary War, a battle that he said had been fixed vividly in his memory as a child by reading Parson Weems's *Life of Washington*. Like Douglas, Lincoln appreciated the fact that Washington's army had suffered for the great cause of national independence, for the right to govern themselves. But:

> I recollect thinking then, boy even though I was, that there must have been something more than common that those men struggled for. I am exceedingly anxious that that thing which they struggled for; that something even more than National Independence; that something that held out a great promise to all the people of the world to all time to come; I am exceedingly anxious that this Union, this Constitution, and the liberties of the people shall be perpetuated in accordance with the original idea for which that struggle was made, and I shall be most happy indeed if I shall be an humble instrument in the hands of the Almighty, and of this, his almost chosen people, for perpetuating the object of that great struggle.[17]

This invocation of the battle of Trenton points towards Lincoln's interpretation of another "great struggle" in the Gettysburg Address, just as that address pointed back in time to the rhetoric of Clay and Webster, to

Washington's Farewell Address, the Constitution, and finally to the Declaration of Independence itself.

When Lincoln delivered his own "Farewell Address" to the people of Springfield in 1861, he remarked that he faced "a task before me greater than that which rested upon Washington."[18] By succeeding in that task, Lincoln implicitly laid claim to a status even greater than that of Washington. Whatever the merits of that contention, we would argue that the Gettysburg Address—with its interpretation of the Declaration of Independence as the core of Union—henceforth superseded (we would not say supplanted) Washington's Farewell Address as the supreme and authoritative expression of the American political community. Lincoln's summary of the "thing" that defined the new "great struggle" had unforgettably captured the essential unity—the common ground of public opinion—that underlay the diversity of American sympathies, interests, and institutions. Without in any way denigrating Washington, Lincoln thus confirmed the place of Jefferson—who, in Lincoln's view, "was, is, and perhaps will continue to be, the most distinguished politician in our history"—as the central figure in the American political tradition.[19]

Still, Lincoln's ultimate success depended on the possibility of an American nation and character that Washington more than any other person had created. It required someone of Lincoln's genius to draw out the full implications of the Declaration of Independence in the midst of the greatest American crisis. Jefferson's other writings and actions could, and did, point some towards disunion. By contrast, Washington's arguments in favor of Union were clear, even to those who did not yet share Lincoln's understanding of the moral purpose of American political life. Washington's legacy could not hold the nation together in 1861. But the popular sentiments in favor of Union that the Address had long inculcated were critical to persuading the North to fight for what would become a new birth of freedom, rather than abandoning the South as a lost cause.

Washington's Foreign Policy Legacy in the Nineteenth Century

After the Civil War, national unity was no longer threatened by sectional differences or party controversies. Accordingly, those portions of the Farewell Address concerning Union and the dangers of factionalism, which had been so important to the Founding generation and its successors, seemed of less immediate significance. However, the other major teachings of the Address, concerning America's relationship to the world, remained the cornerstone of U.S. foreign policy well into the twentieth century.

In *Democracy in America,* Alexis de Tocqueville reflected on the vener-
ated status that the Farewell Address had already attained by the 1830s. He
contended that two men, Washington and Jefferson, had set the direction
of American external policy. Tocqueville quoted extensively from "that
great man's political testament" dealing with the great rule of conduct.
Washington's political conduct, Tocqueville said, was always guided by
these maxims: "He succeeded in keeping his country at peace while all the
rest of the world was at war, and he established it as a fundamental doctrine
that the true interest of America was never to take part in the internal
quarrels of Europe." Tocqueville asserted that Jefferson went still further
and introduced another maxim into American politics: "that the Americans
should never ask for privileges from foreign nations, in order not to be
obliged to grant any in return."[20]

According to Tocqueville, these two principles, "whose evident truth
makes them easily grasped by the multitudes, have greatly simplified the
foreign policy of the United States." Because the United States did not
meddle in European affairs and because there were as yet no powerful
neighbors in the Western Hemisphere, it had, so to speak, "no external
interests at stake. . . . Detached by geography as well as by choice from the
passions of the Old World, it neither needs to protect itself against them
nor to espouse them." Free from hidden obligations, America could profit
from the experience of Europe without having to deal with the "vast heritage of mixed glory and shame, national friendships and national hatreds,
bequeathed by its ancestors. Expectancy is the keynote of American foreign
policy; it consists much more in abstaining than doing."

Tocqueville's assessment of the Farewell Address raised the acute point
of changed circumstances, when America might be required "to do" rather
than "to abstain." In fact, the veneration of the Farewell Address never
presumed a static interpretation of its message in light of emerging international problems and opportunities. Perhaps the most significant early emen-
dation of the Address was that of the Monroe Doctrine in 1823. In a Special
Message to Congress in 1826, President John Quincy Adams, who served
as secretary of state under Monroe, made clear the link in his mind between
the principles of the Monroe Doctrine and those of the Farewell Address,
while still admitting the necessity to move ahead. "Compare our situation
and the circumstances of that time with those of the present day, and what,
from the very words of Washington, would be his counsels to his countrymen now?" Europe, according to Adams, "still has her primary set of interests, with which we have little or a remote relation." The United States'
"distant and detached situation with reference to Europe" remained unal-
tered. But other circumstances had changed over the previous thirty years.

In Washington's time, Adams recalled, the United States was the only independent nation in the Western Hemisphere, surrounded by European colonies, "with which the greater part we had no more intercourse than with the inhabitants of another planet." These colonies had since been transformed into eight independent nations. Since the Farewell Address had been delivered, the population of the United States had "almost trebled" its physical and moral power. Adams was now prepared to say that the period that Washington had predicted as being not far off had indeed arrived, and that

> *America* has a set of primary interests which have none or a remote relation to Europe; that the interference of Europe, therefore, in those concerns should be spontaneously withheld by her upon the same principles that we never interfered with hers, and that if she should interfere, as she may, by measures which may have a great and dangerous recoil upon ourselves, we may be called in defense of our own altars and firesides to take an attitude which would cause our neutrality to be respected, and choose peace or war, as our interest, guided by justice, shall counsel.[21]

The pliability of the Farewell Address—and the degree to which new choices were open to or required of American foreign policy—was constantly a matter of political discourse and debate. On the one hand, there was a strong sense that the traditions of Washington should not be lightly challenged. Henry Clay, for instance, was perhaps his generation's greatest enthusiast for the promotion of liberty abroad, against those (such as John Quincy Adams) who stressed the more cautious aspects of Washington's foreign policy tradition. Still, even Clay knew there were limits. Near the end of his life in 1852, Clay spoke with Louis Kossuth, the Hungarian revolutionary then visiting the United States to appeal for "material aid" for his cause. Clay felt compelled to argue against this request, on the grounds that "by the policy to which we have adhered since the days of Washington, we have prospered beyond precedent—we have done more for the cause of liberty in the world than arms could effect." Clay then went on to paraphrase the Farewell Address:

> We have showed to other nations the way to greatness and happiness; and, if we but continue united as one people, and persevere in the policy which our experience has so clearly and triumphantly vindicated, we may in another quarter of a century furnish an example which the reason of the world cannot resist. But if we should involve ourselves in the tangled web of European politics, in a war in which we could effect nothing, and if in that struggle Hungary should go down, and we should go down with her, where, then, would be the last hope of the friends of freedom

throughout the world? Far better it is for ourselves, for Hungary, and for the cause of liberty, that, adhering to our wise, pacific system, and avoiding the distant wars of Europe, we should keep our lamp burning brightly on this western shore as a light to all nations, than to hazard its utter extinction amid the ruins of fallen or falling republics in Europe.

Clay pointed out to Kossuth that American attempts to intervene in Europe, once having broken Washington's pledge to stay out of those wars, would undoubtedly trigger those advocating monarchical principles to attempt to crush the American experiment. "You have set the example," Clay had the despots of Europe telling America, throwing back the words of the Farewell Address, "You have quit your own to stand on foreign ground."[22]

But other American statesmen differed on this point, and were much more forceful in seeking to overturn the traditions of non-involvement associated with Washington and the Farewell Address. Senator Robert J. Walker of Mississippi, for one, argued in 1851 that the United States ought to impose "her physical and moral power" to aid the Hungarian revolutionaries. Walker was in the decided minority in terms of his proposals to become directly involved in European affairs, as opposed to offering resolutions of sympathy for the cause of freedom. But he offered arguments that paralleled those made decades later about the changing relevance, or irrelevance, of the Farewell Address to American foreign policy.

> I contend, Mr. President, that what was our policy in our infancy and weakness has ceased to be our *true* policy now that we have reached to manhood and strength. And I deny, what is so often asserted, that either Washington or any of the founders of our Republic, ever recommended that the neutral *policy* of our early days should become an established *principle*, to govern the conduct of the country in the days of its maturity and power.

Walker proposed to undertake support for the Hungarians through alliance, if feasible, with Britain, although he would not make American action contingent on cooperation with London. "An alliance on such an occasion would not conflict with the policy or advice of Washington. He never condemned alliances temporary and for the occasion. He only declared that it is your policy to steer clear of *permanent* alliances." For Walker, the danger that despotic powers would intervene in the internal affairs of other nations to suppress republican government was an international concern. "In this case we have the *right* to interpose, and I contend that justice, as well as our interest and security, make it our *duty* to interpose." America, in its weakness at the Founding, did not then possess the strength and consistency necessary to give it command of its own fortunes, but Walker believed "that such time has been gained, and that our country has reached the required condition; and so far from condemning and declining the occasional cooperation of other countries in such a cause, I would approve and accept it, as I would, indeed, invite it."

> Mr. President, of two things I feel certain: first, that the spirit of Russian absolutism, unless prevented by the interposition of constitutional governments, will triumph and prevail in Europe, and ultimately, turn on liberty here and elsewhere; and second, that the only Powers on the broad face of God's earth which can interpose and prevent it, are the United States and England. Separately or in concert, then, we *must* act or fall; or, if not fall, must ultimately suffer and bleed to a degree of depletion tenfold that which our timely interposition would cause.[23]

Washington's Great Rule in the Twentieth Century

The argument between Clay and Walker over the need to reinterpret the Farewell Address to account for changed circumstances reemerged as American policymakers confronted the twentieth century. By this time, the United States had emerged as the world's dominant economic power, and the European and Asiatic balances of power had shifted significantly. Americans began, as Alfred Thayer Mahan put it in his landmark 1890 essay, to look outward. As they did so, they had to come to grips with the seemingly sacrosanct teachings of Washington.

Richard Olney, who as secretary of state under President Grover Cleveland authored the so-called Olney Corollary to the Monroe Doctrine, in particular felt compelled to challenge the traditional interpretation of the Farewell Address. After leaving office, Olney wrote in an 1898 essay that Washington's great rule had been extended "quite in excess of its terms as well as of its true spirit and meaning." Washington himself had, with characteristic caution and wisdom, carefully limited the field and the time covered by the Farewell Address. Olney now claimed that "time has been gained—our institutions have proven to have a stability and to work with a success exceeding all expectation—and though this nation is still young, it has long since ceased to be feeble or to lack the power to command its own fortunes." Of equal importance, the achievements of modern science had "annihilated the time and space that once separated the Old World from the New." The days of telephones and railroads and ocean cables and ocean steamships, according to Olney, had fundamentally changed the world from that of Washington.[24]

With these facts in mind, Olney sought to overthrow the teachings of the Farewell Address, as they had come to be understood:

> Nothing can be more obvious, therefore, than that the conditions for which Washington made his rule no longer exist. The logical, if not the necessary result is that the rule itself should now be considered as nonexistent also. . . . On these grounds, it is possible to regard the isolation rule under consideration as having outlived its usefulness without exposing ourselves to any serious hazards. But it is to be and should be so regarded on affirmative grounds—because the continuance of its supposed authoritativeness is hurtful in its tendency—hurtful in many directions and to large interests.

It was a pitiful ambition for a country as great as the United States to seclude itself from the world at large and to live a life "as insulated and independent as if it were the only country on the foot-stool." For Olney, a "splendid isolation" might have been a worthy cause for a weak nation, when the cause of its independence, dignity, or vital interests required detachment from a hostile world. But isolation at the turn of the twentieth century was nothing but a shirking of the responsibilities of high place and great power. It was simply ignominious. The United States would, sooner or later, "shake off the spell of the Washington legend and cease to act in the role of a sort of international recluse."

But others were not so ready to abandon the traditional interpretation of the Farewell Address. The McKinley administration's decision to seek the annexation of the Philippine Islands after the war with Spain was strongly opposed by anti-imperialists who frequently used the Farewell Address as their point of departure. For example, Senator George Gray of Delaware, a member of the American Peace Commission, warned (unsuccessfully) that "to acquire these islands would be to reverse the accepted continental policy of the country, declared and acted upon throughout our history." Annexation of the Philippines "introduces us into European politics and entangling alliances, against which Washington and all American statesmen have protested." Louisiana Senator Donelson Caffery, in objecting to the characterization of the opponents of Philippine annexation as "little Americans," asked, "When Washington besought his countrymen to avoid all foreign complications and entanglements was he a little American?"[25]

More than a decade later, Woodrow Wilson would attempt an even more ambitious reinterpretation of the Address, in an effort to overcome those who would use the Address to restrict America's involvement in the world and especially in the World War. As early as 1900, Wilson began to lay the groundwork for such a reinterpretation, summarizing Washington's recommendation to his friends and fellow citizens as follows: "I want you to discipline yourselves and stay still and be good boys until you grow up, until you are big enough to stand the competition of foreign countries, until you are big enough to go abroad in the world. . . . Wait until you need not be afraid of foreign influence, and then you shall be ready to take your part in the field of the world."[26]

As America subsequently grappled for the first time in a century with its role and interests in the midst of a great European war, Wilson offered a new interpretation of the Farewell Address and its presumed warning against entangling alliances. As Wilson explained in 1916, "by that I understand him [Washington] to mean avoid being entangled in the ambitions and the national purposes of other nations. It does not mean, if I may be permitted to venture an interpretation of the meaning of that great man, it does not mean that we are to avoid the entanglements of the world, for we are part of the world, and nothing that concerns the whole world can be indifferent to us." Here, Wilson rejected the old doctrine of two spheres, in which Europe and America could and should have separate and distinct interests. In particular, Wilson denied that the causes of European wars were remote to America.

> The world is no longer divided into little circles of interest. The world no longer consists of neighborhoods. The world is linked together in a common life and interests such as humanity never saw before, and the starting of wars can never again be a private and individual matter for nations. What disturbs the life of the whole world is the concern of the whole world.

America's role in the world was "always to hold the force of America to fight"—but fight for what? America would, if necessary, turn outward and fight "not merely for the rights of property, or of national ambition, but for the rights of mankind." For Wilson, "nothing that concerns humanity, nothing that concerns the essential rights of mankind, can be foreign or indifferent to us."[27]

What distinguished America was its disinterestedness on behalf of mankind—not its interestedness, however enlightened. For Wilson, it was in this context that Washington's immortal warning against entangling alliances should be read "with full comprehension and an answering purpose. But only special and limited alliances will entangle; and we recognize and accept the duty of a new day in which we are permitted to hope for a general alliance in which we will avoid entanglements and clear the air of the world for common understandings and the maintenance of common rights."

> But I would gladly assent to a disentangling alliance—an alliance which would disentangle the peoples of the world from those combinations in which they seek their own separate and private interests and unite the people of the world to preserve the peace of the world upon a basis of common right and justice. There is liberty there, not limitation. There is freedom, not entanglement. There is the achievement of its highest things for which the United States has declared its principles.[28]

Wilson's analysis pointed him toward a League of Nations that would guarantee the common rights of mankind. Wilson believed that a system of collective security, based on the league, would supersede the old European balance-of-power system of security that Washington and the Founders had wisely avoided. According to Wilson, the balance-of-power system that Washington had rejected "was a day of every nation taking care of itself and making a partnership with a nation or group of nations to hold the peace of the world steady or dominate the weaker portions of the world. These were the days of alliances. The process of the League of Nations is a process of disentanglement." The League of Nations was the logical culmination of, rather than a departure from, the American diplomatic tradition. "I am proposing, as it were, that the nations should with one accord adopt the doctrine of President Monroe as the doctrine of the world: that no nation should seek to extend its polity over any other nation or people, but that every people should be left free to determine its own polity, its own way of development, unhindered, unthreatened, unafraid, the little along with the great and powerful. . . . There is no entangling alliance in a concert of power."[29]

> The thing he [Washington] longed for was just what we are now about to supply—an arrangement which will disentangle all the alliances in the world. Nothing entangles, nothing enmeshes a man except a selfish combination with someone else. Nothing entangles a nation, hampers it, binds it, except to enter into a combination with some other nation against all the other nations of the world. And this disentanglement of all alliances is now to be accomplished by this Covenant, because one of the covenants is that no nation shall enter into any relationship with another nation inconsistent with the covenants of the League of Nations. Nations promise not to have alliances. Nations promise not to make combinations against each other. Nations agree that there shall be but one combination, and that is the combination of all against the wrongdoer.

Wilson argued that opponents of the League of Nations were establishing "a doctrine of careful selfishness." But "no nation has the right to set up its special interests against the interests and benefits of mankind, least of all this great nation we love. It was set up for the benefit of mankind . . ." An individual American, said Wilson, was often "selfish and confined to his special interests; but take the American in mass, and he is willing to die for an ideal." Americans "believed in righteousness, and we are now ready to make the supreme sacrifice for it—the supreme sacrifice of throwing in our fortunes with the fortunes of men everywhere." Here, then, was Wilson's succinct definition of America's "command of its own fortunes" in the twentieth century: throwing in our fortunes with the rest of mankind.[30]

Wilson's interpretation of the Farewell Address and of the intentions of the Founders was predictably opposed by nationalists and isolationists who rejected his internationalization of the Farewell Address and the Monroe Doctrine. For example, in response to Wilson's "Peace without Victory" speech of January 1917, Senator William Borah, himself a progressive, introduced a resolution that reaffirmed the verities of the Farewell Address and the Monroe Doctrine. Borah would later vote for war with Germany, but he insisted that he was doing so on good Washingtonian grounds: "I join no crusade. I seek or accept no alliances; I obligate this Government to no other power. I make war alone for my countrymen and their rights, for my country and its honor." Those who opposed declaring war on Germany also invoked the traditional standards in their defense: "If we are to choose between the policy of Wilson or the policy of Washington, as for me I will follow Washington."[31]

Opponents of the League of Nations likewise claimed the standard of Washington. Senator Miles Poindexter characterized the division of opinion between what he called innovators and traditionalists. The innovators' view held that "permanent peace can not be secured for the United States or for the rest of the world by the traditional policies of the American Government . . . that we should cast aside, as the refuse of the government, the great policies of the past, and adopt new policies, and make, as they express it, a new order of the world." The opposing view of Poindexter held that "the great men who have formulated public opinion in America in the past, shaped its policies, and achieved its greatness were as sincere and as intelligent advocates of peace, as those who are in charge of American affairs to-day."

> The question is now presented whether we are to adhere to this policy of Washington and Monroe, of cultivating friendly relations with all nations and making entangling alliances with none, or whether we are to enter into a treaty and adopt a constitution of a league which binds us to a greater number, and possibly to all, of the other nations of the world in the most entangling alliance that could ever be conceived, since it binds

us as one of the guardians and guarantors of every right or interest of any of these nations which might be involved in actual or threatened war.

The creation of a League of Nations, in Poindexter's view, would thereby succeed only in

> plunging the world into a new set of controversies, and, by requiring every nation to meddle with every other nation's business, would be bringing about an indefinite series of armed conflicts. 'Mind your own business' is a good motto for an individual, and heretofore it has been the fundamental principle of our foreign policy as a nation. . . . The question now presented is whether or not this high sovereign jurisdiction of the political heirs of Jefferson, Washington, and Lincoln is to be in part surrendered and subjected to the control of strangers and aliens.[32]

The most powerful arguments made against the Wilsonian interpretation of the Farewell Address came from Senator Henry Cabot Lodge, who, like Wilson, was a biographer and admirer of Washington. Lodge was no isolationist. Together with Theodore Roosevelt, he had been a leader in the "large America" movement at the turn of the century, whose intention was to bring the United States onto the world scene. For the large Americans, Washington was the preeminent symbol of American national greatness. In the 1890s, Lodge and Roosevelt had been concerned that the American national character first established by Washington was being weakened by an excessive preoccupation with money and comfort. They wished to harken back to the true and full American nationalism of statesmen like Washington, Thomas Hart Benton, and Lincoln, to point America forward and reinvigorate the national character through, among other things, an assertive (and even martial) American foreign policy. They despised the "small America" view that looked inward, that sought security and international peace through arbitration and good words.

In the context of World War I, Lodge initially supported a policy of American neutrality, but in a very different sense than Wilson. Lodge noted that although Thomas Jefferson had extended Washington's dictum against permanent alliances, neither Jefferson—nor Woodrow Wilson—had accepted the corollary of Washington that "our policy of neutrality, found all its strength in the gradual construction and preservation of an efficient navy." Neutrality for Lodge meant "the full performance of our duties as a neutral and an absolute insistence on our rights as a neutral." When Washington had "declared the country to be neutral he meant that it really should be neutral and in that capacity should not only insist on every neutral right, but should also perform all neutral duties." For Lodge, the old

Republican party of Jefferson, and the Democratic party of Woodrow Wilson, had consistently refused to appreciate Washington's dictum that to have peace one must prepare for war.[33]

As the European war continued, Lodge came to the conclusion that American neutrality and military preparedness were insufficient; the United States must intervene in the war on the grounds that "the cause of the other nations who are fighting Germany has become our cause." As Lodge later explained this conclusion: "Washington declared against permanent alliances. He did not close the door on temporary alliances for particular purposes. Our entry into the great war just closed was entirely in accord with and violated in no respect the policy laid down by Washington. When we went to war with Germany we made no treaties with the nations engaged in the war against the German Government." In 1916, Lodge even declared his openness to post-war international cooperation: "I do not believe that when Washington warned us against permanent alliances he meant for one moment that we should not join with the other civilized nations of the world if a method could be found to diminish war and encourage peace." Lodge, however, subsequently argued that Wilson's proposed League of Nations failed to meet the standards of Washington: "I do not say that agreements may not be made among the nations which stand for ordered freedom and civilization, which will do much to secure and preserve the peace of the world; but no such agreement has yet been presented to us." Lodge would later remark that "there is no lurking place for a league of peace 'supported by the organized forces of mankind' in the sentences of George Washington and Thomas Jefferson . . ."[34]

In his famous February 1919 Senate speech of opposition to the league, Lodge argued that by ratifying the Treaty of Versailles, "we abandon entirely by the proposed constitution the policy laid down in his Farewell Address and the Monroe Doctrine." This was not merely the abandonment of a particular foreign policy; it was the abandonment of true American nationalism in favor of an openness to other, sinister forces that were bound to have an impact on American domestic politics as well as American security.

> Now, in the twinkling of an eye, while passion and emotion reign, the Washington policy is to be entirely laid aside and we are to enter upon a permanent and indissoluble alliance. . . . We are asked to depart now for the first time from the foreign policies of Washington. We are invited to move away from George Washington toward the other end of the line at which stands the sinister figure of Trotsky, the champion of internationalism.[35]

To be sure, Lodge did not understand the principles of Washington to mean that the United States should isolate itself from the world: "Nobody expects to isolate the United States or to make it a hermit nation, which is a sheer absurdity. But there is a wide difference between taking a suitable part and bearing a due responsibility in world affairs and plunging the United States into every controversy and conflict on the face of the globe." The danger, according to Lodge, was that "by meddling in all the differences which may arise among any portion or fragment of humankind we simply fritter away our influence and injure ourselves to no good purpose."

> We shall be of far more value to the world and its peace by occupying, so far as possible, the situation which we have occupied for the last twenty years and by adhering to the policy of Washington and Hamilton, of Jefferson and Monroe, under which we have risen to our present greatness and prosperity. The fact that we have been separated by our consistent policy from the geographical broils of Europe has made us more than any one thing capable of performing the great work which we performed in the war against Germany, and our disinterestedness is of far more value to the world than our eternal meddling in every possible dispute could ever be.[36]

Lodge stated that "I can never be anything else but an American, and I must think of the United States first, and when I think of the United States first in an arrangement like this I am thinking of what is best for the world, for if the United States fails the best hopes of mankind fail with it." Lodge said that he wanted, as Washington had wanted, "an American character" in foreign affairs, a character that could exist only in distinction from Europe.[37]

The foreign policy debate during the lead-in to American involvement in World War II paralleled in many ways the controversies twenty years earlier, including the dispute over the meaning of Washington's great rule of conduct. As the international environment worsened in the 1930s, President Franklin Roosevelt sought to move the United States towards a more activist posture. This tendency raised alarm bells among old-line isolationists and unilateralists. Once again Senator Borah stepped into the breech by reviving discussion of the Farewell Address. The policy of Washington and Jefferson, he said in a 1934 article, had "remained unchallenged and revered" for over one hundred and twenty years. National conflicts of the world had not been superseded by the siren song of internationalism. Borah felt that Americans should be far more worried about domestic than foreign affairs. In dealing with the crisis of the Depression, "our foreign policy therefore should be one best calculated to unite our own people, morally, spiritually, and economically, to inspire them with a sense of national fidelity and personal responsibility." Every civilization had made its contribution to the American civilization; as a consequence, it was dangerously "easy to transfer the racial antipathies and political views and controversies of the Old World into our very midst. Once abandon our aloofness from European controversies, and we bring these controversies into the American home and into our national life." Borah acknowledged that the 1930s was a period in international affairs when democracy and personal liberty (including the exercise of religion) were under general challenge. But: "Our highest service, not only to our own people, but to mankind and to the peace of the world, is transmitting these principles unimpaired to succeeding generations. This is our supreme duty. I believe the foreign policy of Washington and Jefferson and Lincoln will best enable us to meet and discharge that duty."

Borah argued that such a policy was not one of isolationism, "it is freedom of action. It is independence of judgment. It is not isolation, it is free government—there can be no such thing as free government if the people thereof are not free to remain aloof or take part in foreign wars." A people who had "bartered away or surrendered their right to remain neutral in war have surrendered their right to govern." Americans had never been isolationists when it came to matters of trade and commerce—a fact noted in the Farewell Address—nor were Americans indifferent to the effects of natural disasters on other peoples. But, Borah claimed, "in all matters political, in all commitments of any nature or any kind, which encroach in the slightest upon the free and unembarrassed action of our people, or which subscribe their discretion and judgment, we have been free, we have been independent, we have been isolationists. And this, I trust, we shall ever be."[38]

Washington and the Cold War

Following the Japanese attack on Pearl Harbor and the American experience in World War II, there was a marked decline in Washington's political authority relating to matters of foreign policy. The Farewell Address and Washington's great rule of conduct were essentially regarded as relics of the past—or barriers to the future.

President Harry Truman, in an address on foreign policy at the George Washington National Masonic Memorial in February 1950, did not even mention the Farewell Address. Truman admitted to similarities in conditions between his time and that of the first president. Washington, too, had lived in a period of great change, and Truman described Washington's goals as identical to those of America in the late twentieth century—that is, to make the ideal of democratic government work and to defend that ideal against the forces opposed to it. "But our task today is far greater in scope than it was in Washington's time. Not only are we concerned with increasing the freedom, welfare, and opportunity of our people. We are also concerned with the right of other peoples to choose their own form of government, to improve their standards of living, and to decide what kind of life they want to live." Through the progress of science since Washington's time, Truman said, "the nations of the world have been drawn together into a common destiny. Our security and progress are today more closely related than ever before to the advance of freedom and self-government in other lands." Democratic security and progress were threatened as never before by communism, "a modern tyranny far worse than any ancient empire."

Because the world and the threat were much different for Truman than for Washington (even though their tasks remained the same), America must be open to new solutions.

> Just as the thirteen original states found that survival and progress depended on closer association and common effort, so the free nations of the world today must seek their salvation in unity and concerned action. The real strength of the free nations is not to be found in any single country or in any one weapon, but in the combined moral and material strength of the free world as a whole. . . . We shall continue to work with other free nations associated with us in the common defense—for our defense is theirs, and their defense is ours.[39]

That new solution had been outlined in the so-called Truman Doctrine of 1947. The Truman Doctrine was originally articulated for the specific purpose of gaining Congressional support for U.S. aid to Greece and Turkey, but it became the underlying political logic for American foreign policy from the late 1940s until the fall of the Berlin Wall. (Indeed, Truman claimed that it had been the logic behind American efforts to defeat Germany and Japan in World War II.) As Truman saw it, at that moment in world history, every nation was being forced to choose between alternative ways of life—the democratic way and the totalitarian way. It was in the American interest to create "conditions in which we and other nations will be able to work out a way of life free from coercion."

> We shall not realize our objectives, however, unless we are willing to help free people to maintain their free institutions and their national in-

tegrity against aggressive movements that seek to impose upon them totalitarian regimes. . . . The choice is too often not a free one. I believe
that it must be the policy of the United States to support free peoples
who are resisting attempted subjugation by armed minorities or by outside pressures. I believe we must assist free peoples to work out their own
destinies in their own way. . . . The free peoples of the world look to us
for support in maintaining their freedoms. If we falter in our leadership,
we may endanger the peace of the world—and shall surely endanger the
welfare of our own Nation.[40]

To realize the goals of the Truman Doctrine, the president believed
that he would have to first defeat the spirit of American isolationism. In his
memoirs, Truman recalled the strong grip that isolationism had held over
the country after World War II: "Throughout my years in the Senate I
listened each year as one of the senators would read Washington's Farewell
Address. It served little purpose to point out to the isolationists that Washington had advised a method suitable under the conditions of *his* day to
achieve the great end of preserving the nation." Unfortunately, "for the
isolationists this address was like a biblical text. The America First Organization of 1940–41, the Ku Klux Klan, Pelley and his Silver Shirts—they all
quoted the first president in support of their assorted aims." If this sort of
isolationism were revived in the period, Truman believed that the consequences would be severe:

> After World War II it was clear that without American participation there
> would be no power capable of meeting Russia as an equal. If we were to
> turn our back on the world, areas such as Greece, weakened and divided
> as a result of the war, would fall into the Soviet orbit without much effort
> on the part of the Russians. The success of Russia in such areas and our
> avowed lack of interest would lead to the growth of domestic Commu-
> nist parties in such European countries as France and Italy, where they
> were already significant threats. Inaction, withdrawal, "Fortress
> America" notions could only result in handing to the Russians vast areas
> of the globe now denied to them.

For Truman, this was the time for America to step forward at the head
of the Free World. But, Truman believed, "I knew that George Washington's spirit would be invoked against me, and Henry Clay and all the patron
saints of the isolationists." For this reason, Truman did not seek a creative
reinterpretation of the Farewell Address in order to justify greater American
international involvement, as Wilson and others had attempted earlier. If
the Gettysburg Address superseded the Farewell Address in domestic affairs,
the Truman Doctrine can fairly be said to have self-consciously replaced it
in foreign policy. Truman wrote: "I was convinced that the policy I was

about to proclaim was indeed as much required by the conditions of my day as was Washington's by the situation in his era and Monroe's doctrine by the circumstances which he then faced."[41]

Dean Acheson, secretary of state in Truman's second administration, elaborated on the reasons for this shift. According to Acheson, "two contrary and equally unrealistic ideas" about foreign policy had long competed for the American national mind, both springing from earlier history. "From the American phases of the European wars of the eighteenth century—the dominant memory of the Founders of this country—came the doctrine promulgated in the Farewell Address, in 1941 called isolationism." Acheson argued that Washington had taken too narrow a view of these wars, believing that they resulted from "mere dynastic rivalries of no concern to people beginning to think of themselves as 'Americans.'" In fact, according to Acheson, these wars sprang from still deeper causes: specifically, the French drive under a variety of regimes for world hegemony. This drive was manifested in North America, and not just in Europe, as France sought to pin the English colonies between the Atlantic and the eastern slopes of the Alleghenies. In Acheson's view, America had achieved its independence essentially by changing sides in the conflict between French expansionism and English resistance.

When the century-long struggle ended with a British victory in 1815, according to Acheson, "it permitted a century of international peace and of greater technological innovation and economic development than in the whole period since the invention of the sail and the wheel." Britain ruled the seas and, "by putting the sanction of the British fleet behind the Monroe Doctrine . . . made sure that the scattered and divided nine million Americans . . . could attack the enormous task of occupying an unexplored continent free from interference . . ." This experience of isolation, in turn, fostered the second great unrealistic American idea about foreign policy— "the dream of universal law and international enforced peace, embodied and embalmed in the League of Nations and resurrected in the United Nations."[42] Truman, we should note, placed much more faith in the dream of universal law than did Acheson, but both equated the Soviet drive for world hegemony with that of the French more than a century earlier.

Unlike Washington, the new architects of American foreign policy would not make the mistake of assuming that this drive did not affect American security: Europe *did* have a set of primary interests that bore strongly on America, and the causes of European quarrels were not foreign to American concerns. In the minds of the architects of the Truman Doctrine it was better to deal with the causes of European security and insecurity directly rather than struggle later with the consequences of European combinations and collisions, as implied by Washington's great rule. This line of argument led Truman and Acheson to embrace the North Atlantic Treaty and other "entangling alliances."[43]

Under the weight of American international activism after World War II, the Farewell Address faded as an instrument to guide public discourse on American foreign policy. Professor Burton Ira Kaufman noted in 1969: "Washington's Farewell Address is now important only for the insights it affords into the policies and leaders of the Federalist era. In this respect, however, it does remain a classic document in American history"— essentially, nothing more than an antiquarian curiosity.[44]

A good case can be made that the Truman Doctrine and subsequent American policies during the Cold War actually followed the spirit of Washington's legacy. Americans sought to pursue their interests, guided by justice, against a geopolitical and ideological threat to their (and others') safety and happiness. They maintained their essential independence through alliances—which they effectively dominated because of their strength—rather than through political isolation. The fact that Truman and his successors did not explicitly invoke, or attempt to reinterpret, the Farewell Address—as Woodrow Wilson had tried earlier—is by no means insignificant. But neither does this mean that the Address has lost any or all of its relevance, especially as the United States contemplates life after the Cold War.

The Revival of Washington

Over the past several decades, Washington's stature, at least among professional scholars and popular writers, has undergone something of a renaissance. The trend is by no means universal; skeptics of Washington's value, as a man and a statesman, certainly remain. But the possibility of examining the First Citizen seriously is with us again.

The multivolume biographies of Washington by Douglas Southall Freeman, begun in 1948 and completed by his associates in 1957; and by James T. Flexner (1965–1972); have played a central role in this revival. Freeman judged that Washington was and always had been exactly what he appeared to be. Flexner concluded similarly: "My labors have persuaded me that he became one of the noblest and greatest men who ever lived. He was not born that way. . . . He perfected himself gradually through the exercise of his own will and skill." In short, these two biographers agreed that Washington's personal character has indeed stood the test of time. Recently published books on Washington by Richard Brookhiser and Harrison Clark provide considerable depth and insight into Washington's life and personal excellence.[45]

Another group of scholars—ironically, taking their cue from Parson Weems—has focused on the importance as Washington-as-myth. All new governments need symbols to help provide a sense of purpose and coherence, and Washington is said to be the American embodiment of that need. Garry Wills, in the most influential of these works, argued that Washington deliberately made himself into this mythical figure, following the Enlightenment's conception of political heroism. Finally, Glenn A. Phelps and William B. Allen, among others, stressed the seriousness of Washington as a statesman and political thinker.[46]

The renewed respect for Washington as a man of good character, as the quintessential symbol of the American regime, and as a self-conscious statesman and Founder, largely validate the judgment of Washington's contemporaries, as cited in our opening chapter. Scholarly validation of Washington's importance to the Republic should pave the way for the possible renewal of Washington's authority in American political discourse. Any political renewal of the Washingtonian tradition, in turn, must eventually come to grips with the Farewell Address. Surprisingly, little has been done on this score as part of the scholarly revival of Washington (Wills's book being an exception). The path may therefore be open for public officials and ordinary citizens to follow Webster's advice and "reperuse and consider" the Address, to see if in fact it contains "truths important at all times."

6

TRUTHS
IMPORTANT AT ALL TIMES

$\mathcal{A}$t the beginning of this essay we asked a question: Does Washington remain alive in the hearts of his countrymen? If our standards are union and independence, the overriding themes of the Farewell Address, then we must say that Washington's great project of building an American character undeniably succeeded. But times change and worrisome signs and trends are again appearing, as they have throughout American history. In our view, the appearance of these trends gives good reason to reflect again upon Washington's "disinterested warnings"—even as we reserve our right to debate, modify, or reject particular teachings in light of new circumstances (as we think Washington himself would have wanted).

Certainly, the Farewell Address can speak to particular public policy questions in only a limited way. We can speculate endlessly on the position that Washington himself might have taken on a balanced budget, entitlements, school prayer, international trade policy, or the United Nations. But the true value of the Farewell Address lies in its capacity to provide guidance for a new era, one that is equally rich in enormous possibilities and risks for the American character. Above all, Washington and the Farewell Address remind us of the need for public and private virtue, for beliefs held in common, and for the possibility of individual and national greatness.

We cannot help but be attracted to the Plutarchean power of Washington's life, by what Daniel Webster called the "great moral examples" that affect the mind.

> When sublime virtues cease to be abstractions, when they become embodied in human character, and exemplified in human conduct, we should be false to our nature, if we did not indulge in the spontaneous effusions of our gratitude and our admiration. . . . The ingenuous youth of America will hold up to themselves the bright model of Washington's example, and study to be what they behold; they will contemplate his

169

character till all its virtues spread out and display themselves to their de-
lighted vision. . . .[1]

This admiration of Washington and the Farewell Address runs the risk
of going too far, of purely recreating the mythical Washington of cherry
tree fame. To be sure, we naturally seek to overcome the "abstractions"
imposed by time and distance; we are attracted to myths and legends that
lead us to "gratitude and admiration" for great men and women. Parson
Weems's *Washington* is not to be taken lightly; one of its admirers, after all,
was Abraham Lincoln. But to rely on myth—on irrationality—as the primary basis for our political and moral reformation is problematic. It was
decisively not the path taken by the Founders, who insisted that the excellence of the American regime—the American character—was the result of
reflection and choice.

Washington embodied, during his lifetime, the American character.
That is to say, he demonstrated the possibility of and the relationship between public and private virtue in America. Washington's virtues made
him the indispensable man, the actor without whom the political action of
the American Revolution would not have successfully taken place. Washington's career aimed at creating not just an independent country but a
national character that was at once distinctly American and republican. The
idea of a national character presupposed for Washington the idea of a common good, a national interest, a self-sufficient political community or regime based on justice and, ultimately, on the possibility of friendship.
America could and must be something more than a collection of individuals
and interests.

But Washington was also a liberal. That is, he fully recognized the
interested and passionate character of individuals and politics. He believed
as firmly in individual freedom, in the inalienable rights of man, in the
pursuit of economic well-being, in the material fruits of modern science,
as any of the most "modern" Founders. But the interesting and decisive
question for him was this: liberty to do what? Liberty, in either its public
or private aspect, was most decisively not the same as license, the unrestrained pursuit of interest or desire: anarchy was in its own way another
form of tyranny (the negation of liberty), and anarchy would in any case
soon issue in the more traditional form of despotism.

True liberty for Washington made sense and could be sustained only
in the context of a certain type of public, as well as private, life. That life,
that community, was to be republican, manifested in a system of government based, directly or indirectly, on the consent of the governed, a consent formed by an enlightened understanding of the rights of mankind. It

would be a government and a community of laws, where men ruled and were ruled in turn under a Constitution of their own making. But it would be a government of accommodation as well as of laws, because citizens and statesmen appreciated the limits of their own wisdom and the limits of politics itself. Prudence therefore dictated to Washington that the formation of an American and republican character be undertaken indirectly and that an appropriate distance be placed between the community and the individual, between public and private, between religion (that is, conscience) and politics, between the state and society. The distinction was intended to provide proper allowance to the dignity and importance of each element, as each related to individual and national character.

Above all, the Farewell Address directs the American regime toward Union, or unity, rather than diversity. America must be something more than a league of states or regions, a collection of various groups and interests. In the present context, the Address should remind us that whatever tends to make America less than a cohesive sum of its parts—whether multiculturalism, the identification of discrete and insular minorities, or the unreflective devolution of national responsibilities to state and local governments—works to undermine a singular American character. At different times in American history, diversity and localism, appropriately defined, have served as sources of strength; excessive unity and centralization is the stuff of tyranny. But as the national character today—at least rhetorically—tends towards fragmentation, the Farewell Address reminds us of the importance and primacy of the search for a truly common good. At the same time, those who rightly stress the importance of unity and community over the less-than-whole should remember that, in Washington's view, individual liberty—and rights—are the irreducible foundation of decent and moderate politics in a constitutional republic.

The Farewell Address also reminds us that government—or more accurately, politics—still represents an essential mechanism for forming the American character. Certainly, Americans have traditionally held a degree of cynicism about politics and politicians. Rightly directed, this spiritedness of the people, their insistence upon individual liberty, and their suspicion of public officials remain necessary attributes of public opinion in a democracy. But Washington always insisted on the basic unity of the people and their government, and he resisted efforts to divide the two. Critics of particular policies today should not go so far as to encourage a lack of esteem for politics. This will only serve to deny good men and women their rightful reward for public service (that is, honor and the opportunity to do good) and leave the field to those who enter politics for base reasons only. Washington believed that government should be properly energetic, within the limits of its basic purposes; that government should act positively to improve the material and moral conditions of the people and not merely to restrain their vices. In recent decades, government may well have exceeded the prudent bounds of its basic purposes as spelled out in the preamble to the Constitution. Such excesses make laudable current efforts to restore constitutional government. But such efforts should not weaken the dignity and character-building qualities of law and of the law-making process—in contrast to the more modern concept of government as the administration of things. While acknowledging the negative, we must nevertheless carefully retain the positive.

The Farewell Address's admonition against factionalism further reminds us of the continuing importance of public opinion in defining the American character. Since Washington's time, we have discovered that most of the time political parties can act usefully to break the violence of faction and thereby to increase the possibility of statesmanship and justice. But American politics requires more than the moderation of faction and more than the reconciliation of particular interests. From time to time, statesmanship requires that hard choices be placed before the public in order to bring about necessary and fundamental change. Washington did not shy from recommending the best possible constitution, and supporting those who would defend it, even though he knew he could expect substantial and perhaps successful opposition. He did not shy from issuing a Farewell Address that was bound to attract much immediate criticism. Such statesmanship depends on more than a successful electoral strategy that shrewdly utilizes public opinion polls to capitalize upon particular "hot button" issues. It depends on transforming, and reinforcing, public opinion at the most basic level of understanding what America is about. Efforts to shape public opinion need not be unsophisticated; witness the high level of discourse in *The Federalist Papers* or, as we hope we have demonstrated, in the Farewell Address itself. The politics of public opinion must be active, strategic, and comprehensive, rather than defensive, tactical, and narrow. When practiced successfully, as in the case of the *Federalist* and the Farewell Address, the politics of public opinion creates its own grounds for the reconciliation and accommodation of those who did not originally agree.

The Farewell Address teaches that the American character will always depend fundamentally on the proper dispositions and habits of the people. Religion and traditional morality still truly matter to the "mere politician" as well as to pious men and women. Public virtue cannot be expected in a climate of private vice, nor will individual morality flourish in the absence of a sense of civic responsibility. To be sure, the precise relationship between the two has always been difficult to establish. Washington and the

Founders believed that there must be a significant degree of public separation between religion, or individual conscience, and politics and that this separation, properly constituted, actually strengthened both private morality and public virtue. But although private and public are prudently separated in American republicanism, they are by no means unconnected. Washington believed that the greatest contribution that government could make to this relationship was to ensure public justice, especially with respect to the inalienable rights of life, liberty, and the pursuit of happiness. In return, pious men and women of whatever denomination are required to comport themselves as good citizens. Both sides of the current church-state debate should reflect on the need to hold up their end of the bargain.

Finally, the Farewell Address's warning against foreign influence on American domestic politics suggests that as Americans reconsider their public character after the Cold War they are entitled to define for themselves the terms of America's safety and happiness. Of course, to be true to ourselves, we cannot do this by ignoring the safety and happiness of other nations. But without a certain practical distance or detachment from foreign pressures, Americans cannot make good choices about their domestic institutions. The sensitivity that Americans recently displayed when it came to placing their lives, fortune, and sacred honor in the hands of the United Nations was by no means unreasonable. Obviously, the United States is not alone in the world, and true isolationism is impossible. We do owe a decent respect to the opinions of mankind; some changes to our laws and our behavior may prudently be required to deal with so-called transnational problems such as environmental degradation or refugee flows. But not all human opinions are equally valuable or valid. We must maintain Washington's essential distinction between "us" and "them" and decide for ourselves our own right way of life—and resist those who would use the "force of world opinion" or the criticism of other nations and peoples to persuade us to change that way of life. Rather, we should follow Washington's faith that it is our way of life, exceptional in principle if imperfect in practice, that serves as a beacon of hope to all humanity. We may wish to concentrate prudently on reform at home to strengthen this beacon because to the degree that we fail to meet the high standards we set for ourselves we lessen the influence of our principles abroad.

Washington's foreign policy advice remains sound: to pursue American interests, guided by justice, in order to command our own fortunes in the world. We should not accept the common view that the United States must choose to pursue either its interests or justice exclusively. As in Washington's time, we live in a world dominated by power politics and by the pursuit of interest. American foreign policy therefore rightly begins with efforts to secure its basic material interests of security and prosperity. But these interests should be defined and formed through a domestic political process that has justice as its end; to that extent, American interests will accordingly be moderate. Justice should also guide the pursuit of American interests in relation to other peoples, keeping in mind Washington's concise definition of justice ("minding one's own business"). When the United States' interests are not involved, America may be free directly to pursue justice and to serve humanity. But generally speaking, the existence of a definable American interest will be necessary to help the American people determine the occasion for and course of just actions. Injustices in the world are as infinite as American resources are limited. But in any case, a strong America—one in command of its own fortunes—will be in the best position to formulate a policy where interest and justice can be comprehended, a policy that increases our scope for serving ourselves and others.

FAREWELL ADDRESS
September 19, 1796

To the PEOPLE of the United States:

Friends and Fellow-Citizens:

1. The period for a new election of a Citizen, to Administer the Executive Government of the United States, being not far distant, and the time actually arrived, when your thoughts must be employed in designating the person, who is to be cloathed with that important trust, it appears to me proper, especially as it may conduce to a more distinct expression of the public voice, that I should now apprise you of the resolution I have formed, to decline being considered among the number of those, out of whom a choice is to be made.

2. I beg you, at the same time, to do me the justice to be assured, that this resolution has not been taken without a strict regard to all the considerations appertaining to the relation, which binds a dutiful citizen to his country, and that in with drawing the tender of service which silence in my situation might imply, I am influenced by no diminution of zeal for your future interest, no deficiency of grateful respect for your past kindness; but am supported by a full conviction that the step is compatible with both.

3. The acceptance of and continuance hitherto in the office to which your Suffrages have twice called me, have been a uniform sacrifice of inclination to the opinion of duty, and to a deference for what appeared to be your desire. I constantly hoped, that it would have been much earlier in my power, consistently with motives which I was not at liberty to disregard, to return to that retirement, from which I had been reluctantly drawn. The strength of my inclination to do this, previous to the last Election, had even led to the preparation of an address to declare it to you; but mature reflec-

tion on the then perplexed and critical posture of our Affairs with foreign Nations, and the unanimous advice of persons entitled to my confidence, impelled me to abandon the idea.

4. I rejoice that the state of your concerns, external as well as internal, no longer renders the pursuit of inclination incompatible with the sentiment of duty, or propriety; and am persuaded, whatever partiality may be retained for my services, that in the present circumstances of our country, you will not disapprove my determination to retire.

5. The impressions with which I first undertook the arduous trust, were explained on the proper occasion. In the discharge of this trust, I will only say that I have, with good intentions, contributed towards the Organization and Administration of the government, the best exertions of which a very fallible judgment was capable. Not unconscious, in the outset, of the inferiority of my qualifications, experience in my own eyes, perhaps still more in the eyes of others, has strengthned the motives to diffidence of myself; and every day the encreasing weight of years admonishes me more and more that the shade of retirement is as necessary to me as it will be welcome. Satisfied that if any circumstances have given peculiar value to my services, they were temporary, I have the consolation to believe, that while choice and prudence invite me to quit the political scene, patriotism does not forbid it.

6. In looking forward to the moment which is intended to terminate the career of my political life, my feelings do not permit me to suspend the deep acknowledgment of that debt of gratitude wch. I owe to my beloved country, for the many honors it has conferred upon me; still more for the steadfast confidence with which it has supported me; and for the opportunities I have thence enjoyed of manifesting my inviolable attachment, by services faithful and persevering, though in usefulness unequal to my zeal. If benefits have resulted to our country from these services, let it always be remembered to your praise, and as an instructive example in our annals, that, under circumstances in which the Passions, agitated in every direction were liable to mislead, amidst appearances sometimes dubious, vicissitudes of fortune often discouraging, in situations in which not infrequently want of Success has countenanced the spirit of criticism, the constancy of your support was the essential prop of the efforts, and a guarantee of the plans by which they were effected. Profoundly penetrated with this idea, I shall carry it with me to my grave, as a strong incitement to unceasing vows that Heaven may continue to you the choicest tokens of its beneficence; that your Union and brotherly affection may be perpetual; that the free consti-

tution, which is the work of your hands, may be sacredly maintained; that its Administration in every department may be stamped with wisdom and Virtue; that, in fine, the happiness of the people of these States, under the auspices of liberty, may be made complete, by so careful a preservation and so prudent a use of this blessing as will acquire to them the glory of recommending it to the applause, the affection, and adoption of every nation which is yet a stranger to it.

7. Here, perhaps, I ought to stop. But a solicitude for your welfare, which cannot end with my life, and the apprehension of danger, natural to that solicitude, urge me on an occasion like the present, to offer to your solemn contemplation, and to recommend to your frequent review, some sentiments; which are the result of much reflection, of no inconsiderable observation, and which appear to me all important to the permanency of your felicity as a People. These will be offered to you with the more freedom, as you can only see in them the disinterested warnings of a parting friend, who can possibly have no personal motive to biass his counsel. Nor can I forget as an encouragement to it, your indulgent reception of my sentiments on a former and not dissimilar occasion.

8. Interwoven as is the love of liberty with every ligament of your hearts, no recommendation of mine is necessary to fortify or confirm the attachment.

9. The Unity of Government which constitutes you one people is also now dear to you. It is justly so; for it is a main Pillar in the Edifice of your real independence, the support of your tranquility at home; your peace abroad; of your safety; of your prosperity; of that very Liberty which you so highly prize. But as it is easy to foresee, that from different causes and from different quarters, much pains will be taken, many artifices employed, to weaken in your minds the conviction of this truth; as this is the point in your political fortress against which the batteries of internal and external enemies will be most constantly and actively (though often covertly and insidiously) directed, it is of infinite moment, that you should properly estimate the immense value of your national Union to your collective and individual happiness; that you should cherish a cordial, habitual and immovable attachment to it; accustoming yourselves to think and speak of it as of the Palladium of your political safety and prosperity; watching for its preservation with jealous anxiety; discountenancing whatever may suggest even a suspicion that it can in any event be abandoned, and indignantly frowning upon the first dawning of every attempt to alienate any portion of our Country from the rest, or to enfeeble the sacred ties which now link together the various parts.

10. For this you have every inducement of sympathy and interest. Citizens by birth or choice, of a common country, that country has a right to concentrate your affections. The name of AMERICAN, which belongs to you, in your national capacity, must always exalt the just pride of Patriotism, more than any appellation derived from local discriminations. With slight shades of difference, you have the same Religion, Manners, Habits and political Principles. You have in a common cause fought and triumphed together. The independence and liberty you possess are the work of joint councils, and joint efforts; of common dangers, sufferings, and successes.

11. But these considerations, however powerfully they address themselves to your sensibility are greatly outweighed by those which apply more immediately to your Interest. Here every portion of our country finds the most commanding motives for carefully guarding and preserving the Union of the whole.

12. The *North*, in an unrestrained intercourse with the *South*, protected by the equal Laws of a common government, finds in the productions of the latter, great additional resources of Maritime and commercial enterprise and precious materials of manufacturing industry. The *South* in the same intercourse, benefitting by the same Agency of the *North*, sees its agriculture grow and its commerce expand. Turning partly into its own channels the seamen of the *North*, it finds its particular navigation envigorated; and while it contributes, in different ways, to nourish and increase the general mass of the National navigation, it looks forward to the protection of a Maritime strength, to which itself is unequally adapted. The *East*, in a like intercourse with the *West*, already finds, and in the progressive improvement of interior communications, by land and water, will more and more find a valuable vent for the commodities which it brings from abroad, or manufactures at home. The *West* derives from the *East* supplies requisite to its growth and comfort, and what is perhaps of still greater consequence, it must of necessity owe the *secure* enjoyment of indispensable *outlets* for its own productions to the weight, influence, and the future Maritime strength of the Atlantic side of the Union, directed by an indissoluble community of Interest as *one Nation*. Any other tenure by which the *West* can hold this essential advantage, whether derived from its own separate strength, or from an apostate and unnatural connection with any foreign Power, must be intrinsically precarious.

13. While then every part of our country thus feels an immediate and particular Interest in Union, all the parts combined can not fail to find in

the united mass of means and efforts greater strength, greater resource, proportionably greater security from external danger, a less frequent interruption of their Peace by foreign Nations; and, what is of inestimable value! they must derive from Union an exemption from those broils and Wars between themselves, which so frequently afflict neighboring countries, not tied together by the same governments; which their own rivalships alone would be sufficient to produce, but which opposite foreign alliances, attachments and intrigues would stimulate and imbitter. Hence likewise they will avoid the necessity of those overgrown Military establishments, which under any form of Government are inauspicious to liberty, and which are to be regarded as particularly hostile to Republican Liberty: In this sense it is that your Union ought to be considered as a main prop of your liberty, and that the love of the one ought to endear to you the preservation of the other.

14. These considerations speak a persuasive language to every reflecting and virtuous mind, and exhibit the continuance of the UNION as a primary object of Patriotic desire. Is there a doubt whether a common government can embrace so large a sphere? Let experience solve it. To listen to mere speculation in such a case were criminal. We are authorized to hope that a proper organization of the whole, with the auxiliary agency of governments for the respective Subdivisions, will afford a happy issue to the experiment. 'Tis well worth a fair and full experiment. With such powerful and obvious motives to Union, affecting all parts of our country, while experience shall not have demonstrated its impracticability, there will always be reason to distrust the patriotism of those, who in any quarter may endeavor to weaken its bands.

15. In contemplating the causes wch. may disturb our Union, it occurs as matter of serious concern that any ground should have been furnished for characterizing parties by *Geographical* discriminations: *Northern* and *Southern*; *Atlantic* and *Western*; whence designing men may endeavor to excite a belief that there is a real difference of local interests and views. One of the expedients of Party to acquire influence, within particular districts, is to misrepresent the opinions and aims of other Districts. You can not shield yourselves too much against the jealousies and heart burnings which spring from these misrepresentations. They tend to render Alien to each other those who ought to be bound together by fraternal affection. The Inhabitants of our Western country have lately had a useful lesson on this head. They have seen, in the Negotiation by the Executive, and in the unanimous ratification by the Senate, of the Treaty with Spain, and in the universal satisfaction at that event, throughout the United States, a decisive

proof how unfounded were the suspicions propagated among them of a policy in the General Government and in the Atlantic States unfriendly to their Interests in regard to the MISSISSIPPI. They have been witnesses to the formation of two Treaties, that with G: Britain and that with Spain, which secure to them every thing they could desire in respect to our Foreign relations, towards confirming their prosperity. Will it not be their wisdom to rely for the preservation of these advantages on the UNION by which they were procured? Will they not henceforth be deaf to those advisers, if such there are, who would sever them from their Brethren and connect them with Aliens?

16. To the efficacy and permanency of your Union a Government for the whole is indispensable. No Alliances however strict between the parts can be an adequate substitute. They must inevitably experience the infractions and interruptions which all Alliances in all times have experienced. Sensible of this momentous truth, you have improved upon your first essay, by the adoption of a Constitution of Government, better calculated than your former for an intimate Union, and for the efficacious management of your common concerns. This government, the offspring of our own choice uninfluenced and unawed, adopted upon full investigation and mature deliberation, completely free in its principles, in the distribution of its powers, uniting security with energy, and containing within itself a provision for its own amendment, has a just claim to your confidence and your support. Respect for its authority, compliance with its Laws, acquiescence in its measures, are duties enjoined by the fundamental maxims of true Liberty. The basis of our political systems is the right of the people to make and to alter their Constitutions of Government. But the Constitution which at any time exists, 'till changed by an explicit and authentic act of the whole People, is sacredly obligatory upon all. The very idea of the power and the right of the People to establish Government presupposes the duty of every Individual to obey the established Government.

17. All obstructions to the execution of the Laws, all combinations and Associations, under whatever plausible character, with the real design to direct, controul counteract, or awe the regular deliberation and action of the Constituted authorities are destructive of this fundamental principle and of fatal tendency. They serve to organize faction, to give it an artificial and extraordinary force; to put in the place of the delegated will of the Nation, the will of a party; often a small but artful and enterprizing minority of the Community; and, according to the alternate triumphs of different parties, to make the public administration the Mirror of the ill concerted and incongruous projects of faction, rather than the organ of consistent and

wholesome plans digested by common counsels and modified by mutual interests. However combinations or Associations of the above description may now and then answer popular ends, they are likely, in the course of time and things, to become potent engines, by which cunning, ambitious and unprincipled men will be enabled to subvert the Power of the People, and to usurp for themselves the reins of Government; destroying afterwards the very engines which have lifted them to unjust dominion.

18. Towards the preservation of your Government and the permanency of your present happy state, it is requisite, not only that you steadily discountenance irregular oppositions to its acknowledged authority, but also that you resist with care the spirit of innovation upon its principles however specious the pretexts. One method of assault may be to effect, in the forms of the Constitution, alterations which will impair the energy of the system, and thus to undermine what can not be directly overthrown. In all the changes to which you may be invited, remember that time and habit are at least as necessary to fix the true character of Governments, as of other human institutions; that experience is the surest standard, by which to test the real tendency of the existing Constitution of a country; that facility in changes upon the credit of mere hypotheses and opinion exposes to perpetual change, from the endless variety of hypothesis and opinion: and remember, especially, that for the efficient management of your common interests, in a country so extensive as ours, a Government of as much vigor as is consistent with the perfect security of Liberty is indispensable. Liberty itself will find in such a Government, with powers properly distributed and adjusted, its surest Guardian. It is indeed little else than a name, where the Government is too feeble to withstand the enterprises of faction, to confine each member of the Society within the limits prescribed by the laws and to maintain all in the secure and tranquil enjoyment of the rights of person and property.

19. I have already intimated to you the danger of Parties in the State, with particular reference to the founding of them on Geographical discriminations. Let me now take a more comprehensive view, and warn you in the most solemn manner against the baneful effects of the Spirit of Party, generally.

20. This spirit, unfortunately, is inseparable from our nature, having its root in the strongest passions of the human Mind. It exists under different shapes in all Governments, more or less stifled, controuled, or repressed; but in those of the popular form it is seen in its greatest rankness and is truly their worst enemy.

21. The alternate domination of one faction over another, sharpened by the spirit of revenge natural to party dissension, which in different ages and countries has perpetrated the most horrid enormities, is itself a frightful despotism. But this leads at length to a more formal and permanent despotism. The disorders and miseries, which result, gradually incline the minds of men to seek security and repose in the absolute power of an Individual: and sooner or later the chief of some prevailing faction more able or more fortunate than his competitors, turns this disposition to the purposes of his own elevation, on the ruins of Public Liberty.

22. Without looking forward to an extremity of this kind (which nevertheless ought not to be entirely out of sight) the common and continual mischiefs of the spirit of Party are sufficient to make it the interest and duty of a wise People to discourage and restrain it.

23. It serves always to distract the Public Councils and enfeeble the Public administration. It agitates the Community with ill founded jealousies and false alarms, kindles the animosity of one part against another, foments occasionally riot and insurrection. It opens the door to foreign influence and corruption, which find a facilitated access to the government itself through the channels of party passion. Thus the policy and the will of one country, are subjected to the policy and will of another.

24. There is an opinion that parties in free countries are useful checks upon the Administration of the Government and serve to keep alive the spirit of Liberty. This within certain limits is probably true, and in Governments of a Monarchical cast Patriotism may look with indulgence, if not with favour, upon the spirit of party. But in those of the popular character, in Governments purely elective, it is a spirit not to be encouraged. From their natural tendency, it is certain there will always be enough of that spirit for every salutary purpose. And there being constant danger of excess, the effort ought to be, by force of public opinion, to mitigate and assuage it. A fire not to be quenched; it demands a uniform vigilance to prevent its bursting into a flame, lest instead of warming it should consume.

25. It is important, likewise, that the habits of thinking in a free Country should inspire caution in those entrusted with its administration, to confine themselves within their respective Constitutional spheres; avoiding in the exercise of the Powers of one department to encroach upon another. The spirit of encroachment tends to consolidate the powers of all the departments in one, and thus to create whatever the form of government, a real despotism. A just estimate of that love of power, and proneness to abuse it, which predominates in the human heart is sufficient to satisfy us

of the truth of this position. The necessity of reciprocal checks in the exercise of political power; by dividing and distributing it into different depositories, and constituting each the Guardian of the Public Weal against invasions by the others, has been evinced by experiments ancient and modern; some of them in our country and under our own eyes. To preserve them must be as necessary as to institute them. If in the opinion of the People, the distribution or modification of the Constitutional powers be in any particular wrong, let it be corrected by an amendment in the way which the Constitution designates. But let there be no change by usurpation; for though this, in one instance, may be the instrument of good, it is the customary weapon by which free governments are destroyed. The precedent must always greatly overbalance in permanent evil any partial or transient benefit which the use can at any time yield.

26. Of all the dispositions and habits which lead to political prosperity, Religion and morality are indispensable supports. In vain would that man claim the tribute of Patriotism, who should labor to subvert these great Pillars of human happiness, these firmest props of the duties of Men and citizens. The mere Politician, equally with the pious man ought to respect and to cherish them. A volume could not trace all their connections with private and public felicity. Let it simply be asked where is the security for property, for reputation, for life, if the sense of religious obligation *desert* the oaths, which are the instruments of investigation in Courts of Justice? And let us with caution indulge the supposition, that morality can be maintained without religion. Whatever may be conceded to the influence of refined education on minds of peculiar structure, reason and experience both forbid us to expect that National morality can prevail in exclusion of religious principle.

27. 'Tis substantially true that virtue or morality is a necessary spring of popular government. The rule indeed extends with more or less force to every species of free Government. Who that is a sincere friend to it, can look with indifference upon attempts to shake the foundation of the fabric?

28. Promote then as an object of primary importance, Institutions for the general diffusion of knowledge. In proportion as the structure of a government gives force to public opinion, it is essential that public opinion should be enlightened.

29. As a very important source of strength and security, cherish public credit. One method of preserving it is to use it as sparingly as possible: avoiding occasions of expense by cultivating peace, but remembering also that timely disbursements to prepare for danger frequently prevent much

greater disbursements to repel it; avoiding likewise the accumulation of debt, not only by shunning occasions of expence, but by vigorous exertions in time of Peace to discharge the Debts which unavoidable wars have occasioned, not ungenerously throwing upon posterity the burthen which we ourselves ought to bear. The execution of these maxims belongs to your Representatives, but it is necessary that public opinion should cooperate. To facilitate to them the performance of their duty, it is essential that you should practically bear in mind, that towards the payment of debts there must be Revenue; that to have Revenue there must be taxes; that no taxes can be devised which are not more or less inconvenient and unpleasant; that the intrinsic embarrassment inseparable from the selection of the proper objects (which is always a choice of difficulties) ought to be a decisive motive for a candid construction of the Conduct of the Government in making it, and for a spirit of acquiescence in the measures for obtaining Revenue which the public exigencies may at any time dictate.

30. Observe good faith and justice towds. all Nations. Cultivate peace and harmony with all. Religion and morality enjoin this conduct; and can it be that good policy does not equally enjoin it? It will be worthy of a free, enlightened, and, at no distant period, a great Nation to give to mankind the magnanimous and too novel example of a People always guided by an exalted justice and benevolence. Who can doubt that in the course of time and things the fruits of such a plan would richly repay any temporary advantages wch. might be lost by a steady adherence to it? Can it be, that Providence has not connected the permanent felicity of a Nation with its virtue? The experiment, at least, is recommended by every sentiment which ennobles human Nature. Alas! is it rendered impossible by its vices?

31. In the execution of such a plan nothing is more essential than that permanent, inveterate antipathies against particular Nations and passionate attachments for others should be excluded; and that in place of them just and amicable feelings towards all should be cultivated. The Nation, which indulges towards another an habitual hatred, or an habitual fondness, is in some degree a slave. It is a slave to its animosity or to its affection, either of which is sufficient to lead it astray from its duty and its interest. Antipathy in one Nation against another, disposes each more readily to offer insult and injury, to lay hold of slight causes of umbrage, and to be haughty and intractable, when accidental or trifling occasions of dispute occur. Hence frequent collisions, obstinate envenomed and bloody contests. The Nation, prompted by ill will and resentment sometimes impels to War the Government, contrary to the best calculations of policy. The Government sometimes participates in the national propensity, and adopts through passion

what reason would reject; at other times, it makes the animosity of the Nation subservient to projects of hostility instigated by pride, ambition and other sinister and pernicious motives. The peace often, sometimes perhaps the Liberty, of Nations has been the victim.

32. So likewise, a passionate attachment of one Nation for another produces a variety of evils. Sympathy for the favourite nation, facilitating the illusion of an imaginary common interest, in cases where no real common interest exists, and infusing into one the enmities of the other, betrays the former into a participation in the quarrels and Wars of the latter, without adequate inducement or justification: It leads also to concessions to the favourite Nation of priviledges denied to others, which is apt doubly to injure the Nation making the concessions; by unnecessarily parting with what ought to have been retained; and by exciting jealousy, ill will, and a disposition to retaliate, in the parties from whom eql. priviledges are withheld: And it gives to ambitious, corrupted, or deluded citizens (who devote themselves to the favourite Nation) facility to betray, or sacrifice the interests of their own country, without odium, sometimes even with popularity; gilding with the appearances of a virtuous sense of obligation a commendable deference for public opinion, or a laudable zeal for public good, the base or foolish compliances of ambition, corruption or infatuation.

33. As avenues to foreign influence in innumerable ways, such attachments are particularly alarming to the truly enlightened and independent Patriot. How many opportunities do they afford to tamper with domestic factions, to practice the arts of seduction, to mislead public opinion, to influence or awe the public Councils! Such an attachment of a small or weak, towards a great and powerful Nation, dooms the former to be the satellite of the latter.

34. Against the insidious wiles of foreign influence, (I conjure you to believe me, fellow citizens) the jealousy of a free people ought to be *constantly* awake; since history and experience prove that foreign influence is one of the most baneful foes of Republican Government. But that jealousy to be useful must be impartial; else it becomes the instrument of the very influence to be avoided, instead of a defence against it. Excessive partiality for one foreign nation and excessive dislike of another, cause those whom they actuate to see danger only on one side, and serve to veil and even second the arts of influence on the other. Real Patriots, who may resist the intrigues of the favourite are liable to become suspected and odious; while its tools and dupes usurp the applause and confidence of the people, to surrender their interests.

35. The Great rule of conduct for us, in regard to foreign Nations is in extending our commercial relations to have with them as little *political* connection as possible. So far as we have already formed engagements let them be fulfilled, with perfect good faith. Here let us stop.

36. Europe has a set of primary interests, which to us have none or a very remote relation. Hence she must be engaged in frequent controversies, the causes of which are essentially foreign to our concerns. Hence therefore it must be unwise in us to implicate ourselves, by artificial ties, in the ordinary vicissitudes of her politics, or the ordinary combinations and collisions of her friendships, or enmities:

37. Our detached and distant situation invites and enables us to pursue a different course. If we remain one People, under an efficient government, the period is not far off, when we may defy material injury from external annoyance; when we may take such an attitude as will cause the neutrality we may at any time resolve upon to be scrupulously respected; when belligerent nations, under the impossibility of making acquisitions upon us, will not lightly hazard the giving us provocation; when we may choose peace or war, as our interest, guided by our justice shall Counsel.

38. Why forego the advantages of so peculiar a situation? Why quit our own to stand upon foreign ground? Why, by interweaving our destiny with that of any part of Europe, entangle our peace and prosperity in the toils of European Ambition, Rivalship, Interest, Humour or Caprice?

39. 'Tis our true policy to steer clear of permanent Alliances, with any portion of the foreign world. So far, I mean, as we are now at liberty to do it, for let me not be understood as capable of patronizing infidelity to existing engagements (I hold the maxim no less applicable to public than to private affairs that honesty is always the best policy). I repeat it therefore, let those engagements be observed in their genuine sense. But in my opinion, it is unnecessary and would be unwise to extend them.

40. Taking care always to keep ourselves, by suitable establishments on a respectable defensive posture, we may safely trust to temporary alliances for extraordinary emergencies.

41. Harmony, liberal intercourse with all Nations, are recommended by policy, humanity and interest. But even our Commercial policy should hold an equal and impartial hand: neither seeking nor granting exclusive favours or preferences; consulting the natural course of things; diffusing and diversifying by gentle means the streams of Commerce, but forcing nothing; establishing with Powers so disposed; in order to give trade a stable

course, to define the rights of our Merchants, and to enable the Government to support them; conventional rules of intercourse, the best that present circumstances and mutual opinion will permit, but temporary, and liable to be from time to time abandoned or varied, as experience and circumstances shall dictate; constantly keeping in view, that 'tis folly in one Nation to look for disinterested favors from another; that it must pay with a portion of its Independence for whatever it may accept under that character; that by such acceptance, it may place itself in the condition of having given equivalents for nominal favours and yet of being reproached with ingratitude for not giving more. There can be no greater error than to expect, or calculate upon real favours from Nation to Nation. 'Tis an illusion which experience must cure, which a just pride ought to discard.

42. In offering to you, my Countrymen these counsels of an old and affectionate friend, I dare not hope they will make the strong and lasting impression, I could wish; that they will controul the usual current of the passions, or prevent our Nation from running the course which has hitherto marked the Destiny of Nations: But if I may even flatter myself, that they may be productive of some partial benefit, some occasional good; that they may now and then recur to moderate the fury of party spirit, to warn against the mischiefs of foreign Intriegue, to guard against the Impostures of pretended patriotism; this hope will be a full recompense for the solicitude for your welfare, by which they have been dictated.

43. How far in the discharge of my Official duties, I have been guided by the principles which have been delineated, the public Records and other evidences of my conduct must Witness to You and to the world. To myself, the assurance of my own conscience is, that I have at least believed myself to be guided by them.

44. In relation to the still subsisting War in Europe, my Proclamation of the 22d. of April 1793 is the index to my Plan. Sanctioned by your approving voice and by that of Your Representatives in both Houses of Congress, the spirit of that measure has continually governed me; uninfluenced by any attempts to deter or divert me from it.

45. After deliberate examination with the aid of the best lights I could obtain I was well satisfied that our Country, under all the circumstances of the case, had a right to take, and was bound in duty and interest, to take a Neutral position. Having taken it, I determined, as far as should depend upon me, to maintain it with moderation, perseverance and firmness.

46. The considerations, which respect the right to hold this conduct, it is not necessary on this occasion to detail. I will only observe, that ac-

cording to my understanding of the matter, that right, so far from being denied by any of the Belligerent Powers has been virtually admitted by all.

47. The duty of holding a Neutral conduct may be inferred, without any thing more, from the obligation which justice and humanity impose on every Nation, in cases in which it is free to act, to maintain inviolate the relations of Peace and amity towards other Nations.

48. The inducements of interest for observing that conduct will best be referred to your own reflections and experience. With me, a predominant motive has been to endeavor to gain time to our country to settle and mature its yet recent institutions, and to progress without interruption, to that degree of strength and consistency, which is necessary to give it, humanly speaking, the command of its own fortunes.

49. Though in reviewing the incidents of my Administration, I am unconscious of intentional error, I am nevertheless too sensible of my defects not to think it probable that I may have committed many errors. Whatever they may be I fervently beseech the Almighty to avert or mitigate the evils to which they may tend. I shall also carry with me the hope that my Country will never cease to view them with indulgence; and that after forty five years of my life dedicated to its Service, with an upright zeal, the faults of incompetent abilities will be consigned to oblivion, as myself must soon be to the Mansions of rest.

50. Relying on its kindness in this as in other things, and actuated by that fervent love towards it which is so natural to a Man, who views in it the native soil of himself and his progenitors for several Generations; I anticipate with pleasing expectation that retreat, in which I promise myself to realize, without alloy, the sweet enjoyment of partaking, in the midst of my fellow Citizens, the benign influence of good Laws under a free Government, the ever favourite object of my heart, and the happy reward, as I trust, of our mutual cares, labours and dangers.

Notes

Chapter 1

1. The Resolutions of the United States House of Representatives and the statement of the Senate and President John Adams are quoted in John Marshall, *The Life of George Washington* (1801–1805; reprint, Fredericksburg, Va.: The Citizens' Guild of Washington's Boyhood Home, 1926), 5:364, 368 and 369–70. Such sentiment was not reserved to the American continent. Upon learning of Washington's death, Napoleon Bonaparte decreed that the standards and flags of the French army be dressed in mourning crape. The flags of the British Channel Fleet were lowered to half-mast to honor the fallen hero. Talleyrand, the French minister of foreign affairs, calling for a statue of Washington to be erected in Paris, wrote that "a proper veneration for all that is held dear and sacred to mankind, impel us to give expression to our sentiments by taking part in an event which deprives the world of one of its brightest ornaments, and removes to the realm of history one of the noblest lives that ever honored the human race." Henry Cabot Lodge, *George Washington* (1889; reprint, New Rochelle, New York: Arlington House, n.d.), 2.

2. William B. McGroarty, *Washington: First in the Hearts of His Countrymen* (Richmond: Garrett & Massie, 1932), 29.

3. The text of the Farewell Address can be found in *The Writings of George Washington from the Original Manuscript Sources, 1745–1799*, ed. John C. Fitzpatrick (Washington: U.S. Government Printing Office, 1931–1944), 35:214–38. It is also reprinted as an appendix to this volume. The quote is from paragraph 7. We have used the Fitzpatrick collection because it is currently the most widely available collection of Washington's correspondence and writings. A new edition of Washington's papers is being issued by the University Press of Virginia under the editorship of W. W. Abbott.

4. John Quincy Adams to Washington, 11 February 1797, quoted by Samuel Flagg Bemis, *John Quincy Adams and the Foundations of American Foreign Policy* (New York: W. W. Norton & Company, 1973), 64; James Madison to Thomas Jefferson, 8 February 1825, in *The Mind of the Founder: Sources of the Political Thought of James Madison*, ed. Marvin Meyers (Hanover, N.H.: Brandeis University Press, 1981), 348–50; Marshall, *Life of Washington*, 5:279. According to Marshall the Farewell Address, "though long, is thought too valuable to be omitted or abridged." It was reprinted in full, pp. 279–306, in Mason L. Weems, *The Life of Washington* (1807; reprint, Cambridge: Harvard University Press, 1962), 141.

5. Edwin P. Whipple, ed., *The Great Speeches and Orations of Daniel Webster* (Boston: Little, Brown, 1894), 342, 344.

6. Farewell Address, para. 35, 39.

7. First Inaugural Address, 30 April 1789, *Writings of Washington*, 30:294; Farewell Address, para. 27.

8. Quoted by Marshall, *Life of Washington*, 5:370.

Chapter 2

1. See, for instance, Fisher Ames, "Eulogy of Washington," 8 February 1800, *Works of Fisher Ames*, ed. William B. Allen (Indianapolis: Liberty Classics, 1983), 1: 519–38.

2. *The Records of the Federal Convention of 1787*, ed. Max Farrand (New Haven, Conn.: Yale University Press, 1911), 3:302. The delegate was Pierce Butler.

3. Washington to John Armstrong, 25 April 1788, *The Writings of George Washington from the Original Manuscript Sources, 1745–1799*, ed. John C. Fitzpatrick (Washington: U.S. Government Printing Office, 1931–1944) 30: 465.

4. Thomas Jefferson to Dr. Walter Jones, 2 January 1814, *Thomas Jefferson: Writings*, ed. Merrill D. Peterson (New York: Literary Classics of the United States, 1984), 1318–19. On the question of statesmanship, see Leo Strauss, *Natural Right and History* (Chicago: University of Chicago Press, 1953), 161 and passim: "What cannot be decided in advance by universal rules, what can be decided in the critical moment by the most competent and most conscientious statesman on the spot, can be made visible as just, in retrospect, to all." Washington to Major General John Armstrong, 26 March 1781, *Writings of Washington*, 21: 378.

5. Gordon Wood, *The Radicalism of the American Revolution* (New York: Alfred A. Knopf, 1992), 39–40. For an excellent discussion of Washington, honor, and character, see Lorraine Smith Pangle and Thomas L. Pangle, *The Learning of Liberty: The Educational Ideas of the American Founders* (Lawrence: University of Kansas Press, 1993), 231–49; Washington to Alexander Hamilton, 28 August 1788, *Writings of Washington*, 30:67.

6. "Rules of Civility and Decent Behavior in Company and Conversation," *George Washington: A Collection,* ed. W.B. Allen (Indianapolis: Liberty Classics, 1988), 8, 13.

7. Washington to George Steptoe Washington, 23 March 1789, *Writings of Washington*, 30: 248; Washington to George Steptoe Washington, 5 December 1790, *Writings of Washington*, 30: 163; Washington to George Washington Parke Custis, 19 December 1796, *Writings of Washington*, 35: 341.

8. Washington to Warner Lewis, 14 August 1755, *Writings of Washington*, 1: 162; Washington to Mrs. Martha Washington, 18 June 1775, *Writings of Washington*, 3: 294; Washington to Henry Lee, 22 September 1788, *Writings of Washington*, 30: 97.

9. Thomas Jefferson to George Washington, 10 May 1789, *The Writings of Thomas Jefferson*, ed. Paul L. Ford (New York: G. P. Putnam's Sons, 1892–1899), 5: 94–95.

10. Washington, General Orders, 1 January 1776, *Writings of Washington*, 4: 202; Washington to John Bannister, 21 April 1778, *Writings of Washington*, 11: 291.

11. Washington to the President of Congress, 24 September 1776, *Writings of Washington*, 6: 111. It was for this reason that Washington, despite the fears of many colonists, advocated a permanent military establishment instead of relying upon an

untrained and undisciplined militia. Washington, General Orders, 4 July 1775, *Writings of Washington,* 3: 309.

12. Washington, General Orders, 9 July 1776, *Writings of Washington,* 5: 245; Washington, General Orders, 1 January 1776, *Writings of Washington,* 4: 202; Washington, General Orders, 2 July 1776, *Writings of Washington,* 5: 211.

13. Washington, General Orders, 1 January 1776, *Writings of Washington,* 4: 203; Washington to Philip Schuyler, 17 July 1776, *Writings of Washington,* 5: 290–91; Washington to Colonel William Woodford, 10 November 1775, *Writings of Washington,* 4: 80; Washington to the President of Congress, 24 September 1776, *Writings of Washington,* 6: 108–10.

14. Washington, Farewell Orders to the Armies of the United States, 2 November 1783, *Writings of Washington,* 27: 223–27. Emphasis added.

15. Washington, Address to Congress on Resigning His Commission, 23 December 1783, *Writings of Washington,* 27: 284–85; Thomas Jefferson to Washington, 16 April 1784, *Writings of Jefferson,* 3:323–29.

16. Washington to John Augustine Washington, 31 March 1776, *Writings of Washington,* 4: 450.

17. See E. James Ferguson, "Currency Finance: An Interpretation of Colonial Monetary Practices," *William and Mary Quarterly* 10 (April 1953), 151–80 and *The Power of the Purse: A History of American Public Finance, 1776–1790* (Chapel Hill: University of North Carolina Press, 1961); also E. Wayne Carp, *To Starve the Army at Pleasure: Continental Army Administration and American Political Culture, 1775–1783* (Chapel Hill: University of North Carolina Press, 1984). Washington to Alexander Hamilton, 31 March 1783, *Writings of Washington,* 26: 277; Washington to Gouverneur Morris, 4 October 1778, *Writings of Washington,* 13: 21–23.

18. Washington to Benjamin Harrison, 18[–30] December 1778, *Writings of Washington,* 13: 464–67; Washington to Gouverneur Morris, 8 May 1779, *Writings of Washington,* 15: 25; Washington to James Warren, 31 March 1779, *Writings of Washington,* 14: 312.

19. Washington to George Mason, 27 March 1779, *Writings of Washington,* 14: 300–301; Washington to Marquis de Lafayette, 5 April 1783, *Writings of Washington,* 26: 298.

20. Washington to Marquis de Lafayette, 5 April 1783, *Writings of Washington,* 26: 298; Washington to Lieutenant Colonel Tench Tilghman, 24 April 1783, *Writings of Washington,* 26: 359.

21. Washington, Circular to the States, 14 June 1783, *Writings of Washington,* 26: 483–96. Hamilton wrote Washington on 30 September 1783: "At all events, without compliment Sir, It will do you honor with the sensible and well meaning; and ultimately it is to be hoped with the people at large—when the present epidemic frenzy has subsided." *The Papers of Alexander Hamilton,* ed. Harold C. Syrett (New York: Columbia University Press, 1961–1987), 3: 463.

22. Edmund Randolph wrote James Madison on 28 June 1783 that the "arrival of Gen. Washington's circular letter excited this hope [the passage of the impost law] in the minds of the sanguine: but its effect is momentary, and perhaps it will hereafter be accepted by the assembly with disgust. For the murmur is free and general against what is called the unsolicited obtrusion of his advice." See *Writings of Washington,* 26: 491.

23. The phrase "the eyes of the World are turned upon them" is reminiscent

of John Winthrop's famous line (following Matthew 5:14) of 1630: "we must Consider that we shall be as a City upon a Hill, the eyes of all people are upon us." *The Puritans*, ed. Perry Miller and Thomas H. Johnson (New York: Harper & Row, 1963), 1: 199. Washington, General Orders, 2 July 1776, *Writings of Washington*, 5: 211; Alexander Hamilton, James Madison, and John Jay, *Federalist* No. 1, *The Federalist Papers*, ed. Clinton Rossiter (New York: New American Library, 1961), 33.

24. Washington to Governor Robert Hunter Morris, 9 April 1756, *Writings of Washington*, 1: 309. Washington's reference was to the beginning of the French and Indian War (Seven Years' War) of 1756–1763. Benjamin Franklin had proposed a continental union under the British Empire in his Albany Plan two years earlier.

25. Thomas Paine, *The Rights of Man and Other Writings*, ed. Courtlandt Canby (London: Heron Books, 1970), 72.

26. Washington to Lund Washington, 17 December 1778, *Writings of Washington*, 13: 408.

27. Washington to George William Fairfax, 10 July 1783, *Writings of Washington*, 27: 58; Washington to Jonathan Trumbull, Jr., 5 January 1784, *Writings of Washington*, 28: 294; Washington to Marquis de Lafayette, 1 February 1784, *Writings of Washington*, 27: 319; Washington to Governor Benjamin Harrison, 18 January 1784, *Writings of Washington*, 27: 305–306.

28. *Documents of American History*, ed. Henry Steele Commager (Englewood Cliffs, N.J.: Prentice-Hall, 1973), 1: 133.

29. Washington to James Warren, 7 October 1785, *Writings of Washington*, 28: 290.

30. Washington to John Jay, 18 May 1786, *Writings of Washington*, 28: 431–32; Washington to John Jay, 1 August 1786, *Writings of Washington*, 28: 502–503.

31. Thomas Jefferson to William S. Smith, 13 November 1787, *Writings of Jefferson*, 4:467; Washington to Henry Lee, 31 October 1786, *Writings of Washington*, 29: 33–34; Washington to David Humphreys, 26 December 1786, *Writings of Washington*, 29: 125–26.

32. Washington to Marquis de Lafayette, 10 May 1786, *Writings of Washington*, 28: 421–22; Washington to Henry Lee, 31 October 1786, *Writings of Washington*, 29: 33–34.

33. Washington to James Madison, 5 November 1786, *Writings of Washington*, 29: 51–52; Washington to James Madison, 18 November 1786, *Writings of Washington*, 29: 71.

34. Washington to Governor Edmund Randolph, 21 December 1786, *Writings of Washington*, 29: 120; Washington to Henry Knox, 8 March 1787, *Writings of Washington*, 29: 171; Washington to Governor Edmund Randolph, 28 March 1787, *Writings of Washington*, 29: 187; Washington to Henry Knox, 2 April 1787, *Writings of Washington*, 29: 194; Washington to James Madison, 31 March 1787, *Writings of Washington*, 29: 191–92.

35. James Madison to Washington, 16 April 1787, *Papers of James Madison,* ed. Robert Rutland et al. (Charlottesville: University Press of Virginia, 1962–1991), 9:382–87.

36. James Flexner, *George Washington and the New Nation* (Boston: Little, Brown, 1970), 116.

37. Flexner, *George Washington and the New Nation,* 116–17. It had been moved that the number of representatives not exceed one for every thirty thousand

persons, instead of the proposed one for every forty thousand persons. Washington supported the move, and the change was agreed to unanimously. In general, see William B. Allen, "Washington and Franklin: Symbols or Lawmakers," *The Political Science Reviewer* 17 (Fall 1987) and Glenn Phelps, *George Washington and American Constitutionalism* (Lawrence: University of Kansas Press, 1993), 99–109.

38. Washington to Patrick Henry, 24 September 1787, *Writings of Washington*, 29: 278; Washington to James Madison, 10 January 1788, *Writings of Washington*, 29: 372–73; James Monroe to Thomas Jefferson, 12 July 1788, *The Papers of Thomas Jefferson,* ed. Julian P. Boyd et al. (Princeton: Princeton University Press, 1950–), 13: 352.

39. Washington to John Armstrong, 25 April 1788, *Writings of Washington*, 29: 466.

40. Washington to Marquis de Lafayette, 7 February 1788, *Writings of Washington*, 29: 409–10.

41. Because it was never delivered and not included in the earliest edition of Washington's writings, the "discarded inaugural" was cut up by Jared Sparks for autograph samples and exists only in fragmentary form. Although long presumed to be the work of David Humphreys, Washington's personal secretary, recent scholarship has argued persuasively that it is indeed the work of Washington and an important source of his thought. See W. B. Allen, "Washington and Franklin," 109–138. The most extensive collection of the fragments, ordered in a sensible fashion, is to be found in *George Washington: A Collection,* ed. W.B. Allen (Indianapolis: Liberty Classics, 1988), 445–49. Washington, Fragments of the Discarded First Inaugural Address, in *Washington: A Collection*, 448, 454.

42. Washington to Benjamin Lincoln, 29 June 1788, *Writings of Washington*, 30: 11.

43. Mercy Otis Warren, *The History of the American Revolution*, ed. Lester H. Cohen (Indianapolis: Liberty Classics, 1805, reprint 1988), 2: 662.

44. Washington to Benjamin Lincoln, 28 August 1788, *Writings of Washington*, 30: 62–63; Washington to Marquis de Lafayette, 29 January 1789, *Writings of Washington*, 30: 184–85; Washington to Benjamin Lincoln, 31 January 1789, *Writings of Washington*, 30: 189–90; Washington to Thomas Jefferson, 31 August 1788, *Writings of Washington*, 30: 83; Washington to Marquis de Lafayette, 29 January 1789, *Writings of Washington*, 30: 186.

45. Washington to the Mayor, Corporation, and Citizens of Alexandria, 16 April 1789, *Writings of Washington*, 30: 286–87.

46. Washington to James Madison, 5 May 1789, *Writings of Washington*, 30: 310–311.

47. Washington to John Armstrong, 25 April 1788, *Writings of Washington*, 30: 465.

48. *Washington: A Collection*, 464–65; Washington, First Inaugural Address, 30 April 1789, *Writings of Washington*, 30: 291–96.

49. Phelps, *George Washington and American Constitutionalism*, 104–106; Washington to Bushrod Washington, 10 November 1787, *Writings of Washington*, 29: 312.

50. Washington, Plan of American Finance, October 1789, *Writings of Washington*, 30: 454–55; Washington to David Stuart, 15 June 1790, *Writings of Washington*, 31: 52–53.

51. Flexner, *George Washington and the New Nation*, 278–80.

52. Thomas Jefferson, "Opinion on the Constitutionality of a National Bank," 15 February 1791, *Writings of Jefferson*, 5: 284–89; Alexander Hamilton, "Opinion on the Constitutionality of an Act to Establish a National Bank," 23 February 1791, *Papers of Hamilton*, 8: 97–134; Washington to Gouverneur Morris, 28 July 1791, *Writings of Washington*, 31: 329.

53. Washington to Marquis de Lafayette, 29 January 1789, *Writings of Washington*, 30: 186–87; Washington to Hamilton, 14 October 1791, *Writings of Washington*, 31: 389, and Jefferson, "Anas," *Writings of Jefferson*, 1: 163–64.

54. Washington, First Inaugural Address, *Writings of Washington*, 30: 292; Washington to James Wilson, 9 May 1789, *Writings of Washington*, 30: 314.

55. Thomas Jefferson to Washington, 8 May 1791, *Writings of Jefferson*, 5: 328–30.

56. Thomas Jefferson to Washington, 23 May 1792, *Writings of Jefferson*, 6: 1–6; Alexander Hamilton, Speech in the Constitutional Convention on a Plan of Government, 18 June 1787, *Papers of Hamilton*, 4: 178–87; Washington to Hamilton, 29 July 1792, *Writings of Washington*, 32: 95–100; Alexander Hamilton to Washington, 18 August 1792, *Papers of Hamilton*, 12: 228–58.

57. Washington to Hamilton, 26 August 1792, *Writings of Washington*, 32: 132–34; Washington to Jefferson, 23 August 1792, *Writings of Washington*, 32: 130–31.

58. Washington to James Madison, 20 May 1792, *Writings of Washington*, 32: 46; Thomas Jefferson to Washington, 23 May 1792, *Writings of Jefferson*, 6: 1–6; Alexander Hamilton to Washington, 30 July 1792, *Washington's Farewell Address*, ed. Victor Hugo Paltsits (New York: The New York Public Library, 1935), 232–34; James Madison, "Madison's Personal Memorandum Respecting Conversations with Washington about His Proposed Retirement," 5 May 1792, *Washington's Farewell Address*, 215.

59. Washington to Gouverneur Morris, 13 October 1789, *Writings of Washington*, 30: 443; Flexner, *George Washington and the New Nation*, 253.

60. Washington to Gouverneur Morris, 13 October 1789, *Writings of Washington*, 30: 443; Washington to Marquis de Lafayette, 28 July 1791, *Writings of Washington*, 31: 324–25. The Neutrality Proclamation was written by Attorney General Randolph; the document did not include the word "neutrality" in deference to the sentiments of Jefferson. *Documents of American History*, 1: 163.

61. In addition to the above, see Hamilton, "The Cause of France, and the French Revolution," 1794, *Papers of Hamilton*, 17:585–86 and 586–88. Washington to Jefferson, 11 July 1793, *Writings of Washington*, 33: 4; Washington to Alexander Hamilton, 8 May 1796, *Writings of Washington*, 35: 40.

62. The classic study on this subject is Samuel Flagg Bemis, *Jay's Treaty: A Study in Commerce and Diplomacy* (New Haven: Yale University Press, 1962).

63. Washington to Randolph, 31 July 1795, *Writings of Washington*, 34: 266.

64. See Samuel Flagg Bemis, *Pinckney's Treaty: America's Advantage from Europe's Distress, 1783–1800* (New Haven: Yale University Press, 1965).

65. Washington to John Jay, 1–5 November 1794, *Writings of Washington*, 34: 16; Washington to Alexander Hamilton, 3 July 1795, *Writings of Washington*, 34: 227; Joseph Charles, *Origins of the American Party System* (New York: Harper & Row, 1961).

66. Forrest McDonald, *The Presidency of George Washington* (Topeka: University of Kansas Press, 1974), 132–33; Washington to Alexander Hamilton, 26 June 1796, *Writings of Washington*, 35: 103; Thomas Jefferson to James Monroe, 12 June 1796, *Writings of Jefferson*, 7: 80; Thomas Jefferson to Mazzei, 24 April 1796, *Writings of Jefferson*, 7: 76.

67. Washington to Thomas Jefferson, 6 July 1796, *Writings of Washington*, 35: 118–20; Jefferson, "Anas," *Writings of Jefferson*, 1: 168; Alexander Hamilton to Tobias Lear, 2 January 1800, *Papers of Hamilton*, 24: 155. Emphasis added. Hamilton concluded the letter: "If virtue can secure happiness in another world he is happy. In this the Seal is now put upon his glory. It is no longer in jeopardy from the fickleness of fortune."

Chapter 3

1. James T. Flexner, *George Washington, Anguish and Farewell* (Boston: Little, Brown, 1972), 303; *Washington's Farewell Address*, ed. Victor Hugo Paltsits (New York: The New York Public Library, 1935), 67.

2. Washington to James Madison, 20 May 1792, *The Writings of George Washington from the Original Manuscript Sources, 1745–1799*, ed. John C. Fitzpatrick (Washington: U.S. Government Printing Office, 1931–1944), 32: 46–48.

3. There were five "drafts" of the Farewell Address, not counting Washington's extensive letters and directions: 1) the Madison Draft of 1792; 2) the Washington Draft of 1796; 3) the Major Draft (Hamilton); 4) the Draft for Incorporating (Hamilton); and 5) the Final Draft. These texts and important correspondence were published together in the Paltsits volume, making it an indispensable reference for the documents surrounding the Farewell Address. James Madison to President Washington, 20 June 1792, ed. Paltsits, *Washington's Farewell Address*, 227–29.

4. Speaking of the dispute between Hamilton and Jefferson, Washington expressed his wish that "the cup wch. has been presented, may not be snatched from our lips by a discordance of *action* when I am persuaded that there is no discordance in your *views*." Washington to Thomas Jefferson, 18 October 1792, *Writings of Washington*, 32: 186. In the Circular Address, Washington wrote that "honesty will be found on every experiment, to be the best and only true policy." Washington, Circular to the States, 8 June 1783, *Writings of Washington*, 26: 489.

5. Washington to Patrick Henry, 9 October 1795, *Writings of Washington*, 34: 335.

6. Washington to Gouverneur Morris, 22 December 1795, *Writings of Washington*, 34: 401, and Washington to Charles Carroll of Carrollton, 1 May 1796, *Writings of Washington*, 35: 29–31.

7. Washington, Circular to the States, 8 June 1783, *Writings of Washington*, 26: 486.

8. "Washington's First Draft for an Address," enclosed in his letter to Hamilton of 15 May 1796, ed. Paltsits, *Washington's Farewell Address*, 164–73.

9. Washington to Alexander Hamilton, 15 May 1796, *Writings of Washington*, 35: 48–51.

10. "Washington's First Draft for an Address," enclosed in his letter to Hamilton of 15 May 1796, ed. Paltsits, *Washington's Farewell Address*, 164–73. Paltsits

believed that this judgment, first propounded by Jared Sparks, "is sensible and susceptible to proof" (*Washington's Farewell Address*, 39).

11. While he ended with twenty-three numbers, there were only twenty-two points in Hamilton's abstract; there was no eighth point. At the same time, there were twenty-two paragraphs in Washington's draft if the first two explanatory paragraphs are dropped. This analysis agrees with Paltsits's breakdown of the abstract, although Paltsits argued that only some ideas in the seven points were derived from Washington's draft. A close comparison, however, shows that Hamilton derived all his points from Washington's material.

12. Hamilton to Washington, 30 July 1796, ed. Harold C. Syrett (New York: Columbia University Press, 1961–1987), *The Papers of Alexander Hamilton*, 20: 264–65.

13. Washington to Alexander Hamilton, 10 August 1796, *Writings of Washington*, 35: 178; "Hamilton's Draft for Incorporating in Address," enclosed in his letter to Washington of 10 August 1796, ed. Paltsits, *Washington's Farewell Address*, 200–208; Hamilton to Washington, 10 August 1796, *Papers of Hamilton*, 20: 293–94. Emphasis added.

14. Washington to Alexander Hamilton, 25 August 1796, *Writings of Washington*, 35: 190–92.

15. Washington to Alexander Hamilton, 1 September 1796, *Writings of Washington*, 35: 199–200; Hamilton to Washington, 4 September 1796, *Papers of Hamilton*, 20: 316; Hamilton to Washington, 5 September 1796, *Papers of Hamilton*, 20: 317–18.

16. "Washington's Final Manuscript," ed. Paltsits, *Washington's Farewell Address*, 148–49, and "Hamilton's Original Major Draft," ed. Paltsits, *Washington's Farewell Address*, 189–90; "Washington's Final Manuscript," ed. Paltsits, *Washington's Farewell Address*, 156; "Hamilton's Original Major Draft," ed. Paltsits, *Washington's Farewell Address*, 195, and "Washington's Final Manuscript," ed. Paltsits, *Washington's Farewell Address*, 154; "Hamilton's Original Major Draft," ed. Paltsits, *Washington's Farewell Address*, 197, and "Washington's Final Manuscript," ed. Paltsits, *Washington's Farewell Address*, 156; Thomas Paine, *The Rights of Man and Other Writings*, ed. Courtlandt Canby (London: Heron Books, 1970), 25.

17. "Washington's Final Manuscript," ed. Paltsits, *Washington's Farewell Address*, 142, and "Hamilton's Draft for Incorporating," ed. Paltsits, *Washington's Farewell Address*, 201; "Washington's Final Manuscript," ed. Paltsits, *Washington's Farewell Address*, 144; "Washington's Final Manuscript," ed. Paltsits, *Washington's Farewell Address*, 152.

18. "Washington's Final Manuscript," ed. Paltsits, *Washington's Farewell Address*, 151, and "Hamilton's Original Major Draft," ed. Paltsits, *Washington's Farewell Address*, 192.

19. "Washington's Final Manuscript," ed. Paltsits, *Washington's Farewell Address*, 157–58.

20. "Washington's Final Manuscript," ed. Paltsits, *Washington's Farewell Address*, 145, 149; "Washington's Final Manuscript," ed. Paltsits, *Washington's Farewell Address*, 148; "Washington's Final Manuscript," ed. Paltsits, *Washington's Farewell Address*, 159, and "Madison's Form for an Address," ed. Paltsits, *Washington's Farewell Address*, 161.

21. "Certification of David C. Claypoole, 22 February 1826," ed. Paltsits, *Washington's Farewell Address*, 290–92.

22. Referring to the Farewell Address, French Minister Pierre Adet wrote: "It would be useless to speak to you about it. You will have noticed the lies it contains, the insolent tone that governs it, the immorality which characterizes it. You will have no difficulty in recognizing the author of a piece extolling ingratitude, showing it as a virtue necessary to the happiness of states, presenting interest as the only counsel which governments ought to follow in the course of their negotiations, putting aside honor and glory. You will have recognized immediately the doctrine of the former Secretary of the Treasury, Hamilton, and the principles of loyalty that have always directed the Philadelphia Government." Quoted in *Washington's Farewell Address: The View from the 20th Century,* ed. Burton Ira Kaufman (Chicago: Quadrangle Books, 1969), 109. See the 1811 correspondence between John Jay and Richard Peters, ed. Paltsits, *Washington's Farewell Address,* 263–71.

23. Felix Gilbert argues that Hamilton was essentially introducing new material into the draft. Felix Gilbert, *The Beginnings of American Foreign Policy: To the Farewell Address* (New York: Harper & Row, 1961), 127–34; Joseph Charles, *The Origins of the American Party System* (New York: Harper & Row, 1956), 48, 52; Alexander DeConde, *Entangling Alliances: Politics and Diplomacy under George Washington* (Durham: Duke University Press, 1958), 503.

24. Horace Binney, *An Inquiry into the Formation of Washington's Farewell Address* (Philadelphia: n.p., 1859), 50–51; ed. Paltsits, *Washington's Farewell Address,* xv; Samuel Flagg Bemis, "A Foreign Policy of Independence," *American Historical Review* (January 1934): 262; Thomas Jefferson to Justice William Johnson, 12 June 1823, *Thomas Jefferson: Writings,* ed. Merrill D. Peterson (New York: Literary Classics of the United States, 1984), 1472.

25. Alexander Hamilton, *The Defence II,* July 1795, *Papers of Hamilton,* 18: 493–501; Note John Jay's discussion of the providential circumstances that made for "one united people." Alexander Hamilton, James Madison, and John Jay, *Federalist* No. 2, *The Federalist Papers,* ed. Clinton Rossiter (New York: New American Library, 1961), 38.

26. Madison quoted in *The Creation of a Republican Empire,* Bradford Perkins (Cambridge: Cambridge University Press, 1993), 46.

27. Farewell Address, para. 1.

28. Fisher Ames to Oliver Wolcott, 26 September 1796, *Works of Fisher Ames,* ed. William B. Allen (Indianapolis: Liberty Classics, 1983), 2: 1192.

29. Washington to James Madison, 20 May 1792, *Writings of Washington,* 32: 46–48, and Washington to Alexander Hamilton, 15 May 1796, *Writings of Washington,* 35: 48–51; Washington, First Inaugural, 30 April 1789, *Writings of Washington,* 30: 292; Washington to Landon Carter, 17 October 1796, *Writings of Washington,* 35: 246.

30. Farewell Address, para. 2–4.

31. Farewell Address, para. 5; Washington to Henry Knox, 8 March 1787, *Writings of Washington,* 29: 171; Washington to Catherine Macaulay Graham, 9 January 1790, *Writings of Washington,* 30: 495–96.

32. Farewell Address, para. 6.

33. Farewell Address, para. 6.

34. Farewell Address, para. 7.

35. Washington, Circular to the States, 8 June 1783, *Writings of Washington,* 26: 489.

36. Washington to Bryan Fairfax, 24 August 1774, *Writings of Washington*, 3: 232–34; Farewell Address, para. 8; Abraham Lincoln, "Fragment on the Constitution and the Union," January 1861, *The Collected Works of Abraham Lincoln*, ed. Roy P. Basler (New Brunswick: Rutgers University Press, 1953), 4: 168–69.

37. Farewell Address, para. 10; *Federalist* No. 2, 38.

38. Washington to John Banister, 21 April 1778, *Writings of Washington*, 11: 286. Banister was a Virginia delegate to the Continental Congress. Farewell Address, para. 11.

39. Farewell Address, para. 11, 12.

40. Washington to Harry Innes, 2 March 1789, *Writings of Washington*, 30: 215; Washington to Gouverneur Morris, 28 July 1791, *Writings of Washington*, 31: 328.

41. Washington to David Humphreys, 25 July 1785, *Writings of Washington*, 28:202–205. Washington to James Warren, 7 October 1785, *Writings of Washington*, 28: 289–92. Washington to William Irvine, 31 October 1788, *Writings of Washington*, 30: 123.

42. Washington, Discarded Draft of First Inaugural, *Washington: A Collection*, 455–56.

43. Farewell Address, para. 14.

44. Farewell Address, para. 9; Farewell Address, para. 13.

45. Washington to Lieutenant Colonel Tench Tilghman, 24 April 1783, *Writings of Washington*, 26: 359.

46. Washington to David Stuart, 1 July 1787, *Writings of Washington*, 29: 238; Washington to Lafayette, 5 April 1783, *Writings of Washington*, 26: 297–98.

47. Washington to John Augustine Washington, 31 May 1776, *Writings of Washington*, 5: 92; Farewell Address, para. 17, 18.

48. *Federalist* No. 1, 33.

49. Washington to Governor Henry Lee, 26 August 1794, *Writings of Washington*, 33: 475–76; Washington to Burgess Ball, 25 September 1794, *Writings of Washington*, 33: 506–507; Washington, Sixth Annual Message, 19 November 1794, *Writings of Washington*, 34: 28–35.

50. Jefferson, First Inaugural Address, 4 March 1801, *Thomas Jefferson: Writings*, 492–93; Farewell Address, para. 16.

51. See, for example, Washington to Robert Morris, 12 April 1786, *Writings of Washington*, 28: 408; to Marquis de Lafayette, 10 May 1786, *Writings of Washington*, 28: 424; to John Francis Mercer, 9 September 1786, *Writings of Washington*, 29: 5; to Tobias Lear, 6 May 1794, *Writings of Washington*, 33: 358; to Alexander Spotswood, 23 November 1794, *Writings of Washington*, 34: 47–48; to Lawrence Lewis, 4 August 1797, *Writings of Washington*, 36: 2; to Robert Lewis, 18 August 1799, *Writings of Washington*, 37: 338–39; and Washington's Last Will and Testament, 9 July 1799, *Writings of Washington*, 37: 276–77. Of particular interest is James Thomas Flexner, "George Washington and Slavery," in *George Washington, Anguish and Farewell* (Boston: Little, Brown, 1972), 112–25.

52. Farewell Address, para. 15.

53. Farewell Address, para. 19, 20; *Federalist* No. 10, 79.

54. Washington to George Mason, 27 March 1779, *Writings of Washington*, 14: 301; Washington to Gouverneur Morris, 8 May 1779, *Writings of Washington*, 15: 25–26.

55. Washington to David Humphreys, 26 December 1786, *Writings of Washington*, 29: 126; Washington to Bushrod Washington, 10 November 1787, *Writings of Washington*, 29: 309–12; Washington to David Stuart, 30 November 1787, *Writings of Washington*, 29: 323–24; Washington to John Armstrong, 25 April 1788, *Writings of Washington*, 29: 446; Washington to Lafayette, 28 April 1788, *Writings of Washington*, 29: 478; Washington to Benjamin Lincoln, 28 August 1788, *Writings of Washington*, 30: 62–63; Washington to Marquis de Lafayette, 29 January 1789, *Writings of Washington*, 30: 184–85; Washington to Benjamin Lincoln, 31 January 1789, *Writings of Washington*, 30: 190.

56. Washington to Thomas Jefferson, 6 July 1796, *Writings of Washington*, 35: 119; Washington to Governor Jonathan Trumbull, 30 August 1799, *Writings of Washington*, 37: 349.

57. Washington to the Acting Secretary of State, 27 September 1795, *Writings of Washington*, 34: 315; Washington to Marquis de Lafayette, 25 December 1798, *Writings of Washington*, 37: 66; Washington to Patrick Henry, 15 January 1799, *Writings of Washington*, 37: 90.

58. Washington to Governor Henry Lee, 21 July 1793, *Writings of Washington*, 33: 23–24; Thomas Jefferson to Washington, 9 September 1792, *The Writings of Thomas Jefferson*, ed. Paul L. Ford (New York: G. P. Putnam's Sons, 1892–1899) 6: 101–109. Washington to Jefferson, 18 October 1792, *Writings of Washington*, 32: 185–86.

59. Washington to Alexander Hamilton, 29 July 1795, *Writings of Washington*, 34: 264.

60. *Federalist* No. 10, 78; Farewell Address, para. 20–24.

61. See Colleen A. Sheehan, "The Politics of Public Opinion: James Madison's 'Notes of Government,'" *William and Mary Quarterly* 49 (1992): 609–27; Charles R. Kesler, "*Federalist* 10 and American Republicanism," and William B. Allen, "Justice and the General Good: *Federalist* 51," in *Saving the Revolution: The Federalist Papers and the American Founding*, ed. Charles R. Kesler (New York: The Free Press, 1987), 13–39 and 131–149. Farewell Address, para. 24.

62. Washington, Fragments of the Discarded First Inaugural Address, *Washington: A Collection*, 448, 454.

63. Farewell Address, para. 25.

64. *Federalist* No. 55, 346.

65. Washington to George Washington Parke Custis, 19 December 1796, *Writings of Washington*, 35: 341; Washington, Thanksgiving Proclamation, 3 October 1789, *Writings of Washington*, 30: 427–28.

66. Farewell Address, para. 26, 27.

67. Washington to the Roman Catholics in the United States of America, 15 March 1790, *Washington: A Collection*, 547; Washington to the General Assembly of Presbyterian Churches, May 1789, *Washington: A Collection*, 533; Washington to the Hebrew Congregation in Newport, August 1790, *Washington: A Collection*, 548. Emphasis added.

68. Washington to Hamilton, 1 September 1796, *Writings of Washington*, 35: 199–200; Hamilton to Washington, 4 September 1796, *The Papers of Hamilton*, 20: 316; Hamilton to Washington, 5 September 1796, *The Papers of Hamilton*, 20: 317–18.

69. Washington, Eighth Annual Message, 7 December 1796, *Writings of Washington*, 35: 316–17.

70. Washington to Nicholas Pike, 20 June 1788, *Writings of Washington*, 30: 2–3; Washington to George Chapman, 15 December 1784, *Writings of Washington*, 28: 13–14.

71. Washington to Edmund Randolph, 30 July 1785, *Writings of Washington*, 28: 214–15. In the 1790s, Washington hoped these shares would be the seed-money for his idea of a national university. Washington to the Trustees of the Alexandria Academy, 17 December 1785, *Writings of Washington*, 28: 356–58. It is interesting to note that when Washington (in his will) freed his slaves upon his wife's death, the young slaves were to be held until age twenty-five so that they could be taught to read and write. In addition to his work with William and Mary College, Washington received five honorary Doctor of Laws degrees, from Harvard, Yale, Pennsylvania, Washington College, and Brown. Both facts are noted in Eugene Miller, *Washington's Discourses on Education*, unpublished manuscript.

72. Washington to the Commissioners of the District of Columbia, 28 January 1795, *Writings of Washington*, 34: 106; Washington to Thomas Jefferson, 15 March 1795, *Writings of Washington*, 34: 149; Washington to Hamilton, 1 September 1796, *Writings of Washington*, 35: 199–200.

73. Washington, First Annual Message, 8 January 1790, *Writings of Washington*, 30: 493.

74. Farewell Address, para. 30.

75. Farewell Address, para. 31–34.

76. Farewell Address, para. 37, 41, 44–47; Washington to Patrick Henry, 9 October 1795, *Writings of Washington*, 35: 335. Emphasis in original.

77. Farewell Address, para. 49.

78. "Nor could it be expected that my sentiments and opinions would have much weight on the minds of my countrymen—they have been neglected, tho' given as a last legacy in the most solemn manner." Washington to John Jay, 1 August 1786, *Writings of Washington*, 28: 502–503.

79. Farewell Address, para. 42.

80. John Marshall, *The Life of George Washington* (1801–1805; reprint Fredericksburg, Va.: The Citizens' Guild of Washington's Boyhood Home, 1926), 5: 377; Abraham Lincoln, "Address before the Young Men's Lyceum of Springfield, Illinois," 27 January 1838, *The Collected Works of Abraham Lincoln*, ed. Roy P. Basler (New Brunswick: Rutgers University Press, 1953), 1: 115.

81. Farewell Address, para. 50; Washington to the Citizens of Alexandria and Its Neighbors, 23 March 1797, *Writings of Washington*, 35: 423.

82. Farewell Address, para. 2, 7, 42, 50.

83. Compare the photographic reproduction of the first page of "Madison's Form for an Address as Drafted by Him for Washington," ed. Paltsits, *Washington's Farewell Address*, 161, and a similar reproduction of the first page of "Washington's First Draft for an Address," ed. Paltsits, *Washington's Farewell Address*, 165. Farewell Address, para. 43.

84. Washington to the Mayor, Corporation, and Citizens of Alexandria, 16 April 1789, *Writings of Washington*, 30: 286; Washington, First Inaugural Address, 30 April 1789, *Writings of Washington*, 30: 291; Washington, Second Inaugural Address, 4 March 1793, *Writings of Washington*, 32: 374; Washington to Bushrod Washington, 15 January 1783, *Writings of Washington*, 26: 39.

85. Abraham Lincoln, First Inaugural, 4 March 1861, *Works of Lincoln*, 4: 271.

86. John Carroll, "A Discourse on General Washington: Delivered in the Catholic Church of St. Peter, in Baltimore," 22 February 1800, *The John Carroll Papers*, ed. Thomas O'Brien Hanley (Notre Dame: University of Notre Dame Press, 1976), 2: 308; Farewell Address, para. 50.

Chapter 4

1. The text of the Farewell Address can be found in *The Writings of George Washington from the Original Manuscript Sources, 1745–1799*, ed. John C. Fitzpatrick (Washington: U.S. Government Printing Office, 1931–1944), 35:214–38. It is also reprinted as an appendix to this volume. The quote is from paragraph 3.

2. Washington to Hamilton, 25 August 1796, *Writings of Washington*, 35:190–91. In this same letter, Washington also stated that his first draft of the Address "was designed in a more especiall manner for the Yeomanry of this Country."

3. Farewell Address, para. 3. Washington to Thomas Jefferson, 6 July 1796, *Writings of Washington*, 35:119–20; Jefferson to James Monroe, 4 June 1793, *The Writings of Thomas Jefferson*, ed. Paul L. Ford (New York: G. P. Putnam's Sons, 1892–1899), 6: 282.

4. Stanley Elkins and Eric McKitrick, *The Age of Federalism* (New York: Oxford University Press, 1993), 336.

5. Bradford Perkins, *The Creation of a Republican Empire, 1776–1865* (New York: Cambridge University Press, 1993), 90.

6. Washington's characterization of the Hamilton–Jefferson "coalition" is recorded in Jefferson, "Anas," *Writings of Thomas Jefferson*, 1:215. The unhappy fate of Edmund Randolph can be followed in John J. Reardon, *Edmund Randolph: A Biography* (New York: Macmillan, 1975), 307–34. For a discussion of Monroe's actions, which suggests that Washington's concerns were not unjustified, see Harry Ammon, *James Monroe: The Quest for National Identity* (Charlottesville: University Press of Virginia, 1971), especially chapter 8. With respect to Washington's conclusion that "to bring a man into office, of consequence knowingly whose political tenets are adverse to the measures which the *general* government are pursuing . . . would be a sort of political Suicide," see Washington to Thomas Pinckney, 27 September 1795, *Writings of George Washington*, 34:315.

7. Washington to Jefferson, 6 July 1796, *Writings of Washington*, 35:119–20.

8. First Inaugural Address, 4 March 1801, *Thomas Jefferson: Writings*, ed. Merrill D. Peterson (New York: The Library of America, 1984), 494.

9. Washington to Madison, 31 March 1787, *Writings of Washington*, 29:188–92.

10. Farewell Address, para. 48. Emphasis added. Washington to Marquis de Lafayette, 29 January 1789, *Writings of George Washington*, 30:186–87.

11. Samuel Flagg Bemis, "Washington's Farewell Address: A Foreign Policy of Independence," *American Historical Review* 39 no. 2 (1934): 252–68.

12. See, for example, Aristotle, *Nichomachean Ethics*, 1097b2–21; Aristotle, *Politics*, 1252b27–1253a7.

13. Farewell Address, para. 9; Jefferson to Judge Spencer Roane, 6 September 1819, *Jefferson: Writings*, 1426.

14. *The Papers of Alexander Hamilton*, ed. Harold C. Syrett et al. (New York:

Columbia University Press, 1961–1987), 4:140. For more reflections on this point, see Harry V. Jaffa, *The Conditions of Freedom* (Baltimore: Johns Hopkins University Press, 1975), 108–109. For a stimulating, if different, perspective, see Paul A. Rahe, *Inventions of Prudence: Constituting the American Regime* (Chapel Hill: University of North Carolina Press, 1993).

15. Washington to Governor Arthur Fenner, 4 June 1790, *Writings of Washington*, 31:47–48.

16. First Inaugural Address, 30 April 1789, *Writings of Washington*, 30:293; Alexander Hamilton, James Madison, and John Jay, *Federalist* No. 8, *The Federalist Papers*, ed. Clinton Rossiter (New York: New American Library, 1961), 67.

17. Farewell Address, para. 37. Emphasis added.

18. Washington to Sir Edward Newenham, 29 August 1788, *Writings of Washington*, 30:71–72; Fragments of the Discarded First Inaugural Address, April 1789, *George Washington: A Collection,* ed. W.B. Allen (Indianapolis: Liberty Classics, 1988), 454–55. The idea of national greatness, as something other than an increase in power, is considered in Gerald Stourzh, *Alexander Hamilton and the Idea of Representative Government* (Stanford: Stanford University Press, 1970), 171–205.

19. Farewell Address, para. 30.

20. Madison to James Monroe, 5 October 1786, *The Papers of James Madison*, ed. Robert A. Rutland, et al. (Charlottesville: University Press of Virginia, 1962–1991), 9:141.

21. Farewell Address, para. 12–13.

22. *Federalist* No. 6, 59; Circular to the States, 14 June 1783, *Writings of Washington*, 26:486; Washington to Tench Tilghman, 24 April 1783, *Writings of Washington*, 26:358–59. Emphasis in original.

23. See, for example, Washington to Henry Knox, 8 March 1787, *Writings of Washington*, 29:171. "It is among the evils, and perhaps not the smallest, of democratical governments, that the people must *feel*, before they will *see*. When this happens, they are roused to action; hence it is that this form of governments [*sic*] is so slow."

24. Farewell Address, para. 13. On these points, see the analysis in *Federalist* No. 5, 50–53; No. 8, 66–71; and No. 41, 255–64.

25. Madison to Monroe, 6 October 1786, *Papers of Madison*, 9:141.

26. Farewell Address, para. 33.

27. Farewell Address, para. 31; Washington to Bryan Fairfax, 24 August 1774, *Writings of Washington,* 3:237–42.

28. Farewell Address, para. 31.

29. Hamilton to Edward Carrington, 26 May 1792, *Papers of Hamilton*, 11:439.

30. Felix Gilbert, *To the Farewell Address: Ideas of Early American Foreign Policy* (Princeton: Princeton University Press, 1961), 100–103.

31. Washington to Patrick Henry, 9 October 1795, *Writings of Washington*, 34:335; Washington to William Heath, 20 May 1797, *Writings of Washington*, 35:449.

32. Farewell Address, para. 31, 32.

33. Washington to Benjamin Harrison, 18 January 1784, *Writings of Washington*, 27:305–307.

34. For evidence of Washington's extensive grievances against the British, see Washington to Gouverneur Morris, 22 December 1795, *Writings of Washington*,

34:399–403. For a summary of Washington's attitude towards the British and his implicit differences with Hamilton, see Stanley Elkins and Eric McKitrick, *The Age of Federalism*, 126–27.

35. Farewell Address, para. 32.

36. Farewell Address, para. 32, 34.

37. Washington to Jefferson, 6 July 1796, *Writings of George Washington*, 35:119–20.

38. This open letter to Washington, dated 1795, can be found in *The Thomas Paine Reader*, ed. Michael Foot and Isaac Kramnick (New York: Penguin Books, 1987), 490–502. The quote is on p. 502.

39. Washington to Timothy Pickering, 27 July 1795, *Writings of Washington*, 34:251; Washington's First Draft for an Address, 15 May 1796, in Victor Hugo Paltsits, ed., *Washington's Farewell Address* (New York: New York Public Library, 1935), 171.

40. Farewell Address, para. 34.

41. Washington to Gouverneur Morris, 20 October 1792, *Writings of Washington*, 32:189–90.

42. John Beckley to James Madison, 20 June 1796, *Papers of Madison*, 16:373.

43. Washington to Edmund Randolph, 22 July 1795, *Writings of Washington*, 34:244.

44. Jefferson to Elbridge Gerry, 21 June 1797, *Writings of Jefferson*, 7:149–50. The Gallatin address is in *Annals of Congress*, 5th Cong., 1,118–43. Gallatin also advocated "a fixed determination to prevent the increase of the national expenditure." Similar conclusions about the even-handedness of Washington's intentions with respect to Britain and France were reached by Garry Wills, *Cincinnatus: George Washington and the Enlightenment* (Garden City, NY: Doubleday, 1984), 89; and Forrest McDonald, *Alexander Hamilton: A Biography* (New York: W.W. Norton, 1979), 322.

45. Farewell Address, para. 35. See Wills, *Cincinnatus: George Washington and the Enlightenment*, 90–91. The reference to "enlightened statesmen" is from *Federalist* No. 10, 80.

46. Farewell Address, para. 35, 36, 38, 39. Hamilton's earlier analysis of the political and geographic separation between Europe and America may be found in *Federalist* No. 11, 90–91. Washington's First Draft of an Address, 15 May 1796, ed. Paltsits, *Washington's Farewell Address,* 169.

47. Washington to Jefferson, 31 August 1788, *Writings of Washington*, 30: 82; Washington to Sir Edward Newenham, 29 August 1788, *Writings of Washington*, 30:70–71; Jefferson to Monroe, 11 July 1790, *Writings of Jefferson*, 5:198; Washington to Gouverneur Morris, 28 July 1791, *Writings of Washington*, 31:327.

48. Fifth Annual Message, 3 December 1793, *Writings of Washington*, 33:163–69; Washington to Gouverneur Morris, 28 July 1791, *Writings of Washington*, 31:327–28.

49. Washington to Henry Laurens, 14 November 1778, *Writings of Washington*, 13:254–57. For an account of the Continental Congress's deference to the French, see J. Fred Rippy and Angie Debo, "The Historical Background of the American Policy of Isolation," *Smith College Studies in History* 9 (April-July 1924): 111–112.

50. Farewell Address, para. 37, 39; Washington to Gouverneur Morris, 22 December 1795, *Writings of Washington*, 34:401. See also First Draft for an Address,

15 May 1796, ed. Paltsits, *Washington's Farewell Address*, 170. This work uses "our interest, guided by *our* justice" following the Fitzpatrick version of the Farewell Address. Some versions read "our interest, guided by justice."

51. Third Annual Message, 25 October 1791, *Writings of Washington*, 31:396–404; Fifth Annual Message, 3 December 1793, *Writings of Washington*, 33:163–69.

52. Jefferson, First Inaugural Address, 4 March 1801, *Thomas Jefferson: Writings*, 493. Jefferson's statement was made specifically in the context of domestic threats to the Union and Constitution, but there is no doubt that he believed that it had equal validity to foreign threats as well.

53. Farewell Address, para. 29; Washington to Joseph Reed, 28 May 1780, *Writings of Washington*, 18:434–40.

54. For a discussion of these elements of the Jefferson-Madison approach to foreign and economic policy, see in particular Lance Banning, *The Jeffersonian Persuasion: Evolution of a Party Ideology* (Ithaca: Cornell University Press, 1979); Drew R. McCoy, *The Elusive Republic: Political Economy in Jeffersonian America* (Chapel Hill: University of North Carolina Press, 1980); Robert W. Tucker and David C. Hendrickson, *Empire of Liberty: The Statecraft of Thomas Jefferson* (New York: Oxford University Press, 1990); and Doron S. Ben-Atar, *The Origins of Jeffersonian Commercial Policy and Diplomacy* (New York: St. Martin's Press, 1993).

55. Farewell Address, para. 26, 27, 30; Jefferson to Madison, 28 August 1789, *Writings of Jefferson*, 5:111; Fragments of the Discarded First Inaugural Address, April 1789, *Washington: A Collection*, 456.

56. Farewell Address, para. 6, 30.

57. Fragments of the Discarded First Inaugural Address, April 1789, *Washington: A Collection*, 456.

58. Reply to an Address by the Legislature of Pennsylvania, September 1789, *Writings of Washington*, 30:395, ft. 13.

59. Reply to an Address by the Legislature of Pennsylvania, September 1789, *Writings of Washington*, 30:395, ft. 13; Wilson, Remarks to the Pennsylvania Ratifying Convention, 24 November 1787, *The Documentary History of the Ratification of the Constitution*, ed. Merrill Jensen et al. (Madison: University of Wisconsin Press, 1976), 2:350–63.

60. Farewell Address, para. 30.

61. Washington to the Mechanical Society of Baltimore, 7 June 1793, *Writings of Washington*, 32:490.

62. Washington to the Inhabitants of Alexandria, 4 July 1793, *Writings of Washington*, 33:3–4; Washington to the Mechanical Society of Baltimore, 7 June 1793, *Writings of Washington*, 32:490.

63. Hamilton, *The Defence* No. 8, 15 August 1795, *Papers of Hamilton*, 19:139.

64. Farewell Address, para. 41; Washington to Henry Laurens, 14 November 1778, *Writings of Washington*, 13:254–57.

65. Jefferson, Second Inaugural Address, 4 March 1805, *Thomas Jefferson: Writings*, 518. In a letter to Lafayette, Jefferson had expressed this view as follows: "nations ought to be governed according to their interest; but I am convinced that it is in their interest, in the long run, to be grateful, faithful to their engagements even in the worst of circumstances, and honorable and generous always." Jefferson to Lafayette, 2 April 1790, *Writings of Jefferson*, 5:152. Washington, as we have seen, would not have agreed that gratitude—if defined as a sacrifice of one's own true

interests—ought to guide this or any other nation. But otherwise Jefferson and Washington were of the same mind.

66. Aristotle, *Nichomachean Ethics*, 1155a17–29; Washington to Lafayette, 15 August 1786, *Writings of Washington*, 28:518–22; Washington to Andrew Hamilton, 4 May 1792, *Writings of Washington*, 32:34.

67. Washington to Robert Brooke, 16 March 1795, *Writings of Washington*, 34:149–50.

68. Washington to Francis Vanderkemp, 28 May 1788, *Writings of Washington*, 29:504–505; Washington to John Adams, 15 November 1794, *Writings of Washington*, 34:23.

69. Farewell Address, para. 36.

70. Farewell Address, para. 36; Washington to Hamilton, 7 May 1793, *Writings of Washington*, 32:451.

71. Farewell Address, para. 44.

72. Washington to Doctor James Anderson, 24 December 1795, *Writings of Washington*, 34:407

73. Farewell Address, para. 47; Washington to the Mechanical Society of Baltimore, 7 June 1793, *Writings of Washington*, 32:490; Washington to the Merchants and Traders of the City of Philadelphia, 17 May 1793, *Writings of Washington*, 32:460–61. For an intriguing examination of Hamilton's views, see Stephen Peter Rosen, "Alexander Hamilton and the Domestic Uses of International Law," *Diplomatic History* 5 (Summer 1981): 183–202.

74. *Federalist* No. 11, 87; *Federalist* No. 4, 47. Emphases in original.

75. Farewell Address, para. 37.

76. Washington to Henry Knox, 10 January 1788, *Writings of Washington*, 29:378; Washington to Jefferson, 1 January 1788, *Writings of Washington*, 29:350–51.

77. Washington to Madison, 31 March 1787, *Writings of Washington*, 29:189; Sixth Annual Message, 19 November 1794, *Writings of Washington*, 34:28–37.

78. Samuel Flagg Bemis, *Pinckney's Treaty: America's Advantage from Europe's Distress, 1783–1800*, rev. ed. (New Haven: Yale University Press, 1960); Washington to Jefferson, 1 January 1788, *Writings of Washington*, 29:350–51; Washington to Gouverneur Morris, 28 July 1791, *Writings of Washington*, 31:327–28; Washington to Comte de Rochambeau, 29 January 1789, *Writings of Washington*, 30:187.

79. Washington to Diego de Gardoqui, 1 December 1786, *Writings of Washington*, 29:98; Washington to Eleonor François Elie, Comte De Moustier, 26 March 1788, *Writings of Washington*, 29:448; Washington to Gouverneur Morris, 28 July 1791, *Writings of Washington*, 31:327–28. On this point, see Edmund S. Morgan, *The Genius of George Washington* (New York: W.W. Norton, 1980), 24.

80. Farewell Address, para. 35; Washington's First Draft of an Address, 15 May 1796, ed. Paltsits, *Washington's Farewell Address*, 169.

81. Washington to Henry Laurens, 14 November 1778, *Writings of Washington*, 13:254–57.

82. Washington to the Senate, 17 September 1789, *Writings of Washington*, 30:406; Washington to David Humphreys, 20 July 1791, *Writings of Washington*, 31:320; Washington to Edmund Randolph, 10 October 1791, *Writings of Washington*, 31:386.

83. Farewell Address, para. 41; Washington to Lafayette, 15 August 1786,

Writings of Washington, 28:518–22; Washington to Jefferson, 30 May 1787, *Writings of Washington*, 29:219–20.

84. Farewell Address, para. 41.

85. Washington to Chevalier de la Luzerne, 17 February 1788, *Writings of Washington*, 29:405; Washington to Eleonor François Elie, Comte De Moustier, 26 March 1788, *Writings of Washington*, 29:448–49; Washington to Lafayette, 28 April 1788, *Writings of Washington*, 29:477; Washington to David Stuart, 26 July 1789, *Writings of Washington*, 30:363. Madison's proposals for commercial discrimination are conveniently discussed in Elkins and McKitrick, *The Age of Federalism*, chapters 2 and 9.

86. Washington to James Warren, 7 October 1785, *Writings of Washington*, 28:289–92; Washington to Jefferson, 29 March 1784, *Writings of Washington*, 27:373–77; Washington to Benjamin Harrison, 10 October 1784, *Writings of Washington*, 27:471–80. Emphasis in original.

87. Fragments of the Discarded First Inaugural Address, April 1789, *Washington: A Collection*, 454.

88. Hamilton, Remarks on the Treaty of Amity Commerce and Navigation lately made between the United States and Great Britain, 9–11 July 1795, *Papers of Hamilton*, 18:451–52.

89. Hamilton, *The Defence*, No. 7, 12 August 1795, *Papers of Hamilton*, 19:116.

90. Washington to Lafayette, 15 August 1786, *Writings of Washington*, 28:518–22.

91. Washington to Lafayette, 15 August 1786, *Writings of Washington*, 28:518–22; Washington to Lafayette, 10 January 1788, *Writings of Washington*, 29:374–75.

92. Washington to Marquis de Chastellux, 25 April–1 May 1788, *Writings of Washington*, 29:484–85.

93. Washington to Reverend John Lathrop, *Writings of Washington*, 22 June 1788, 30:5.

94. Washington to Lafayette, 28 July 1791, *Writings of Washington,* 31:326; Seventh Annual Address, 7 December 1795, *Writings of Washington*, 34:386–93.

95. Sixth Annual Address, 19 November 1794, *Writings of Washington*, 34:28–37. With respect to Washington's confidence in the people, see, for example, Washington to Rufus King, 25 June 1797, *Writings of Washington*, 35:475; and Washington to David Humphreys, 26 June 1797, *Writings of Washington*, 35:481.

96. Washington to Charles Carroll, 1 May 1796, *Writings of Washington*, 35:30; Washington to Edmund Pendleton, 22 January 1795, *Writings of Washington*, 34:97–99; Madison, Political Observations, 20 April 1795, *Papers of Madison*, 15:518; Washington to Gouverneur Morris, 22 December 1795, *Writings of Washington*, 34:401; Washington's First Draft of an Address, 15 May 1796, ed. Paltsits, *Washington's Farewell Address*, 170; Hamilton, *The Defence* No. 5, 5 August 1795, *Papers of Hamilton* 19:90. Hamilton was also concerned that, based on Republican threats to sequester or confiscate individual American debts owed to British citizens, a war with Great Britain would compound the usual deleterious effects of any conflict between nations. "It was to be feared that in the fermentation of certain wild options, those wise just & temperate maxims which will for ever constitute the true security & felicity of a state would be overruled & that a war upon credit, eventually upon the general principles of public order might aggravate and embitter

the ordinary calamities of foreign war. The confiscation of debts due to the enemy might have been the first step of this destructive process. From one violation of justice to another the passage is easy." Hamilton, *The Defence* No. 18, 6 October 1795, *Papers of Hamilton,* 19:300.

97. Washington to Gouverneur Morris, 25 March 1793, *Writings of Washington,* 32:402–403.

98. Fragments of the Discarded First Inaugural Address, April 1789, *Washington: A Collection,* 454.

99. Washington to the President of the National Assembly of France (in reply to communication of 10 June 1790), 27 January 1791, *Writings of Washington,* 31:206.

100. Washington to Monroe, 25 August 1796, *Writings of Washington,* 35:189–90.

101. Washington to Henry Lee, 26 August 1794, *Writings of Washington,* 33:474–79. Emphasis in original. This was in response to a letter from Lee, who reported that Jefferson had been asked whether it was possible that Washington had attached himself to Great Britain and that he was now governed by British influence. Jefferson was said by Lee to have responded "that there was no danger of your being biased by considerations of that sort so long as you were influenced by wise advisers, or advice, which you at present had."

102. Washington to Eleonor François Elie, Comte De Moustier, 26 March 1788, *Writings of Washington* 29:447–48; *An Autobiographical Sketch by John Marshall,* ed. John S. Adams (Ann Arbor: University of Michigan Press, 1937), 13.

103. Jefferson to Gouverneur Morris, 20 April 1793, *Writings of Jefferson,* 6:217; Washington to Monroe, 25 August 1796, *Writings of Washington,* 35:189–90. On the agreement between Jefferson and Hamilton of the need for the United States to avoid war—however much they disagreed on the means to do so—see Tucker and Hendrickson, *Empire of Liberty,* 38–40.

104. Alexis de Tocqueville, *The Old Regime and the French Revolution,* chapter 3.

105. Jefferson, "Anas," *Writings of Jefferson,* 1:231.

106. Washington to Sir Edward Newenham, 22 June 1792, *Writings of Washington,* 32:73; Fisher Ames, Eulogy of Washington, 8 February 1800, *Works of Fisher Ames,* ed. William B. Allen (Indianapolis: Liberty Classics, 1983), 1:532; Washington to Charles Cotesworth Pinkney, 8 July 1796, *Writings of Washington,* 35:130.

107. Washington to Jefferson, 1 January 1788, *Writings of Washington,* 29:350; Washington to Hector St. John de Crèvecoeur, 10 April 1789, *Writings of Washington,* 30:281; Washington to David Humphreys, 20 July 1791, *Writings of Washington,* 30:320–21.

108. Washington to Lafayette, 19 June 1788, *Writings of Washington,* 29:524; Washington to Gouverneur Morris, 13 October 1789, *Writings of Washington,* 30:443.

109. Washington to Gouverneur Morris, 13 October 1789, *Writings of Washington,* 30:443; Washington to Marquis de la Luzerne, 29 April 1790, *Writings of Washington,* 31:40–41.

110. Washington to Lafayette, 10 June 1792, *Writings of Washington,* 32:54; Washington to Marquis de la Luzerne, 29 April 1790, *Writings of Washington,* 31:40–41.

111. Circular to the States, 14 June 1783, *Writings of Washington*, 26:489.

112. Reply to the French Minister, 1 January 1796, *Writings of Washington*, 34:413–14. Washington's exoterically effusive praise of France must also be viewed in light of the circumstances. Earlier, the American minister to France, James Monroe, had presented an American flag to the French National Convention, which displayed it in a permanent place of honor in their meeting hall. (Monroe had been officially reprimanded for expressing his pro-French sentiments on this occasion.) In receiving the French flag in return, Washington announced that it would be deposited in the archives of the United States and hence not displayed publicly. See James Thomas Flexner, *George Washington: Anguish and Farewell* (Boston: Little, Brown, 1972), 256–57. Washington's message to the French minister can thus be understood as deflecting any criticism by Republicans of this sign of coolness towards France. But we think that Washington's message, read carefully, in fact reflected his true perspective on the French Revolution.

113. Reply to the French Minister, 1 January 1796, *Writings of Washington*, 34:413–14.

114. Reply to an Address by the Legislature of Pennsylvania, September 1789, *Writings of Washington*, 30:395, ft. 13.

115. Washington to the Inhabitants of the City of New London, 2 September 1793, *Writings of Washington*, 33:80.

Chapter 5

1. Thomas Jefferson to Washington, 23 May 1792, *The Writings of Thomas Jefferson*, ed. Paul L. Ford (New York: G. P. Putnam's Sons, 1892–1899), 6:1–2.

2. Van Buren to the Minister to Columbia, 9 June 1829, quoted in *A Digest of International Law*, ed. John Bassett Moore (Washington, DC: U.S. Government Printing Office, 1906), 6:14–15. These tenets were also representative of the Monroe Doctrine, which was the logical extension of the Farewell Address into the affairs of the Western Hemisphere.

3. Rufus King to John Quincy Adams, 10 November 1796, *The Life and Correspondence of Rufus King*, ed. Charles R. King (New York: G. P. Putnam's Sons, 1894–1900), 1:104; John Quincy Adams to Johan Luzac, 25 November 1796, W.C. Ford, ed., *Writings of John Quincy Adams* (New York: The Macmillan Company, 1913–1917), 2:50.

4. James Madison to James Monroe, 29 September 1796, *The Papers of James Madison*, ed. Robert A. Rutland et al. (Charlottesville: University Press of Virginia, 1962–1991), 16:403.

5. Monroe to Madison, 1 January 1797, *Papers of Madison*, 16:443.

6. John Quincy Adams to Joseph Pitcairn, 31 January 1797, *Writings of John Quincy Adams*, 2:95–96; Jefferson to Elbridge Gerry, 21 June 1797, *Writings of Jefferson*, 7:149–50. The George Clinton pamphlet is cited by John Zvesper, *Political Philosophy and Rhetoric: A Study in the Origins of American Party Politics* (Cambridge: Cambridge University Press, 1977), 164.

7. Jefferson, "Anas," *Writings of Thomas Jefferson*, 1:165; First Inaugural Address, 4 March 1801, *Thomas Jefferson: Writings*, ed. Merrill D. Peterson (New York:

The Library of America, 1984), 495; Jefferson to Dr. Walter Jones, 2 January 1814, *Thomas Jefferson: Writings*, 1320.

8. Madison to Jefferson, 8 February 1825, *The Mind of the Founder: Sources of the Political Thought of James Madison*, ed. Marvin Meyers, rev. ed. (Hanover, N.H.: Brandeis University Press, 1981), 350; Jefferson, Minutes of the Board of Visitors, University of Virginia, 4 March 1825, *Thomas Jefferson: Writings*, 479–81. For a discussion of the larger meaning of this correspondence, see Harry V. Jaffa, *How to Think about the American Revolution: A Bicentennial Celebration* (Durham, NC: Carolina Academic Press, 1978), 97–104.

9. *National Intelligencer*, 28 April 1812, 5 and 7 May 1812. This series of editorials was established to have been written by Monroe in Irving R. Brant, *James Madison: The President, 1809–1912* (Indianapolis: Bobbs-Merrill, 1956), 434, 449–50.

10. Irving H. Bartlett, *Daniel Webster* (New York: W. W. Norton, 1978), 120.

11. This and the following quotes are taken from Webster, "The Character of Washington," 22 February 1832, in *The Great Speeches and Orations of Daniel Webster*, ed. Edwin P. Whipple (Boston: Little, Brown, 1882), 339–46.

12. Merrill D. Peterson, *The Great Triumvirate: Webster, Clay and Calhoun* (New York: Oxford University Press, 1987), 455–56.

13. Calhoun, Speech on the Admission of California and the General State of Union, 4 March 1850, in *Union and Liberty: The Political Philosophy of John C. Calhoun*, ed. Ross M. Lence (Indianapolis: Liberty Fund, 1992), 590–91.

14. Third Joint Debate, Jonesboro, 15 September 1858, in *The Lincoln-Douglas Debates of 1858*, ed. Robert W. Johannsen (New York: Oxford University Press, 1965), 116–31.

15. Third Joint Debate, *Lincoln-Douglas Debates*, 116–31. See also Douglas, First Joint Debate, Ottawa, 21 August 1858, *Lincoln-Douglas Debates*, 37–48.

16. Address at Cooper Union, New York City, 27 February 1860, in *The Collected Works of Abraham Lincoln*, ed. Roy P. Basler (New Brunswick: Rutgers University Press, 1953), 3:527, 550.

17. Address to the New Jersey Senate at Trenton, New Jersey, 21 February 1861, *Collected Works of Lincoln*, 4:235–36.

18. Farewell Address at Springfield, Illinois, 11 February 1861, *Collected Works of Lincoln*, 4:190.

19. Speech at Peoria, Illinois, 16 October 1854, *Collected Works of Lincoln*, 2:249.

20. This and the following quotes are from Alexis de Tocqueville, *Democracy in America*, trans. George Lawrence (New York: HarperPerennial, 1969), 226–30.

21. John Quincy Adams, Special Message, 15 March 1826, *Messages and Papers of the Presidents*, ed. James D. Richardson (1896–1899): 2:337.

22. Speech to Louis Kossuth, 9 January 1852, in *The Papers of Henry Clay*, ed. Melba Porter Hay (Lexington: The University Press of Kentucky, 1991), 10:944–46.

23. *Congressional Globe*, 32nd Cong., 1st session, pt. 1:105. Emphasis in original.

24. This and subsequent quotations are from Richard Olney, "International Isolation of the United States," *Atlantic Monthly* 81 (May 1898): 577–88.

25. Gray to Secretary of State John Hay, 25 October 1898, *Papers Relating to*

the Foreign Relations of the United States, 1898 (Washington, DC: U.S. Government Printing Office, 1901), 934; *Congressional Record*, 55th Cong., 3d session, pt. 1:501.

26. Speech before the Puritan Society of New York City, 22 December 1900, in *The Papers of Woodrow Wilson*, ed. Arthur S. Link et al. (Princeton: Princeton University Press, 1966–1994), 12:52–58.

27. A Memorial Day Address, 30 May 1916, *Papers of Wilson*, 37:123–28; An Address in Omaha, 5 October 1916, *Papers of Wilson*, 38:343–49.

28. An Address at the Metropolitan Opera House, 27 September 1918, *Papers of Wilson*, 51:127–33.

29. Special Address to the Senate, 22 January 1917, *Papers of Wilson*, 40:533–39.

30. An Address at the Metropolitan Opera House, 4 March 1919, *Papers of Wilson*, 55:413–21.

31. Senate Resolution 329 in *Congressional Record*, 64th Cong., 2d sess., 1808; Borah quoted in Ralph Stone, *The Irreconcilables: The Fight against the League of Nations* (Lexington: University of Kentucky Press, 1970), 14; Congressman Lundeen of Minnesota quoted in *Congressional Record*, 65th Cong., 1st sess., 362.

32. *Congressional Record*, 65th Cong, 3d sess., 3746–47.

33. Henry Cabot Lodge, *A Frontier Town and Other Essays* (New York: Charles Scribner, 1906), 269; Lodge, *The Life and Letters of George Cabot* (Boston: Little, Brown and Company, 1877), 461; Lodge, Speech at Norwell, Massachusetts, 4 September 1915, quoted in William C. Widenor, *Henry Cabot Lodge and the Search for an American Foreign Policy* (Berkeley: University of California Press, 1980), 203; Lodge, *War Addresses* (Boston: Houghton Mifflin, 1917), 122.

34. Lodge, *War Addresses*, 299; Lodge, *The Senate and the League of Nations* (New York: Charles Scribner's Sons, 1925), 132, 230, 260, 296.

35. Lodge, *The Senate and the League of Nations*, 260–61.

36. Lodge, *The Senate and the League of Nations*, 405.

37. Lodge, Speech on the League of Nations, 12 August 1919, in Daniel Boorstin, ed., *An American Primer* (Chicago: University of Chicago Press, 1966), 790; *Boston Evening Transcript*, 14 October 1920, quoted in Widenor, *Henry Cabot Lodge*, 317.

38. William E. Borah, "American Foreign Policy in a Nationalistic World," *Foreign Affairs* 12 (special supplement, January 1934), iii–xii.

39. *Public Papers of the Presidents of the United States: Harry S Truman, 1950* (Washington, DC: U.S. Government Printing Office, 1965), 171–75.

40. *Public Papers of the Presidents of the United States: Harry S Truman, 1947* (Washington, DC: U.S. Government Printing Office, 1963), 178–79.

41. Harry S Truman, *Memoirs*, vol. 2: *Years of Trial and Hope, 1946–1952* (New York: Doubleday, 1956), 101–102. Emphasis in original.

42. Dean Acheson, *Present at the Creation* (New York: W.W. Norton, 1969), 6–7.

43. Those representing the so-called realist school of international relations, such as Hans Morgenthau and George Kennan, believed that, even under Truman and Acheson, the Wilsonian perspective had badly distorted American foreign policy by making it impossible to distinguish between vital and peripheral American national interests. Washington and the Founders, by contrast, were portrayed by the realists as hard-headed statesmen who established and defended the indepen-

dence of the United States by manipulating—even covertly supporting—the European balance of power. For Hans Morgenthau, "*The Federalist* and Washington's Farewell Address are their classic expression." Even when apparently more moralistic American statesmen (such as Thomas Jefferson and John Quincy Adams) subsequently assumed control of American foreign policy, the influence of Washingtonian realism persisted, "under the cover of those moral principles with which from Jefferson onward American statesmen have liked to justify their moves on the international scene." However, according to Morgenthau, the utopianism exemplified by Woodrow Wilson had led Americans to cease to use moral principles to justify their enduring national interests; instead, the concept of national interest became opposed to that of morality. Such utopianism, in different forms, resulted both in American isolationism and in immoderate efforts to make the world safe for democracy. Hans J. Morgenthau, *In Defense of the National Interest: A Critical Examination of American Foreign Policy* (New York: Alfred A. Knopf, 1951), 3–28.

44. Burton Ira Kaufman, ed., *Washington's Farewell Address: The View from the 20th Century* (Chicago: Quadrangle Books, 1969), 115.

45. Douglas Southall Freeman, *George Washington: A Biography*, 7 vols. (New York: Scribner's, 1948–1957); James T. Flexner, *George Washington*, 4 vols. (Boston: Little, Brown, 1965–1972). The quote is from volume 1, p. 5. Richard Brookhiser, *Founding Father: Rediscovering Washington* (New York: Free Press, 1996); Harrison Clark, *All Cloudless Glory: The Life of George Washington from Youth to Yorktown* (Washington: Regnery Publishing, 1995).

46. Garry Wills, *Cincinnatus: George Washington and the Enlightenment* (Garden City, N.Y.: Doubleday, 1984). This approach might be said to have begun with Marcus Cunliffe, *George Washington, Man and Monument* (1958; reprint, New York: New American Library, 1982). Less complimentary to Washington in his mythical role is Barry Swartz, *George Washington: The Making of an American Symbol* (New York: Free Press, 1987). For Washington's political purpose and stature, see Glenn A. Phelps, *George Washington and American Constitutionalism* (Lawrence: University of Kansas Press, 1993); and William B. Allen, "Washington and Franklin: Symbols or Lawmakers?" *Political Science Reviewer* 17 (Fall 1987).

Chapter 6

1. Edwin P. Whipple, ed., *The Great Speeches and Orations of Daniel Webster* (Boston: Little, Brown, 1882), 339–46.

Index

A

Acheson, Dean, 166–67, 210n43
Adams, John, ix, xi-xii, 1, 7, 35, 38, 58, 117
Adams, John Quincy, 2–3, 143–44, 152–53, 211n43
Adet, Pierre, 196–97n22
Allen, William B., 168
alliances (foreign), 3, 48, 51, 53, 57, 62, 72, 94, 99, 108, 110, 123, 129, 154, 156–59, 161, 167
American Revolution, 13–16, 20–21, 35–36, 57, 62, 64, 68, 99–101, 108, 110, 112, 114, 116, 118, 124, 134–35, 146, 150, 170
Ames, Fisher, 58, 133
anti-Federalism, 30, 38, 68, 73
Aristotle, 60, 88, 117
Articles of Confederation, 17–18, 23, 24, 26–27, 34, 35, 67, 76, 94, 108, 120

B

Bache, Benjamin, 75
Bemis, Samuel Flagg, 56, 95, 121
Benton, Thomas Hart, 160
Binney, Horace, 56
Blount, William, 106
Bonaparte, Napoleon, 189n1
Borah, William, 159, 162–63
Brookhiser, Richard, 167–68
Burke, Edmund, 38

C

Caffery, Donelson, 156
Calhoun, John C., 148

Carlyle, Thomas, x, xvi
Carroll, Charles, 48
Carroll, John, 88
character. *See* national (American) character
Charles, Joseph, 55
Circular Address to the States of 1783 (Washington), 6, 19–23, 24, 56, 61–67, 85, 99, 111, 126, 141
citizenship, xviii, 5, 16, 21, 23, 29, 31, 45, 62, 69, 80, 84–89, 91, 95–96, 117, 126, 133
Clark, Harrison, 168
Clay, Henry, 147–48, 150, 153–55, 165
Clinton, George, 144
commerce, x, 20, 48, 51, 57, 63, 65–67, 96–99, 104, 108, 111–12, 118, 120–21, 123–29, 132, 137, 146, 163, 170
common (or public) good, 15, 17–18, 23, 61, 65, 71, 73, 96, 101, 104, 170
Constitution of the United States, xi-xii, xv, xvii, 2, 28–30, 31, 33, 34, 40, 46–49, 59–62, 65, 67–70, 73–75, 77, 85–86, 88–89, 96, 100, 128, 142, 145, 148, 150–51, 171–72
Constitutional Convention, xv, xvii, 9–10, 26–28, 34, 38, 142

D

Davis, Jefferson, 147
Declaration of Independence, 2, 63, 70, 113, 123, 142, 144, 149–50
DeConde, Alexander, 55
Democratic Party, 149, 161
Douglas, Stephen, 148–50

E

education, 12, 16, 52–53, 76, 78–82, 117
Elkins, Stanley, 92

F

factions, 37, 39, 48, 54, 69–76, 92, 94, 100–103, 107–8, 133–34, 143, 145, 151, 172. *See also* parties (political)
Federalist Papers, 2, 4, 20, 28, 36, 50, 57, 64, 69, 71, 75–77, 99–100, 119, 124, 144, 172
Federalist Party, xv, 37, 39, 44, 71, 74–75, 93–94, 101, 107, 111–12, 132, 143–45
First Inaugural Address (Washington), 5, 32–33, 37, 48, 54, 56, 58–59, 113, 144; discarded First Inaugural Address, 29–30, 66, 76, 97, 129, 193n41
Flexner, James T., 167
France, 40–45, 55, 66, 84, 92–93, 101–8, 110, 116, 118, 122–24, 128–29, 131–37, 143–44, 165–66, 189n1, 203n49. *See also* French Revolution
Franklin, Benjamin, ix–xi
Frederick the Great (of Prussia), 102
freedom. *See* liberty
Freeman, Douglas Southall, 167
French Revolution, xv, 40–41, 43, 69, 107, 130–37, 208n112
Freneau, Philip, 38, 74
friendship, 17, 45, 82, 86–89, 105, 108, 109, 117–18, 123, 152, 170

G

Gallatin, Albert, 107, 203n44
Gardoqui, Diego, 121
Genet, Edmund Charles, 41, 69–70
Germany, 159, 161–62, 164
Gettysburg Address, 2, 21, 85, 150–51, 165. *See also* Lincoln, Abraham
Gilbert, Felix, 55, 102, 197n23

Gray, George, 156
Great Britain, 36, 37, 38, 40–44, 53, 55, 62–63, 66, 84, 92, 99, 101–4, 106–8, 110, 112, 114, 116, 118, 120–23, 131–33, 143–45, 148, 154–55, 166, 189n1
Greece, 95, 164–65

H

Hamilton, Alexander, xii, xv, 5, 15, 24, 35–41, 43–44, 71, 75, 80, 87, 92–93, 96, 99, 102, 104, 116, 118–19, 125, 129, 142, 144, 162, 195n4, 203n46, 206–7n96; and the Farewell Address, 47, 49–57, 91, 93, 195n3, 196n11. See also *Federalist Papers*
Harrison, Benjamin, 104
Hayne, Robert, 145
Heath, William, 103
Henry, Patrick, 28, 48, 84, 103
Holland, 40
Humphreys, David, 193n41
Hungary, 154–55

I

Italy, 165

J

Jackson, Andrew, x, 142
Japan, 163–64
Jay, John, 24, 35, 41, 43, 50, 55, 57, 64, 119, 197n25. *See also* Jay's Treaty
Jay's Treaty, 42, 43, 57, 65, 71, 100, 107, 124–25, 145
Jefferson, Thomas, x–xii, xiv–xvi, 3, 5, 10–11, 13, 16, 25, 28, 35–41, 43–44, 48–49, 56, 58, 70–71, 74–75, 92–95, 102, 104–5, 108, 111–13, 116, 118, 121, 125, 133–34, 141, 144, 150, 152, 160–63, 194n60, 195n4, 204n65, 207n101, 211n43
justice, 2, 4, 6, 11, 22, 31, 48, 61–63, 76, 78, 82–84, 86–87, 91, 96, 102,

104, 108, 110–13, 115–23, 126, 128, 137–39, 145, 153, 158, 167, 170, 173–74

K

Kaufman, Burton Ira, 167
Kennan, George, 210n43
King, Rufus, 143
Knox, Henry, 26, 35, 37, 39
Kossuth, Louis, 153–54

L

Lafayette, Marquis de, xvi, 23, 28–29, 31, 37, 40, 74, 94, 123, 126, 135, 149
Laurens, Henry, 122
League of Nations, 158–61, 166
Lee, Henry, 1, 12, 132
Lee, Richard Henry, 106
liberty, xvi, 2, 14–15, 21, 25–26, 33, 41, 46, 53, 62–68, 70, 72, 75, 81–83, 86–88, 96, 100, 102, 105, 113–14, 117, 130–39, 145, 148, 150, 153, 158, 161, 163–65, 171, 173
Lincoln, Abraham, x, 6, 63, 67, 85–86, 88, 148–51, 160, 163, 170. *See also* Gettysburg Address
Locke, John, xvi, 10, 144
Lodge, Henry Cabot, 160–62

M

Machiavelli, Niccolo, 95
Madison, James, xv, 1, 3, 26, 27, 31, 35–41, 56–57, 60, 71, 74–76, 77, 93, 97, 100, 102, 104, 124, 128, 143–45, 195n3; and the Farewell Address, 46–47, 49–52. See also *Federalist Papers*
Mahan, Alfred Thayer, 155
Marshall, John, 1, 3, 85, 132
McKinley, William, 156
McKitrick, Eric, 92
Monroe, James, 28, 40, 92–93, 107,

131, 143, 145, 152, 162, 201n6, 208n112. *See also* Monroe Doctrine
Monroe Doctrine, 152, 155, 158–59, 161, 166, 208n2
morality, 5, 7, 10–12, 20–21, 29–30, 33, 52–54, 60, 76, 78–80, 82, 86, 95, 100, 115–16, 120, 146, 153, 163, 169, 172–73. *See also* religion
Morgan, Edmund, xvi, 122
Morgenthau, Hans, 210–11n43
Morris, Gouverneur, 27, 48, 65, 106, 108, 110, 121, 129, 132, 134
Morris, Robert, 35

N

national (American) character, xviii, 3–6, 10, 13, 18–19, 21–22, 26, 30–31, 39–40, 62, 68, 71, 76, 84–85, 94, 101, 104–6, 108–10, 115, 117, 120, 126, 128–29, 131–33, 135–39, 141, 148–50, 160, 162, 169–73
neutrality, 34, 40–41, 44, 54, 84, 92–93, 98, 118–20, 128, 131–33, 154, 160–61, 163, 194n60
Neutrality Proclamation of 1793, 40, 49, 92–93, 118, 194n1
Nietzsche, Friedrich, xvi

O

Olney, Richard, 155–56

P

Paine, Thomas, 22, 38, 53, 57, 105
Paltsits, Victor Hugo, 56
parties (political), xviii, 34, 37, 42–44, 48–49, 51, 53, 58, 62, 71–76, 85, 89, 92–93, 105, 107, 149, 172. *See also* factions
patriotism, 14, 32, 59, 64, 66–67, 85, 87, 98, 135, 147
Perkins, Bradford, 92
Phelps, Glenn A., 168
Pickering, Timothy, 74

Pinckney, Charles Cotesworth, 45, 143

Pinckney, Thomas, 42. *See also* Pinckney's Treaty

Pinckney's Treaty, 42, 65, 71, 100, 125

Plutarch, 6, 141, 169

Poindexter, Miles, 159–60

Poland, 134

Portugal, 104

Prussia, 102–3

public opinion, 29, 39, 71, 75–76, 80,
91, 99, 101–2, 105, 112, 117, 142,
150, 172

$\mathcal{R}$

Randolph, Edmund, 26, 27, 35, 37, 39,
42, 194n60

religion, 1, 5, 7, 14–15, 20, 23, 27, 30,
32–33, 52–54, 59, 64, 67, 76, 78–
80, 83–84, 113, 117, 119, 122, 126,
133, 137, 146–47, 163, 171–73

Republican Party (of Jefferson), xv, 37,
39, 43, 44, 66, 68, 71, 75, 93–94,
101, 103, 107, 111–12, 124, 128,
132, 143–44, 161

reputation, 11–13, 15, 49, 109–10, 116,
120

rights, 4–6, 14, 20, 21, 28–29, 73, 80,
82, 91, 102, 119, 134, 136, 138, 147,
157, 170

Roosevelt, Franklin Delano, x, 58, 162

Roosevelt, Theodore, 160

Rush, Benjamin, ix

Russia, 155, 165–66

$\mathcal{S}$

Shay's Rebellion, 25–26, 73

Sidney, Algernon, 144

slavery, xiv, 42, 71, 83, 101–2, 114,
148–50, 200n71

Soviet Union. *See* Russia

Spain, 40, 42, 66, 100, 121–22, 156

Sparks, Jared, 194n41, 196n10

$\mathcal{T}$

Talleyrand, 189n1

Tocqueville, Alexis de, 133, 152

Treaty of Versailles, 161

Truman, Harry S, x, 163–67, 210n43.
See also Truman Doctrine

Truman Doctrine, 164–67

Turkey, 164

$\mathcal{U}$

Union, 3, 16, 18, 21–24, 30, 39, 47–48,
52–53, 60, 62–67, 71, 74, 76, 78,
82, 85–89, 96–100, 122, 137, 142,
145–51, 171

United Nations, 166, 173

$\mathcal{V}$

Van Buren, Martin, 142

virtue, 2, 4–6, 12, 16–17, 23–24, 29–
31, 33, 60, 66, 77–81, 83, 95–97,
113, 115, 117, 130, 143, 145, 169–
70, 172–73, 195n67

$\mathcal{W}$

Walker, Robert, 154–55

Washington, George. *See* Circular Address to the States of 1783; First Inaugural Address

Webster, Daniel, x, 3, 7, 145–47, 150,
168–69

Weems, Mason (Parson), 3, 150, 168,
170

Wills, Garry, 168

Wilson, James, 38, 114

Wilson, Woodrow, 157–61, 165, 167,
210–11n43

Winthrop, John, 20

Wolcott, Oliver, 58

About the Authors

Matthew Spalding is director of lectures and educational programs at the Heritage Foundation in Washington, D.C. He is also a contributing editor of *Policy Review: The Journal of American Citizenship*. He has a Ph.D. in government from the Claremont Graduate School, where he wrote his dissertation on George Washington. In addition to having taught American government at George Mason University, he has written extensively on the American Founding and the political thought of the Founding era.

Patrick J. Garrity is a staff member with the Los Alamos National Laboratory and a senior fellow at the Claremont Institute. He has been a fellow at the Foreign Policy Institute of the Johns Hopkins University School of Advanced International Studies, a visting teaching professor at the Naval Postgraduate School, and a research fellow at the Center for Strategic and International Studies. He has co-edited two books, *Nuclear Weapons in the Changing World: Perspectives from Europe, Asia, and North America* and *Regional Security Issues*, and has contributed an essay, "Foreign Policy in the Federalist Papers," to *Saving the Revolution: The Federalist Papers and the American Founding*, edited by Charles R. Kesler.